ALASKA BUSH PILOT

Memoirs of 'Dok-tor Nik-sik'

ALASKA BUSH PILOT

Memoirs of 'Dok-tor Nik-sik'

Keith Hooker, M.D.
and M. Dawn Bentley

To order additional copies of this book, contact:
Xlibris Corporation
1-888-795-4274
www.Xlibris.com
Orders@Xlibris.com
71561

CONTENTS

PROLOGUE AND DEDICATION

Keith Speaks

Looking back over the pages of my early journals prompted this book. . . I wanted a permanent record of that particular time in my life for my descendants. Personally, I got real sick of seeing my own name in print over and over, when Dawn would run the chapters past me, but I guess that can't be avoided when writing a book like this.

When Phyllis and I moved to Alaska, we took our two little boys; while up there, we had two little girls. After returning to the Lower 48, four more kids came along. *All* of their births , I feel, are too sacred and private to appear in this context.

Kyle, Kit, Kelly, Kiana, Keena, Karma, Kassie, Kory: you are my true wealth and treasure. . . you are honorable and fine and good. . . each one of you. . . and I am extremely proud to be your father. The grandchildren are amazing; I feel as much love for each of them as I did for their parents. Our family is Eternal and it's the greatest blessing in my life. This book is dedicated to you. . . . .

Dawn's Turn

What a unique opportunity I've had to get to know this guy, Keith Hooker! He chose a profession where he directly and profoundly serves others and has done this over his lifetime. Simply put, he is a great person and a humble one. . . I am proud to call him 'Sonny Boy'! Invaluable in this endeavor was my hubby Clemont and my friend Karen Terkelsen. . . they alternately raved and criticized. . . just enough of each to keep me motivated and humble. Megan Leigh has been absolutely crucial in the creation of this book. She has been Editor in Chief, Project manager, Chauffeur, Photo Lab Tech and PC Support. . . all quid pro quo of a nature yet-undetermined.

. . . and to MY children and grandchildren, *my* autobiography is in the works, kids: be afraid. . . be very afraid!

DISCLAIMER

There are more words in Keith's journals not included for different reasons; some, like the births of two of his children, were too personal and private for publication. This 'Forward' will not be read by Keith until after the book is printed, for you see, he has been uncomfortable during this whole process of writing his memoirs, 'putting on airs', in his words, to consider having this kind of work made public. It is, however, written in first-person style, using existing notes from his Alaska journals plus additional clarification on cassette tapes. His last words on the last tape, the one dated 14 October 2009, follow here . . . . verbatim. There is no 'artistic license' on my part as I feel they are too precious to edit . . . . these are his words:

"My motivation and wish in keeping these notes in the years of 1966 through 1970 and the pictures I felt compelled to take during that time were not made clear to me. But now, my goal in writing this is for my kids to know me a little better than they do now and some of the things I've done and where their ancestry came from and what kind of a guy their dad, or grandpa was or is, and when we meet in the next world we'll have something to talk over. I hope it'll motivate my kids to get out and be adventuresome. Probably my purpose of this book is, I was aware when I was up there (Alaska) that it was a pretty unique opportunity so I took thousands of pictures and met as many people as I could and never turned down a trip or opportunity to go someplace or do something. If there was a trip to be taken, I was the first one in line. It's got me a lot of things, in trouble a few times! Feeling, for many years, that I was still not 'good enough' as some other people, and feeling like I was looking up from a lower platform than others, has been an ongoing impression for me, (but) I plan to continue serving my fellowman in whatever capacity and for however many years I have the strength to do so. I have survived 8 airplane crashes and two bouts with cancer and I am still going . . . . each day is a joy and I live it to the fullest. So that's my (reason) in writing this, and if anyone else finds this interesting, well, I'll be flattered . . . ."

CHAPTER 1

WHAT ARE YOU DOING . . .
THE REST OF YOUR LIFE?

It was 1966 and the longest and most unpopular war in the history of America was being waged in Vietnam. It was every-day news. The reports were not easy to listen to, even when spoken in the somber and measured tones of Walter Cronkite. A running count of the American Military death tolls appeared in a little box on the screen during some news reports. Cold numbers that represented warm young lives, blasted and packed into body bags and flown home . . . a running count multiplied by brokenhearted loved ones who were left desolated by grief. Natural disasters, worldwide sickness and starvation, and man's inhumanity to man . . . these horrors, too, made their way into the daily news. The world was full to the top and brimming over and whether the wars in southeast Asia were a sin and a blunder, or a necessary and noble cause, there was nothing I could do about all of the suffering and death in any humanitarian sense . . . except what I *was* doing.

So, on the way home from the large Hospital which was my workplace and where I was finishing my first year of Internship, I stopped at the mailbox in front of the apartment complex that had been home to my wife Phyllis and our two little energetic, under-three boys Kyle and Kit and me for the past 2 years. Nothing out of the ordinary or of life-changing importance was expected in the mail at that time. Gingerly, I grabbed the handle because the August sun that was beating down on Riverside County had made it hot enough to fry my fingers. Inside, there was an envelope with an impressive return address, bearing the title of the United States of America.

At that time, receiving Greetings from Uncle Sam was universal cause for concern to most young men between the ages of 18 to 29. I expected *The Letter* to come eventually, as there was outright drafting of single doctors of the right age-range and even married Docs with families were being called to go in for basic training, just in case the conflict accelerated, I guess.

Because I had planned for this and knew what to do, it didn't cause a shock. I was 26 years old, married 4 years and was close to finishing my internship, and so reasoned with those items tucked in my belt I was nearly draft-proof! Regardless of my politics or my feelings about the war, I didn't want to be drafted . . . . no *wants* to be drafted . . . .

Back in my first year of college at Arizona State, I planned on a major in Engineering but the classes put me to sleep and my grades reflected it, so I switched majors in the second year. While studying in the library, I'd gotten hold of several books that lit the fire of my future profession within me. Three of the best were 'Burma Surgeon,' by Seagraves, 'The Night They Burned the Mountain' by Doctor Tom Dooley and the writings, of course, of Albert Schweitzer about his life's work as a missionary-doctor in Africa. The last three years in Med school had been the best of my life. I was working 10-12 hour days completing my Internship at the hospital, then going almost directly back to work as a scrub nurse in any surgical department that needed me and *then* night-janitor-ing as well, in order to make enough income to keep training to be a doctor. The last 3 years found me managing to juggle all of that with little more than four hours sleep a night . . . well, not just night . . . I could sleep anytime I had a chance to catch 15 minutes for a power nap. Still can. The four years I spent in Medical School at the University of Oregon were the best of my life.

Even now, 44 years after graduation, I can still feel the heat from the glowing coals . . . the strong and constant glow generated by those powerful books and their inspired authors, and the influence they had on me. Occasionally, during the 80-hour weeks put in at

Emergency Room services at the Utah Valley Regional Hospital in Provo, Utah, it still warms my heart . . . .

My lifelong career as a doctor hadn't been foreseen from the beginning of my life, by any means. Born at a very young age in a town you've never heard of called Primghar, Iowa, my hometown was awash in history, which, to outsiders anyway, is very interesting . . . the first time you hear it. It was founded by eight families who had traveled by wagon train to that spot in the fall of 1872, and when one night, talking around their fires, they decided they'd had enough and even the promises of distant California gold fields was not alluring enough to get them to go one more mile. That part of the country they were in looked just fine to them, so, they unhitched their teams from the wagons and began to put down roots.

When it came time to name the little town they established and make it the County seat, it was decided that the best way to honor the eight founding families would be to take the first letter of each of their last names and juggle them around until they made a plausible, semi-pronounceable town-type name. It remained and it is original. I'd been born there and still have relatives there; my father owned the local lumberyard and sold Real Estate on the side and my mother worked fulltime, too.

We were, I guess you could say, firmly middle-class in our lifestyle but living in the 1940's and '50's was different in a sense that is hard to describe. One thing different, was having and spending of money in our family was certainly not like I see it done by families today. On the occasions when my father would sell a house he had listed, we would make a celebration out of me getting on my trusty bicycle and riding down to the Dairy Queen for hamburgers. Blame it on the 'Depression Mentality' that most grownups of that era could hark back to as an example of thrifty habits. We weren't wealthy but we weren't poor; I was both taught *and* shown the merits of hard work and I never wanted for anything . . . my parents were good and kind and my memories of childhood are all happy ones . . . a little brother or two would have been neat, though. Too late now for that, I suppose . . . .

Growing up in that idyllic setting formed my love for the outdoors; there was peace and satisfaction in simple diversions. We called that farmland spot in the northwest corner of the state 'home' until my mother's health necessitated change to a drier climate, so we moved to Phoenix when I was about 12. I finished eighth grade and graduated high school there, then decided on Arizona State as my Alma Mater. It was there in Tempe that my first mental blueprints of the future I was planning to build began to come together.

Going to college, working as a janitor at night, also selling blood to the blood bank, and working as a part-time stock-boy, too, kept me out of trouble . . . *and,* I was able to leap tall buildings with a single bound! One night, a chance comment caused a life-changing move for me. Seems I was janitor-ing one of the campus buildings I worked at night, cleaning out ashtrays and sweeping up and so forth, when I mentioned off-handedly to Rex Maughn, my friend and fellow-janitor, that I wished everyone who used the building was Mormon, then we wouldn't have any more disgusting ashtrays to clean up. He replied with something like the universal question often asked by members of the Church of Jesus Christ of Latter Day Saints, "What you know about the Mormon Church? Would you like to know more?"

There were a number of LDS people in that part of Arizona in the early 1960's and I had a positive opinion of most of the ones I had gotten to know, but it took me a long time to investigate the church to my satisfaction. I even researched popular *anti*-Mormon literature from the library. Good old Rex stayed patient and loyal throughout my long conversion and gave me some great advice when he told me to 'start with the basic's.' He said, "If you cannot believe and accept the Joseph Smith story of the restored Gospel as it was taught by Jesus Christ, then you will never have a complete testimony of the Church."

His friendship was a constant and his advice was sound; I'm grateful that I took the time I did to know in my heart that it was true. It's served me well over the last 40+ years since my baptism, performed by my friend Rex, by the way. If a person is converted to the *people* of the Church, or to the *missionaries* of the Church, or even the music or something else fleeting, a weak testimony will not stand up to trials of faith. Because nearly everyone goes through trials at one point or another, only the firm belief in the Joseph Smith story will stay the test of time. If *that* is true, it's all true . . .

A blind date led me to my introduction to the former Miss Phoenix, the lovely Phyllis Gunderson, and we began to build another foundation for my future. She was LDS and had been raised in a good, conservative home; seriously dating the way we were, I didn't want anyone to ever think that I joined the Church just because of another person and that I didn't have a testimony myself.

I took my time and studied it until I knew in my heart that it was true. We married in my Senior year of college and her Freshman year, after dating a long time via Ma Bell and the US Post Office's 3-cent stamps. You see, I was really hammered with finances because of my expensive pre-Med classes and so forth; money was tight for both of us, so we couldn't afford to see each other or even call on the phone back and forth from Oregon to Arizona as often as we would have liked. We took turns calling, about once every 2 weeks or so, but we wrote almost daily. Without the everyday physical presence of each other, our love developed in a more esoteric and spiritual fashion. I found her to be beautiful outside and inside, too; we had common goals and interests, and she would prove to have three qualities that would be of imminent importance in order to be Mrs. Keith Hooker: long-suffering patience, a sense of humor and, the most important: she was a real good sport!

Marrying her in the Temple for all Eternity began the transition from where I'd started out to the Dream Life I imagined for my family and myself. Having my companion and, later, our offspring along for the ride was delicious frosting on a very nice cake. She believed in me and wanted the same life that I wanted; most importantly, she stayed around when that perfect life popped out all over with imperfections, which it would prove to do with great regularity over the next few decades!

Now, here we were, just a few years after the first big step of marriage, ready to leap out into the fray. Everyday life with Phyllis and our boys still seemed like it was happening to someone else, every time I held still long enough to analyze my life.

The mirror told me in 1966 that I was a gangly, over-grown, bespectacled, gosling-type German-ancestor-ed-chump whose big hands and feet often ended up going in different directions while my febrile mind was being saturated with as much medical learning as it could hold. Fulltime work, then school, then home, had been the three unevenly dissected pieces of the pie that was my day. Sometimes it felt like my hectic life was snapping in the wind like a big flag on a windy day.

So, on the day *The Letter* had directed, I took time off and dropped down to the local Draft Board, walked in and registered my name on the proffered clip board, then sat on a sticky metal chair surrounded by a jumble of widely-assorted sweaty young men, the pride of our Country and the cream of American youth. I wasn't too nervous, as I felt pretty sure I'd get a deferment, but some of the others in the overly-air-conditioned room didn't look real confident. I was even looking forward to announcing my intentions to whatever military bureaucrat would be handling my deferment, for, now that I was very near finishing up my Internship in Los Angeles, I was certain that the Public Health Service would be sending me on my dream assignment in Alaska! I had filled out all paperwork, completed all forms and sat through all interviews, so I thought that there was very little that they'd have to say to me in that recruiting office that I didn't already know. When my name was called, I stood up, approached the desk and opened my mouth to speak as I tried to hand my papers to the steely-eyed Military figure sitting behind an equally steely desk but he just stood up and came around toward me, ignoring the outstretched hand that was holding my Golden Fleece. Then, he turned me around by the shoulder and aimed me none-to-gently toward another overly-air-conditioned medium size room which was nearly filled with another whole set of nervous young men, little different from the first roomful.

The smell of sweat permeated everything there, too, and even liberal additions of Right Guard Spray Deodorant and the occasional whiff of Jade East could not hide it. I took a chair and waited again as I had waited in the first room. When four other unfortunates entered and filled the last chairs, the large-size Mute holding the clipboard glanced at the clock, stood at the front of the crowd and broke his silence as he spoke in a loud, authoritative voice.

"You will now stand," . . . . he waited until we did, " . . . and then remove all of your clothing, folding it neatly and placing the clothing items on the seat of the chair you were formerly occupying. Put any paperwork you have brought along on top of your clothing and stand at attention." He then stood in what I believe was called an

"At Ease" position and waited for us to comply. Some of the more, shall we say, 'sheltered' young men hesitated but for those of us for whom human nudity was no big deal, myself included, well, we just stripped and stood and waited. It was clear to me that no one was interested in my documents, or anyone else's for the moment, anyway. They stood guard on top of my little pile of clothes.

"Now aren't you glad you wore clean underwear?" . . . . the unspoken voices of myriad mothers spiked through the air and hung there . . . she was right. You never knew . . . .

It appeared there were about 50 of us, I reckoned as I glanced around me. The paperwork on all the chairs looked pretty much alike and that fact made me think that we, The Elect 50, might just be here for the same reason: medical assignments, and that I was no more or no less special than my erstwhile nekkid companions.

"Now, pick up your paperwork and form a circle," our leader instructed and we did so. Then, as if on some silent command, the door opened and in came four Doctor-looking guys with white lab coats . . . they had clipboards too. They began at the 12 o'clock position with the desk as high noon; one set of three started to go around clockwise and the other one, counter-clockwise and as they began going around our circle, they asked a barrage of questions and randomly probed, poked and peered at each subject in turn. I could hear all that was being said, although the nearest Doc had started a couple of guys ahead of me. I was positioned at about 10 minutes after noon (or midnight). I was not sure which.

When the spokesman of the four got to me, I started to explain that I was an Intern and that my paperwork relieved me of any possibility of needing a physical but he just said, "Bend over," without even making eye-contact. Well, I knew that the doctors doing the physicals were there because they had to be and even though they seemed to know we were Docs-in-Training and therefore future kindred spirits, it didn't seem to matter or improve their attitudes; they were all business and no bedside manner at all!

Now, I didn't expect to be woo-ed for crying out loud, but a spark of humanity would have been nice, especially because we were standing there in only the covering God gave us and that alone was disconcerting enough. Their manner was brusque and mechanical for the most part . . . things I planned *never* to do; of course, I *was* a bit idealistic . . . nearly out of a grueling Internship in the City of Angels where I had met darn few angels and had 'way too much of the 'city' part.

We were treated not much different from a bunch of lab monkeys, instead of being prepared by Uncle Sam's finest for our life's work of helping and healing the masses but in the meantime, we stood there, none too happy about it, in a chilly room on cold linoleum. In times such as that, believe me, there is no *good* place to be looking, so, averting my eyes so as not look as if I was looking at anything, I kept my eyes on one guy that was meandering around behind the circle, nodding to himself and making notes on his clipboard. There was another guy about 3 feet in front of us, too, asking all the questions. What the one giving the 'eye tests' could see at that range was beyond me, especially since I am 6'4" and he was about 5'4".

After some time it seemed that every one of us passed whatever the cursory inspection had ascertained and it was over and permission was given to put our underwear back on (at least!) then each name was called quickly. All left the room except me. I was directed into yet another cold little room where, after unsuccessfully trying to don more than just underwear, another Doc looked closely at the scar on my right knee and inquired thereof . . . . he did take my papers, however! Finally! . . . and handed them off to another uniformed person. Then he directed me through a bunch of calisthenics while still partially dressed. Can't imagine that was lovely to look upon and it sure wasn't a paramount moment in MY life either.

Whether I passed or not, I never learned, nor even what 'passed' meant at that juncture. I just dressed, took the sheaf of orders that was handed to me, made sure I had the originals plus the other mysterious packets and files that had been given over to me along the way and adjourned to a quiet spot nearby and began to read the words that would determine my future. EUREKA!!!

I would be on Medical Assignment out of Anchorage! Congress had appropriated something like $1 million (in 1960's money, which in today's economy might buy a weeks' groceries and a tank full of gas) for the war on TB, then after finishing the last two months of my internship in Riverside, it was time to go train for my upcoming assignment.

So, I folded my frame into our little VW beetle and prepared to head south to Atlanta for 2 weeks of TB training. Kisses and hugs goodbye and with the expected tears, I left Phyllis and the boys to wait in Phoenix and visit the folks while I trained. Phyllis had much more to do than just wait, as she made all the arrangements to close the apartment plus a million-and-one other details pertaining to the next few years of our lives.

The University of Georgia in Rome was the premier facility in America, focusing on TB and was home to the Tuberculosis Division of Health Services. The specialized training on the treatment and elimination tuberculosis was the best in the nation and the University also worked in conjunction with the prestigious Centers for Disease Control in Atlanta. The in-depth education I was going to get there would affect my life for the next few years but what exactly that would be was unbeknownst to me at the time.

When I reached Atlanta and reported for duty, the first detour in the road of my sure and certain future lay in wait for me. I was informed that the Alaska post of my dreams was not open anymore, and I had been *mis*-informed before, due to a clerical error. As the days of training passed, I learned that I would be sent eventually to either Des Moines Iowa, very near to where I had grown up, or, the Tri-City Queens Hospital in New York, or some place in Nebraska I had never even heard of, and which sounded about as exciting as watching paint dry.

My mind was in a fog and I didn't know what to think, so I didn't. I just put all thoughts of Alaska out of my mind and immersed myself in the specialized training offered me in Atlanta. Phyllis was telling me long-distance on our weekly phone calls, that, after all, I would be doing what I wanted to do: be a doctor, so what difference did the location make? Not all the Happy Talk in the world would change the fact that Alaska had been our fondest hope and would have been the reward for my years of training. It was a huge disappointment.

We both knew that where I would be stationed made a huge difference in her life, too. We had sacrificed so much time, money, and energy over the last year of my internship so that I could learn everything possible, thinking that I might have to face a myriad of problems in Alaska, 'way out in the boonies. All these thoughts and more swirled about in my mind and the only clarity I felt was when I was alone in my dorm-type accommodations on my knees in prayer. Then, I would open my mind and heart and soul to my Father, and in return, I was given peace of mind . . . . mostly.

The last day of 2-week training dawned clear and bright and brought with it news that was too good to be believed, for, by the time I was finished in Atlanta, the Alaska post had opened up again, and we never heard the reason why or how, but I received the appointment! Gee whiz! Do ya' think it was maybe the power of prayer???? Hmmmm? *

Sincere prayer and the pledging of many oaths . . . even bargaining with the Lord had played a big part in my constant daily mental ritual and I knew that Phyllis was praying, too. I found out later that Phyllis had taught our little boys to pray, "please, Father in Heaven, make it so we can go to Alaska . . ." Of course, at their tender ages and with their developing enunciation, it sounded more like they were asking "Peez Fodder, bwess Daddy an'peez, we wanna goes to Owassa." As long as it worked . . . . and I knew HE could understand them anyway.

Prayer and luck were involved, I'm sure, and they both served me well in this appointment; with the war going on, despite the fact that Health Department's wages were not all that good, newly-hatched Docs were scurrying to get in to Health Department jobs and that even included jobs in Alaska! Figuring it was a choice between bullets and frostbite, Alaska was lookin' good and lookin' good to many people besides me! I had made application for this particular position months before, but it was still a miracle and a great blessing to have landed in the very area we wanted. Ecstatic, I drove back to Phoenix, picked up an equally ecstatic Phyllis and two totally unconcerned little boys and prepared to head North to Owassa! Our expedition had begun!

We still had only the Volkswagen Beetle at that time and we loaded it with what warm clothes we had. Phyllis the Serene had bought the little boys the warmest clothes she could find in August in Phoenix. This was yet another example of her enormous *faith:* she had been confident we would be going north and had prepared as best she could. The next few weeks were hectic; we packed, unpacked, rearranged, and finally filled up every nook and cranny of the little beast with the necessities of life.

Most of what we called 'our good things', wedding presents and items we didn't want to bring to Alaska . . . china, golf clubs, tents, scuba gear . . . stuff like that, were put in storage for another time and place. We filled the VW and loaded it with whatever would be practical and warm!

* NOTE: I had originally left out the part where prayer and fasting were involved; Phyllis and I were not the only ones doing the double-duty, high-powered praying. Our family members were praying, too, but perhaps, it occurred to us long after we had come back from Alaska, that just maybe there were other prayers going up! Other 'pray-er's', requesting that we DIDN'T move ourselves and out two little boys all the way-and-the-heck up to Alaska . . . . maybe those prayers negated the other prayers . . . and . . . . well, the Lord must have known the best path for us. He always does.

No lover of cold weather, Phyllis put on her long johns as soon as we hit the Canadian border.

We had picked up our travel allowance in San Francisco just prior to leaving. Phyllis had proposed that we just fly and buy everything we needed when we got to Alaska, but I felt that we would need to keep our trustworthy vehicle and besides, I wanted to see the country . . . I had been cooped up so long, it felt great to be outdoors, even if it was in an unbelievably over-packed V-dub. I won that battle . . . . we said goodbye to the 100-degree weather and headed north! . . . to Alaska . . . ! (Well, technically, northwest with the California detour) but *north,* nonetheless) to Alaska! Hooray!

We reached the Canadian Border August 13, 1966; it was getting noticeably colder so we bought some sleeping bags from an outdoor outfitter store in an unremembered town on the way. The next day, we hit Mile-marker Zero on the Alcan Highway at Dawson Creek. One of the first memorable things we saw was a huge bear draped over a jeep parked at a service station. It was dead of course, but that didn't make it look any smaller to Phyllis. She had a morbid fear of b-e-a-r-s, despite her longing to live in the wilderness. She took one long look at it, turned to me and pleaded, "I hear the bears get even bigger further north . . . please, please let's ditch the car and fly from here!" Too late now.

The countryside was beautiful, however it rained quite often and beginning on the first day, but that turned out to be a blessing on the Alcan Highway as it kept the miserable dust down so that we could breathe air that we could not actually see or taste for a change! The gravel road was awful . . . like a poorly maintained detour for the whole 1200 miles. We could make only about 200 miles per day and since that was about the average, regardless of the type vehicles traversing it, we got acquainted with our fellow travelers. The few and far-between gas stations had more and more familiar faces, and we smiled and were smiled at back by a remarkably diverse collection of folks traveling in the same direction, and at the same breathtaking speed as we were. We engaged in idle chatter with them while waiting for the gas tanks to fill, or the time it took to purchase whatever necessities the little ones needed to sustain them for another 100 miles.

We met teachers, construction workers, environmentalists, loggers, or people going up for other types of employment who already had a home waiting there and would live either in Anchorage or in one of the smaller Eskimo villages. We all felt like we had made fast friends—very fast. It was rather like a 20th century wagon train . . . all the glowing faces, filled with wonder and the promise of a new life, a life not overshadowed by the polarity and discord of the Lower 48, and nurtured under the expanse of breathtaking scenery, enveloped by the crisp, clean Alaskan sky. Yeah. Right.

The last 50-mile stretch of road was just plain awful: when we thought it could get no worse, we got off the Canadian Alcan and onto the American section. This part was being torn up to be re-surfaced in the name of Highway Improvement. In fact, Phyllis drove right through one of those 'improvements', which just happened to be a barricade, disguising itself as a pile of rocks that caved in the front of our VW. Nothing was damaged much except her ego . . . our little 'Dub' just kept moving on down the road . . . .

Contrary to doubts that we would arrive with our sanities (or marriage) intact, we got into Anchorage about midnight after 10 days on the road. It was still daylight. Did I mention we had brought our two little darlings?? . . . . one in diapers . . . oh, yes, I guess I did. Oh, and lest we forget, this was back in the Stone Age *before* disposable diapers! Sorry Kit and Kyle, but I doubt if you boys retained much in the way of memories of that time, either. If you're lucky . . . .

We found a modest (read 'cheap') motel in Anchorage and stayed there for a few days until we could find our way around and some place to rent. We were really short of money as it had taken about all of the travel allowance we had picked up in San Francisco just to get what we had needed and to get us up to Alaska. We didn't want to borrow, having gone all the way through Medical school and my Internship without borrowing any money. Too chancy for me was the usual route that aspiring doctors took, borrowing to the hilt and then finding themselves $20K (1960's dollars) or more in debt at age 25 and with no job yet . . . . scary.

Renting an apartment in Anchorage turned out to be a mistake: we were politely invited to vacate our first apartment, due to the enthusiasm and gusto with which our two little boys embraced life . . . (which is a nice way of saying they were really noisy!) and it became obvious that apartment living just wasn't for us. We found a neat little house for rent on two acres of beautiful land. It cost $275 a month, which was exorbitant, but we really loved that place. It was close to the Hospital, too. Over the course of fall and winter, the snow got 6 feet deep around our domicile and the pipes froze with great regularity when "we" forgot to leave a tap running, costing $18 for a sort-of-plumber to come blow-torch them, *each* and *every* time we left the house . . . .

Oh, but it was worth it: sometimes we would see moose walking around in the yard. Once, I got my camera and went running up behind one old bull taking flash pictures of him. I was chasing after him in my down underwear and little else and must have looked like a freak to the neighbors.

We made a skating rink in the back yard by flooding it with the garden hose and had a ball skating and teaching the boys how. Finally, a home . . . . a pleasant and comfortable and safe home. It lent an air of stability that was soothing and settling and healing for Phyllis and the boys, as well. We were a family now: Doc and Family and we were aimed in the direction we knew was right for us. From this lighthouse, I could wander out and the beam of light that was and is my family would guide me back home . . . back home.

CHAPTER 2

. . . AND NOW, FOR THE REAL REASON
WE FIND OURSELVES HERE

My official assignment was to the State Health Department at Anchorage as a TB control officer. My duties were to "detect and treat tuberculosis among the indigent population, including but not limited to the Eskimos, Aleuts and Indians and all of the Alaskan natives."

There were widespread and severe health problems; I had read all the limited material I could on the subject and it was true. I was soon to find out in person, that due to widespread over-crowding in the homes and other key issues, the spread of TB was rampant. There are always hotbeds of TB in situations of poverty, malnutrition, crowding, and less-than-adequate sanitation, *wherever* they may be in the world.

Tuberculosis is a slow-developing condition; some germs multiply every twenty minutes, with staph germs, maybe every hour or so, but TB multiplies once every twenty-four hours. With this slow growth, people don't usually get very sick at first because the body can tolerate slow changes and adapts to them. If something grows in a hurry, it lets its presence be known with physical distress and the victim seeks help. Tuberculosis gets into a person's system usually from inhaling a 'bug' coughed out of somebody else's lungs and if this is the first exposure, there won't be anything more that just a cold-type syndrome. After a bit, the person will be sick for a little while and then the TB will isolate, usually in the lungs. This is very common in children and young people and most of the time that's it and it just stops right there. If one gets a real aggressive case, however, it ends up causing pneumonia—tuberculin pneumonia—and this is very difficult to clear up.

From ancient times, there was no active treatment; wealthy patients would just lie around, usually in a sanatorium (under the best of circumstances) with plenty of rest and fresh air, maybe spending 20 years in bed. In the poverty-stricken population, the patient just wasted away and died, and in great numbers too at particular times in history.

The antibiotics isoniazide, ethambutol, para amino salycilic acid and streptomycin were the Big Four when I was treating it in Alaska, and thanks to modern medicine, they changed all of that. TB was still serious but generally not fatal if diagnosed and treated early.

The disease had been brought over to Alaska by Russian explorers in the 1600's when they originally set up trading posts for the fur industry in Alaska. This, too, seemed par for the course, for whenever a new land gets "discovered" and then "conquered" and then "civilized", it soon sees it's original inhabitants scooted over and bunched up and pushed out of the way. These things are followed by social programs and actions to replace what was taken, depending on the geographic locale. Then, the 'nurturing' governmental agencies systematically strip customs and life-styles and inundate family life, making the "new and improved" people more in keeping with the label 'Civilized'.

Enough soapbox. Back to TB . . . .

It's a very old disease: there are mummies dating back 4000 years that have tuberculosis of the spine. The Hunchback of Notre Dame probably had TB in addition to other problems. It was called consumption, in some forms, back in the Middle Ages and was so common among the high social circles, too, that it became stylish and the pale and languid look that accompanied it was greatly sought after. Oh, now really! Does that sound odd? Stop rolling your eyes! That's not so unusual! Remember Twiggy? From the 1960's? . . . and most of the present fashion models?

Ten years before I came up, I found out that almost *every* kid starting school had a positive TB test, which means they *had been exposed* to the TB bacteria! If they were exposed, they were much more likely to get tuberculosis pneumonia and this left what are called 'cavities' in the lungs. They're contagious and they cause a person to hack and spit all the time, making it *really* contagious and it spreads like wildfire. After treating a patient in the hospital, they were sent home, following two clear consecutive sputum tests and we checked the patient every month thereafter and treated him for up to two years, to be sure. If the patient went home to a crowded house full of relatives who were all hacking and spitting, re-infection was almost certain.

In a town called Emmonak, there was one man, Tony Sugar, who had us trailing him for two years. He didn't know, of course, and we didn't know who he was yet; some people just went back and forth, from village to village, infecting people. We figured after it all came out that there had been at least 18 cases of active TB that we could trace to Tony Sugar. He was the 'Typhoid Mary' of the Arctic.

The skin test is a neat way to assess; if it is negative, the person has never been exposed to TB. We would go around and put in the shots in the kids' arms and check the results in forty-eight hours to 72-hours. If we then found positive skin tests, we would start looking for the person who was infecting them. They were called converters; and it was a little like detective work, as the converters needed to be traced and found and treated.

In some of the villages, over *half* of the adults had spent time in a hospital with TB! Facilities simply ran out of beds and room in Alaska. At one point in the 1950's, many, many patients were transported down the 48 states to Chicago, Seattle, Denver, and other places. It was a terrible period for the native people as they not only had a hard time adapting to white man's food, but some simply died of homesickness. TB caused social problems, for some young people had been literally without parenting for a span of years, and they grew up kind of by themselves and on their own, without guidance or family togetherness. What tragedies it caused, socially as well as physically, and for so many generations after!

It was a good time for me to arrive when I did; Doctor Bob Frazier, who was a chest specialist, together with several other doctors, had set up the very active TB Department of Anchorage. The rate of TB cases per capita in the US proper was around fourteen or fifteen per 100,000, where as Alaska actually had a rate of nearly 350 per 100,000!

Now, we are talking of about a lot of people being really sick! The last year I was there, the rate had dropped to around 40-50 cases per thousand, which, although above the national average, was actually below some of the ghetto numbers in NYC and Detroit and the like. We just stomped all over it!

Actually, just to be specific here, I didn't work for the State Health department but was 'loaned' to them by the Communicable Disease Center in Alaska, which was a division of the Health Service. Although I was stationed in Anchorage those first two years, I didn't really spend much time in Anchorage . . . mostly I traveled out to the small villages which were really under the Division of Indian Health.

The two years I was TB Officer in Anchorage were really good; I planned my own trips and had a credit card to pay for my travel; I went wherever I wanted and I never had to answer to anybody except the Atlanta Office of the CDC. As long as I was doing my job and my reports showed that TB rates were going down, everything was copasetic.

Back during my internship the year before, I had put in several months doing different rotations, including some extra training in dental surgery and anesthesiology. I could perform basic dental work and extractions as well as regional anesthetizing and felt marginally competent. During my internship, I would run down to the ER every chance I had and got involved in whatever was going on down there, learning as much of anything I could when my regular work was completed. I tried to soak up as much as I could because I didn't want to get into serious trouble when I *did* get out into the remote villages I hoped to be practicing in and wanted to be proficient enough to handle whatever came across.

What an incredible time it was: we were young and healthy and we were going to a place we'd dreamed of going and we, Phyllis and I, would be doing the things that we had dreamed of *doing*, too. It was my chosen profession to go out and do Good Things outside the home and earn money to support my family and it was Phyllis' chosen profession to be a full-time mother and contribute to the world by producing fine, upstanding citizens.

We were both idealistic and still are to some degree today. Older, wiser, some dreams have died as have some loved ones, but the idealism remains . . . .

Our religion teaches that service to others is of paramount importance and finally I got to be a Doc and really *help* people. I did not, and still do not, feel much kinship for people who just continue to go to school, getting degree after degree, and never actually get out and help people . . . especially if the person is going to school on scholarships. I have always felt I owed a debt to society as I had been blessed with the means to train to be a physician, treat people, and save lives and I darned well better get out there and *heal!!* I've been blessed far beyond my capacity, and I feel, in all humility, that my life has had a purpose and a mission. Never did I feel that more than when I was a doctor in Alaska . . . .

Ain't life great! We were in Alaska and the whole, vast, frozen state was just waiting for me to tackle it head-on! Oh, yeah . . . I was young and idealistic and I wanted to save the world.

"ROMOLO TOMBLOO, A LOVELY LADY FROM GAMBEL VILLAGE, ON ST. LAWRENCE ISLAND." NOTE THE FACIAL TATOOING WHICH WAS COMMON THEN.

"TYPICAL VILLAGE ELDER ON HIS SNOW MACHINE"

CHAPTER 3

IN THE BEGINNING . . .

The first thing I did after getting my family settled was to go about organizing my office. I really wasn't considered a *practicing* physician at the Hospital in Anchorage because I wouldn't be spending much of my time there . . . mostly I'd be out in the field. I got established there, just going around meeting people and learning what was going on and where things were and who was who and what was what. I went without a phone at first and that was a hassle (pre-cell phone days!) so one of the guys on staff that I had got to know took pity on me and knew someone who called someone else and said "Hey, we have a new Doc here and he needs a phone."

And that was that.

Sharing the building office space at the hospital was a Civil Service guy who was stationed with the Air Force Base in Anchorage. He was a pompous fellow and it appeared that he didn't play well with others and it *also* appeared his ill-tempered manner did not serve him well, because he'd been there 6 months and had not made any friends, it seemed . . . just the opposite, as I was to find out.

The service personnel who had to work with him and work around his obnoxious attitude used their little power trips in the only way they could, so, the regional telephone service had put him on "installation-pending" status which must be just what it sounds like. It was like he had been 'on hold' for half a year and he was NOT taking it well. You can just imagine the calls he made to

Customer Service and the nastier he got, the more time stretched on. The bunch of hospital personnel I worked with and who I was really starting to know and enjoy, gleefully relayed this information to me. Vicious and delicious!

Several of us were sitting at a big table in the cafeteria a few weeks after my arrival and because it was a public area, he sat down with us, and we had no choice than to listen to him rant on and on with his usual load of grief. I got an itch to aggravate him, so I waited until there was a lull in the conversation and made a comment that, "Boy, the telephone service is really slow around here . . . you know, it took me two whole days to get a private line," I said, emphasizing the 'private' part . . . .

He absolutely went into orbit and started raving about these so-and-so's, blank-idy-blank doctors who got their phones right away while really important people with LOTS of business to transact, like him, had to wait and wait! I put on my best Innocent Face and commiserated with him, much to the amusement of the cafeteria audience . . . .

~~~~~~~~~~~~

My journal tells me that on November 10th of 1966 I made my very first village trip to a place called Alakanuk; it's a little over a 1000 miles from Anchorage toward the west and a bit north. One thousand miles . . . on . . . 'rounds' . . . . wow!

So, on this first trip into the field, four of us docs packed into a 180 which is a pretty good trick, especially if one of the six was *me* and with my size. Each of the rural clinics that I was going to would have an SUD doctor—called the Service Unit Director; he administered a small hospital along with the duties of a Head Doctor. At Tanana, the Doc was Kent Jones and his wife was Becky. These clinics had living quarters, but it was customary to invite the visiting doctor to dinner and this little social function was enjoyed by all of us.

As we sat down to dinner, Kent said he would say the blessing, which was not uncommon, but when he ended the prayer with "In the name of Jesus Christ, Amen". I looked up and said, "Well, I'll be darned, you guys must be Mormon!" It turned out, they *were* from Utah so we had a lot to talk about that evening. My boss got tired and excused himself and went to bed which turned out to be he opposite of our future trips when 'we' stayed up as long as 'he' was in charge of the conversation and it was me who wound up in a corner trying to stay awake.

The trip home was normal and uninteresting . . . the Elastic (Alaska) Airlines gave a normal flight, ending in a twenty-mile-an-hour crosswind landing. It was not exactly what I had imagined but I was still positive and eager to continue.

The next trip placed me in Fairbanks, to see my first clinic. This was handled differently than the usual clinics, however, as the patients were *flown in* from surrounding villages which was actually cheaper and handier than going out, packing all of the necessary equipment to see maybe ten people in five outlying, remote villages. Most often, these were inactive TB cases that had been out of the hospital less than a year who needed follow-up care and reminders to take their medicine and follow the cleanliness guidelines that would keep them healthy. This trip, I was flown out and back the same day and it was a pleasantly routine trip: on time, no engine fires or failures, no landing gear mishaps or anything. I found out that frequent fliers liked to say that Elastic Airlines had 'two turnings and two burnings,' as far as the engines went.

~~~~~~~~~~~~~~

My memories of that first year were orchestrated by the voices crying out, 'The Doctor is here!' Everyone was very welcoming and excited and I was really in my element. It was a rewarding experience and it was working in the first villages and all the others that satisfied my desire to serve others. On my first trip to the little community of Alakanuk, Frank Damien was the Health Aid and he came out and picked me up from the plane with a Snow machine. It was about a half-mile from the landing strip to the clinic and I had a lot of gear to haul in . . . I think he enjoyed my visit, too: the Doc was there and Frank was the official spokesman. The villagers could not speak enough English, so he translated.

The decision that gave me the most trouble in the first months of my Alaska assignment was that I was faced with, in many instances, whether to send my patients to a larger hospital or not. Tanana Hospital was responsible for the health and hospital needs of a large number of people . . . figures vary from six to ten thousand villagers, and they were all wards of the government, especially in the medical sense, as they had free health care. Travel money came out of the budgets of the local doctors but it was never enough.

At the end of every fiscal year on June 30, typically, the travel budget had run out in April or May or even sooner; the patients had a choice, after they got through with their hospitalization, one being waiting there if we had plenty of beds and food but had no money to get them home. Or, they could find their own way home. Some patients would come into Tanana and just wait around in the town . . . staying with friends or family . . . and wait until the next budget-year rolled around! It cost from thirty to seventy-five dollars to buy a patient a seat on a mail plane and about $300 to charter a plane to transport him. It was a sticky problem deciding fairly whether the patient would be best handled at home, by the clinic, or should the patient be sent to the hospital for more expert and constant care.

In the early clinics, I would soon find that I felt swamped and it seemed there was always a waiting-room-full of 50 people or more . . . a capacity crowd . . . and seemingly the same 50 people we saw day after day . . . waiting. Translating was so tedious, it made the whole process as slow as molasses for everyone. The older people spoke very little English or, I soon found out, didn't want to because they were bashful. They all smelled like fish. People had chests full of pneumonia for which I prescribed Ampicillin, but did not hospitalize, as I probably would have done anywhere else, because the hospital was just not a good idea in so many cases. They lived, for the most part, lives so grim that any diversion was grasped eagerly, even a medical visit, but going to stay at a faraway Hospital was NOT a viable option for every patient.

According to monetary standards of that day, I must have used and dispersed close to $1000 in medical supplies at every little village, for which no patient paid a dime and yet, there was never enough to treat everything completely. The fact was that I used bum stuff from anywhere I could find it, from friends in the business in Anchorage, manufacturer's samples, or I'd go to the

Hospital and try to beg, borrow or steal stuff out of the pharmacy for these people. I sometimes relate to the television program M.A.S.H on cable, as many of their maneuvering escapades remind me of what it was like for me back then: manipulating the system to get what was necessary for my needs. Bottom line always: THE PATIENT!

Alakanue was the place that I made my first house call; I took a Health Aide named Francis, and although at first, he was unwilling to go, as I was interfering with his mink trapping. But he got paid for being an Aide and so he did. The patient lived in a one-room house across the slough from the tiny clinic. I followed Francis; he just opened the door and walked right in. I banged my head on the doorframe, announcing our presence. There was only one small room with two tiny, high windows and it had little cot-like beds all around two walls, with one larger bed in the middle.

The apparent man of the house was sloshing clothes around in a bucket without visible scrubber or soap. I could see that there were several kids scattered about but they hardly looked up when we came stumbling in, my glasses fogged up from the moist heat. After a moment, the mist cleared, I could see the patient was lying in the bigger bed and I was told that she had been in a lot of abdominal pain for 3 days . . . initially that sounded like a ruptured appendix. After the initial exam, my diagnosis was confirmed, so I started her on a high dosage of antibiotics to be continued, and also arranged for her to be sent to the hospital, along with another woman I had seen in the clinic earlier that day who had a case of active tuberculosis. There was another woman who came to the clinic that day and I thought that she either had a brain tumor or was just crazy . . . I couldn't tell which and wasn't willing to take a chance. It had been a busy day.

~~~~~~~~~~~~~

It was appalling for me, at first, to go to areas and into homes where *all* the children had sore and infected ears and there was an obvious lack of knowledge some grownups had about the problem. I finally understood that when it takes so much time to provide a family with just the essentials, people with large families and large responsibilities don't have much left to give, especially if they are not in the best of health, either. Self-perpetuating misery! Providing medical care in some places, I found, involved teaching as well as treating.

Right away on this first trip, I found out word had gotten around that I was Mormon; I guess it was because I was the only person in the area drinking Kool-Aid instead of coffee for breakfast and using hot water for bouillon cubes and cocoa. My religion didn't seem to matter much after the first introduction though; people just were glad to get help.

Also learned on this Maiden Voyage about the loathsome but essential honeypots found in almost every house I visited. Think about it: you can't dig down through the permafrost layer that is only a foot or so under the ground, for an outhouse, and the little villages had no such thing as a sewer or even septic system, of course. Many 'towns' consisted of just a dozen huts. The only option was the option they used, called honeypots or honey buckets; they are generally made from 5-gallon metal or heavy plastic buckets with or without a one-piece toilet seat or wooden frame for sitting. The top was cut out of the bucket, the seat mounted, an inch or two of Pine Sol was poured in the bottom and it was ready for service. I still can't stand the smell of Pine Sol to this day as it brings back too many stomach-churning exposures to the nasty things. There wasn't really anything else to be done, however. People did what they could. Problem was, although they were taken outside when they got full, daily or weekly, depending on the number of folks using them, they were dumped out onto the icepack, as there were no municipal resources for proper disposal in almost all areas. In the spring, when the ice broke up, it carried the gory cargo out to sea. Everyone prayed sincerely for a good east wind to hurry it along, too! A west wind would blow the mess back on to the beach, and the rest of the warm weather is made miserable thereafter . . . .

Some friends we made, who we came to know quite well, were living in a remodeled mobile home, and had this particular convenience. You can imagine that there's much drawing of straws to decide who gets to haul it out and *no one* is in a hurry to be the one who gets the privilege to do the dirty deed. One time, the story goes, it was the man of the houses' turn to take it out . . . he lost the draw or whatever. Now, up in the far North, the ice is super slick because the dry and granular snow blows across it almost constantly and polishes it so well that it is almost impossible to walk across without cramp-ons on your shoes; those are the straps-with-metal-claw things mountain climbers use. You see where this story is going, don't you??? Well, this fine fellow came around the corner of the trailer house, toting his load of woe and probably thinking about something else. He hit the ice, he hit the skids, and the honeybucket went straight up . . . then the honeybucket went straight down and it showered all over the unfortunate guy.

Instantly, he was covered, sort of like those ice cream cones dipped in chocolate! Because it was 30 degrees below zero with a strong wind, the contents 'set' almost immediately and he was coated in a most unpleasant 'crust' from head to toe. He went creeping and crackling up to the closest door but his wife wouldn't let him in the front room so he made his way around to the back porch and she met him there. He stripped off his stiff clothes, and then, because the chill factor was probably 100-degrees below zero, she yanked him in to soak in a hot bathtub and turned on the exhaust fan. For an hour. It took at least that long, they told us, to get him thawed out and aired out. The clothes were not salvageable and ended up a sacrifice to the 'Great Spirit of the Honeybucket' and they just kicked some snow over the spot where the deed had been done . . . or undone . . . and tried to forget all about it . . . until spring thaw . . . .

~~~~~~~~~~~~~

The Yukon River is 1,500 miles long and it brings down a tremendous amount of driftwood from the Alaskan Interior regions, back up toward British Columbia. A huge amount is deposited along the mouth of the river even though lots of it still goes out to sea. The villagers along the seaside use the ever-replenishing driftwood for firewood. At a village called Emmonak, it seemed that the 400 or so resident's burn frozen willows when the driftwood was scarce or too frozen solid to use. The willows will burn because the ice in them is crystallized; this was a very isolated and primitive village, obviously, barely living above the subsistence level.

My first house call there was about three miles down the road from the village of Emmonak, near a frozen lagoon; I got there using a Skidoo snow machine. I ended up performing a rectal exam on an old, bedridden woman who lived alone in a wretched hut; she had a horrible case of hemorrhoids and bathing for her was just not possible. This visit might be considered one of the low points in my medical career as there were just so many things wrong and so little I could do . . . I could only treat her problem and leave ample supplies for later. She was not 'ill enough' to admit to the hospital, plus taking her out of her home and into the confines of a hospital setting would not have been a positive thing nor appropriate under the circumstances. So, I was limited to making notes to refer her situation to some social service network who could perhaps improve her standard of living. It was hard to shut the door and leave that pitiful old lady, who I could only hope would feel a *little* better for the care I had been able to give her.

Helping the sick and injured in the ER and treating patients where they live are poles apart . . . there was so little I could do for her . . . I had done my best but it threw a dark cloud over the rest of my rounds . . . it probably wasn't a great day for her, either.

One high point of the trip to that particular village is that I met a Mr. Clem who subsequently became my good and valued friend. I learned a lot from him; he was very wise and so knowledgeable about many things; he made fishnets and fashioned them in such a way that he could break up the ice on the lagoon and place the nets underwater and then just pull them in every evening. While I was there, he pulled in three good-size fish which he called 'Shee' fish; they were very tasty, reminding me of halibut. He managed to keep his family fed all winter with these fish and I was to catch and eat many more during my months in Alaska.

∿∿∿∿∿∿∿∿∿∿∿∿

V.I.S.T.A., which stands for Volunteer in Service to America, was very popular at that time and volunteers were high in number in many of the places I visited, wherever they were located. The impression my many contacts with the 'vistas' left me was that they were usually young women and men who were idealistic and seemed to advocate free-thinking-free-sex-free-love-and-get-what-you-can-and-have-a-good-time-doing-it-far-away-from-home-where-you-can-do-what-you-want . . . with attitude. The sexual apostasy that the popularity of 'the Pill' afforded in the 1960's got packed along in the duffle bags of the kids, it appeared and they seemed to be taking full advantage of it. For most of them, it was the first time they had been away from home and parents for such an extended time, and they acted accordingly. Whoopee!

Perhaps I am being a bit cynical . . . I have to admit that some of them were pretty good kids and they sure were not into it for the money. In Alakanuk, for instance, they initiated and then oversaw the Head Start Program. That was a Very Good Thing at that time and in that place. They were freebies to the town and all the villagers had to do was to put them up and put up with them. One town elder told me, "One thing we gotta do is make sure they don't get lost and freeze to death." That seemed pretty straight-forward.

In the even-smaller villages that had no facilities, the visiting doctors like me stayed with the BIA teachers. At this time, the Bureau of Indian Affairs was just turning the schools over to the State of Alaska but most of the schools were still under the Bureau of Indian Affairs. There were also schools run by various Churches like the Catholic, Friends, Episcopal . . . they all sponsored schools in the larger villages. Generally, the teachers were fine but I met some really weird misfits who had come up to teach either as missionary work or they were running away from a garden-variety of personal problems . . . just like many isolated or sparsely-inhabited places, it seems.

~~~~~~~~~~~~~

Alakanuk had a population of around 300 and is a good-size village, and that is where I 'solo-ed' and set up my first clinic. At that time, it felt to me like I was at the end of the world . . . I'd traveled at 160 miles-per-hour, direct air, across a featureless landscape and as I looked down at the town preparatory to landing, I could just make out a few houses and a snow-covered airstrip. It was snowing heavily still and we came to a scree-e-e-eching halt right on the banks of the Yukon, looking right down into the water!

What a great start! I was elated! So far, this was what I'd envisioned it to be. The flying didn't bother me . . . I had always enjoyed it and usually used the time for power-naps, but it took two hours to unload and transport over 800 pounds of equipment to the village itself. I never saw a plane so loaded in all my life: the idea seemed to be that if you could get the stuff in, you could get it up. I'd been musing during the flight that if we DID crash, how were they going to separate the body parts from the cargo load? . . . it would just be a great big jumbled pile of whatever.

Being totally green on this first assignment and not knowing what to expect, I was grateful for the Public Health Nurse who came along. She had been there before; her name was Lisolotte Offergeld and she was 110% German! Officious in action, she was a compact little blond around 50 years old. She was a very good TB nurse with a lot of experience and was a great help to me on that first trip and many trips after that.

Each of my trips would prove to be different and although TB was the central reason for my being there, my visits ran the gamut from setting up a whole, entire clinic from scratch, complete with individual patient files, to serving every medical need that happened to be in the village. Also, there would be 'need-specific' trips that were only for either observing/recording/treating/prevention/education. Things like that.

On this trip, we were setting up a full-fledged mobile clinic; our duties were simple and straightforward: after reading and reviewing all the charts and records on every patient we had scheduled to see, out we went to see them! Copious and careful notes were made and updated and exams were taken of each patient and usually we were called on to 'look at' other members of the household while we were there.

There was to be a lot of traveling to get to the villages and I was enjoying that, too, even with the numerous problems we ran into . . . well, not problems so much as unexpected challenges . . . sure, that would be more accurate. I was the new guy and felt I had to adjust to some degree to the ways of the others, who had been there longer, but I had the medical *responsibility*, and the buck now stopped with me. I found out as I got more and more accustomed to it all, that eventually, I would be responsible for making all the arrangements to get from point A to point B on every trip, checking to see that there was the correct equipment in the right quantities; it was a bit overwhelming at first.

While I was certainly not a kid, being all of 25 for crying out loud, the whole process was so new that I did have feelings of inadequacy quite often. But the realization that if IT did not get done, IT was my fault, and that fact kept me in a constant state of concern over the IT's . . . but that uneasiness went away after a while and I came to find out I was, after all, capable and responsible enough to handle IT all! Eventually.

There was a rather simple-sounding formula for the TB treatment I was supposed to render, too: when the Eskimo patients in the hospital could produce two sputum samples that were clear of the TB bacteria, they could be released to go back home. Not all of the TB patients came in to the Hospital, though; if it was a primary case and was non-contagious, we treated them in the villages. Much better option, obviously, if it was applied correctly and followed up on.

The journal entries that I kept up while in Alaska are the foundation for this book; some of the entries weren't dated . . . just stories I stuck in when something that I felt was of note happened. The next few pages are bits and pieces of the Alaska I learned to love.

. . . . AND THEN, GOD CREATED THE MOSQUITO. As my first month in Alaska moved quickly towards fall and winter, a Good Thing happened: the mosquitoes started slacking off—everyone sure loved the wind up there, because of the resulting disappearance of the horrid little varmints. Blew them away to Hell, hopefully, as far as everyone unanimously agreed! This tiny-in-size irritant actually took on mammoth proportions for both man and beast, and was a very difficult adjustment that sure proved hard for me to acclimate.

In the summer, those flying pests were so bad that even when a person was covered in OFF, or whatever the choice in bug repellant happened to be, the mosquitoes wouldn't land, that was true, and you rarely got bit, that was true, but, they would still hover so close—without landing—that often they'd be inhaled accidentally, through mouth and/or nose. To get any sleep when out in the boonies, I had to spray not only myself thoroughly but the mosquito netting as well; it would still give me the creeps having to lie there and watch a couple zillion of them land on the netting and keep trying their dead-level best to crawl through . . .

Stories abound that large animals like moose or caribou were sometimes driven crazy and would just surge across the tundra and jump into lakes or lagoons to try and get away from virtual clouds of the horrible little bloodsuckers. This, I had heard about but the next little factoid was new to me: flying low in an airplane through clouds of mosquitoes can result in having to land and clean out the air intake or, even deadly loss of power and an unexpected landing! Yup, all the yarns I heard about the mosquitoes proved to be the truth and not fiction or exaggeration. In addition to the mosquitoes and too obnoxious to be left out are the gnats which *look* like small mosquitoes but without a stinger; I guess Nature tells them to buzz around warm-blooded prey but since they do not sting, they just hover . . . it makes them more maddening than the biting ones, almost.

COLD: The first winter we were there, the cold came in hard and fast and although we expected it, the cold just really socked in and stayed bitter. The depth of the frigid temperatures can't be described . . . it has to be experienced. I had *my* first experience with the damage severe weather can do to the human body and the toll it takes on the unprepared. Seems a couple of young fellows who were traveling on their snow machines found out the truth. A comment someone made that stuck with me was that 'you could *travel* a lot further in a snow machine than you could *walk back* in a day'. Some folks believed Snowmobiles were not as good as dogs, for although you can go further, if you get lost and have to bivouac, you can't cuddle up to your snowmobile . . . or eat it, like you could a dog. Everything had its advantages I guess.

Anyway, these guys were 'way out somewhere hunting and their machines broke down and they hadn't told anyone where they were going, so they found themselves in a bit of a predicament. To make it worse, they were dressed in white man's clothes: cloth shirts and pants and leather boots; they also lacked the skills to stay alive. They got wet and didn't know how to dry out correctly. They didn't pack food or supplies or anything to make a fire because it was only supposed to be a day trip. In short, even though they were born and raised in Alaska, they were not much better off than if a city slicker got dumped in the middle of nowhere . . . really *cold* nowhere.

When they were finally found, one of the guy's legs was frozen *solid* up past his knees; I don't recall how much had to be amputated to keep him alive, but it was drastic. He was flown straight to the big hospital in Anchorage; I heard people comment that if they had an older native guy with them, they would have been alright because the old guys knew how to cope with the severities. Both of the boys had serious injuries, which would then affect them for the rest of their lives, all because they were young and cocky know-it-alls!

~~~~~~~~~~~~~~

MISSIONARIES: When Christian missionaries first came to Alaska from wherever they originated, some of the earliest convinced the natives they were all going to hell if they didn't stop living 'underground', in their efficient, earth-sheltered homes, so the practical and safe method of digging down a little and building up a little went away and traditional huts and wood houses were built. A lot of the Eskimo culture was destroyed when the above-ground homes were built after that . . . they were almost impossible to heat effectively, also and there was a constant threat of fire and everything going up in smoke. That happened much too often.

DON WE NOW . . . : The clothing that most Alaskan folks wore for generations had gone under some tremendous changes when we got there, we learned. In some of the pictures we took, the long, below-the-knee parkas were still being worn. A lot of the decoration on the clothing the Alaskan people crafted was not only attractive but practical as well. The most common parka hoods were lined with wolf fur with a dark trim of wolverine, which had coarse hairs that did not hold the frost as much. Often, men and women alike wore a calico or denim covering over the parka because there was really no way to clean the parka and since it was a work garment, worn when they were fishing and hunting, it was apt to get very soiled. And very fragrant.

The workmanship on the clothing was really wonderful: the stitching was as fine as to be almost invisible and the mukluks were waterproof and no matter how much water you got into, they stayed dry. My treasures of mukluks, moose-skin bottoms and caribou tops that I wore with liners, along with my underwear, were enough and that was all I wore, generally, and stayed perfectly cozy. The caribou liners have the hair on which is hollow and makes almost perfect insulation.

We really bought a lot of stuff over the course of time we spent there but I wish that if I had another whole life to live, I could be a museum curator up there. So many of the arts and crafts we bought were truly treasures and continue to give us much satisfaction even now, showing them to friends and family. They will all go the children and the grandchildren, and some should go to museums.

We have a nice assortment of items we collected. One is a beautiful red fox parka ruff; I have a seal skin with a picture on it, too, that I really like . . . the curing process is interesting: they would take the sealskin and leave it in water for about a week, then hang it outside for about a year where it would hang and flap in the wind and get wet and dry, alternately. Eventually, it was totally cured and looked like white velvet of the highest grade. Then, someone with artistic ability would draw on it. The one I have was made by a young artist, just beginning his career, and whose name I cannot come up with . . . it's one of my favorite possessions; I really cherish it. Early on, I saw many 'new, authentic artifacts' for sale that fooled some people into thinking they had a really old item when it was actually manufactured to look that way . . . .

~~~~~~~~~~~~

Another thing I found really interesting early on in my tenure is the story of the village of Anaktuvik Pass; now, this was a very ancient and primitive place. The life the 200 or so inhabitants endured must have been satisfying, as they seemed to stay and simply replenish their numbers, all while intermarrying and occasionally bringing new blood to the settlement, keeping the status-quo, while still living almost like one big family.

Well, a teacher who was sent up there was concerned at the level of 'social and economic deprivation' she saw (her words), so she initiated classes that taught the natives how to stretch skins on a frame and make masks. When the skins were seasoned and dry, they would form and paint them; each family had its own distinctive mask . . . kind of like a copyright or a Coat of Arms, and many were produced and sold for upwards of $30, at 1960's prices!

It turned out that there was a tremendous market for them: they called them 'dancing masks'. The tourists that saw them in the craft stores in the larger cities all over Alaska were excited to find them because they thought they were like the dancing masks of the Indians in the Southwest, who really DID dance with masks. Eskimos never danced with masks, but, oh well . . . . they sold! And they put Anaktuvik Pass on the map.

One interesting gadget is called 'idiot strings', although I don't know the Eskimo wording. To lose a mitten or glove up there might mean the loss of a hand; the contraption was comprised of long "strings" that came around the body of the wearer, like a harness almost, and attached to the mitten cuff so if they were dropped they were not lost . . . they were essential. I used to know how to tie them properly but I've forgotten.

Then, there is an Eskimo yo-yo, which was a string about a yard—long with a ball of fur at each end. The trick was to grasp it somewhere in the middle and twirl one ball one way and the other in the opposite direction. There is definitely a skill to this and I learned it once and it's a lot of fun, because the average person can watch how it it's done but have a hard time mastering it without the 'secret' of handling it, like a yo-yo!

~~~~~~~~~~~~~

Sometimes, it was necessary to go and pick up patients who lived in far-off villages, places that were still primitive to some degree, even in the 1960's. They needed to come into the TB clinics for treatment for cases that had gone too far for home treatment. Some of these people from far-flung outlying hamlets, had perhaps been in airplanes but few had seen cars or 'regular' houses. Once, on one of these retrieval trips, I jumped down out of the plane when we landed and the four patient-passengers hopped out too and followed me, but when I got into the Travel-All to take them into the hospital, they just stood there and looked at it. Finally, it dawned on me that they didn't know how to open the door, so I got out and showed them and then helped them in. All of this was accomplished in a pidgin sort of sign language, as they did not speak English and, although I was in Alaska for four years, learning all of the dozens of dialects that were spoken there was not something I was able to do. Well, when we all got to the clinic, it was the first large building they had been in and their eyes got big as they looked and looked! I went to get someone who could stay with them and take care of them and when I returned, they had moved all the chairs back and were sitting on the floor on their outer clothes, just like they world do at home.

Once, I flew out to pick up a young kid because the Village Health Aide had called in and said he was having severe belly pain and she could not treat it there. I flew out and got him in the plane and back to Kotzebue; when we landed, I exited the plane by jumping, but before I could turn around to help him out, he jumped, too, and he had a raging case of appendicitis! I had diagnosed it correctly, and it really must have hurt like anything, jarring up all of that inflammatory mass in his belly! I understood that the Eskimo people seemingly had high thresholds of pain but what a stoic he was and so young! Turns out, not only did I have to take out his highly inflamed organ, but a good bit of the lower intestine, too, but he survived and thrived!

A lot of my diagnosis relied on x-ray clarification; I had a portable x-ray machine that usually traveled with me everywhere and I would set it up in a closet or a tent I brought for just that purpose if there wasn't another small, dark place where it would work. Most of the villages had power generators for electricity but that was all there was, so when I took a picture, everyone knew it, for the whole village would go dark for a few moments!

Sometimes, I had to take a transformer with me to make up for whatever the machine would need; a lot of the bigger schools had generators, too. Back then, with the smaller generators, you had to leave a light on because you had to draw the power off when it was not being utilized.

Some villages just turned off the power plant if they were running short on fuel for it. At eight or nine at night, almost all of the towns would turn it off, regardless.

Some of the towns had privately-owned generators; I think the store-owner in the town of Marshall had one which he ran at about 110 volts instead of 120. That burned out the globes pretty fast, but then, he had globes for sale in his store. Hmmmm. That struck me as rather odd. Profitable, I guess, for him.

~~~~~~~~~~~~~~

The little things I had taken for granted all of my life sure grew in value as did my appreciation of them. At Point Hope, as in many places I would visit, there was no running water, so I would take my cup and put in about a half-cup of water and use that to brush my teeth. I know that B.A. (before Alaska), I would just let it run in the bowl, using probably at least a gallon.

~~~~~~~~~~~~~~

Point Hope was my destination for one trip. After flying in, despite the rotten late-September weather, I arrived at this desolate-appearing, miss-named little hamlet. Some of my first contacts were the Health Aides, who I met when I got to the Clinic. They had a nice office, well-stocked and clean. There were only two employees present that first day when I knew there were 3, but I was told that the third woman's husband got drunk the night before and got thrown in jail, so she had to leave and bail him out. Turns out, I soon found, that alcoholism is a big problem around there; the same story as in so many . . . too many . . . communities in economically deprived areas. Instead of saving the hard-to-earn money and spending it wisely, the men in the family would buy a bottle of illegal hooch for $20, which was a good day's wages at that time, and down it all and get in trouble, which cost even more money to fix.

During the time I was there in this particular village, the average man worked sporadically, if at all, maybe as a baggage handler for the airport or he just got by on hunting. Whiskey was illegal, so the bootleggers were the richest men in town. It was easy to get a bottle almost anywhere, I heard. I would imagine that it's difficult to stay in a marriage when one partner is a continual liability instead of an asset. A common problem, across all national, economic, social and racial lines, though, isn't it? An old story with almost always a bad ending. Alcohol has been the downfall of many, many millions of people, worldwide, and from the beginnings of recorded history. What a shame and a waste.

"Three men drowned yesterday." (my journal reads). They were coming back from Cape Lisburne; one was the husband of Ethel Timothy, one of the Health Aides that I work with. The saddest experience I have had since moving here. The whole village turned out for the funeral. Afterwards, I saw 43 patients.

Death and healing . . . . death and healing . . . .

"MAKING A HOUSE CALL ON THE YUKON RIVER"

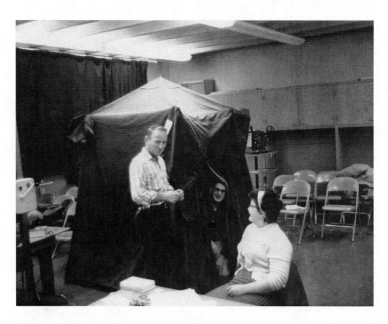

"THE TB TEAM: THE X-RAY TENT AND NURSE-TECHNICIANS"

CHAPTER 4

ARCHEOLOGY and ALASKAN VILLAGES

The town of Kotzebue is old, several thousand years old, and is a well-known archeological site. Ancient people came from up-river on the Kobuk and Noatak rivers where the game was plentiful;. . . lots of moose, elk and many caribou and there was also a mountain of jade . . . a valuable bartering item. Salmon would pass by this point on the river on their way upstream to spawn, the voyage etched on their DNA memory cells. Historically for unknown centuries in the past, summer saw the whole valley filled with tents, a well-populated temporary city and since the wind blew most of the time, the ever-present mosquito problem lessened and was made bearable.

There were many attractive features to this area that have apparently been here for time immemorial; the people who lived in Siberia to the west would travel down the coast in the summer and meet with other tribes and family groups and exchange wares and knowledge, learn and teach skills, and intermingle. The people from along the coast would bring goods like walrus tusks, muktuk, and preserved seal, whale and fish meat. The Siberians probably brought a variety of what they had to offer and those from up the rivers would bring jade for making tools and weapons and caribou and cured and dried moose meat, bones and skins as well as desirable furs of wolf, fox, wolverine and other inland species.

It has been researched and proven that some of the different groups would stay in the area all summer long. It takes 1000 pounds of salmon to keep a dog sled team for the winter, so the salmon were caught in nets and dried there and were not only economically fruitful but life-essential. In the fall, camp would break up and the up-river people would return home in time for the hunt, but there were natives that stayed in Kotzebue year 'round, living in their earth-sheltered dwellings. Even today, the Eskimos are still digging artifacts out of these old house pits and (unfortunately) selling them to the tourists who fly up to visit a unique town that is situated above the Arctic Circle.

If you subscribe to the Continental Drift theory, and you must if you have ever seen a world map in your life, you can sort of scoot things around and see how they fit together once. The water around Point Hope isn't very deep and stays relatively shallow all the way across to Siberia. You can visually slide the two landmasses together and see, too, that there are many cultural and sociological similarities between the people on each side. The Siberians did the crossing over from their side, it's thought. The Eskimos seemed emotionally and temperamentally less aggressive and adventuresome than the inland Indians and during many historical periods, there was actually a great deal of animosity between the two cultures.

We knew of three Indians in Anchorage when we first got there, who had married Eskimos. When the resulting kids would go out to school and intermingle, they would become acquainted, and, as young people do, get married. But the Indian people did not have a very warm reception among the Eskimo people at this time in history; socially they were outcasts. Eskimo mothers would threaten their children with giving them to the Indians; conversely, Indian mothers would use the same tactic on their kids . . . threats to give them to the Eskimos. It saddened me to see racial intolerance in this vast and hostile environment when it would make more sense for everyone to just get along, for the common good of all. Not so.

Tides were low at Kotzebue because ocean currents were held back at Bering Strait, and Kotzebue was on an inland sound. Therefore, the early Eskimos lived on the beach, close to the water. Archeologists had discovered that the beaches would build up and form ridges, the ocean would recede and another ridge would start building. The Eskimos, dependent on the sea for their living, moved, century to century, down the succeeding beach lines; the older ridges dated all the way back as the Denbigh culture, some 8,000 years prior.

This had only been a theory until an island site, a portage on the Kobuk River, was discovered where the layers of occupation had been laid down interspersed with layers of flood sediment and wind blown dust; carbon-dating was then applied to the artifacts. This island site was named Onion Portage and its layers lay on a curve of the Kobuk River where the caribou had always migrated, spring and fall.

Through the centuries, hunting camps were established at Onion Portage where the hunters killed the caribou and dried the meat for winter. Artifacts and carbon dating established that these strata of occupation, separated by layers of river sand from floods to a depth of over 30 feet, could be correlated with the beach ridges at Kotzebue and a system of dating worked out for both sides.

It was fun and interesting for Phyllis and me to read about Alaskan history while we were in the middle of it; the best book we found was 'Ancient Men of the Arctic' by J. Louis Giddings, and it was thrilling to see historical vestiges right before our eyes. When artifacts were offered to us for sale, we bought them as there was no museum or University department that wanted the more common items, so they were sold to us. One nurse brought me a trephinger which is an instrument early healers used to poke holes in the heads of their suffering patients to let the evil spirits out; once in a while, I'm sure it worked. If you get a blood clot on the brain and a medicine man or woman comes along and pokes a hole through your skull and a bunch of blood comes out and your headache all goes away, it's worked. I just wonder what size malpractice insurance rates they paid.

All medical knowledge could be said to have evolved from humble beginnings and then on to advanced technology, just like acupuncture in China, for example. I took a course in acupuncture once and the instructor said the puncture points behind the knee for back pain was probably discovered when someone had a chronic backache and got shot in the back of the knee by an arrow and the pain in his back went away. Many valuable things were discovered accidentally and the skills applied afterwards. The Aztecs operated on skulls and ancient skeletons show *healed* intricate operations on the skull, which are not always successful even today!

At the Kotzebue Airport, the Weins Airline people had a replica built of a typical ancient house to present what they probably looked like thousands of years ago. There was a hole in the top, which, would be covered in winter with semi-transparent gut to let the light in and the smoke out. Most of the archeological digs at that time were at the Krusenstern site across the sound from Kotzebue.

Both Krusenstern and Otto Von Kotzebue were Russian explorers who had sailed here in the nineteenth century, Kotzebue's journey being in 1816. As he neared shore, it's told that the natives ran along the beach, and then two boats full of warriors came out towards the ship waving spears and making hostile gestures. The Russians pointed guns at them but this didn't seem to impress the Eskimos, who had never seen firearms but when the sailors brought out swords, he Eskimos dropped back and the ship sailed away safely.

Captain James Cook had sailed past in 1778, and Vitas Bering had piloted these waters back in 1728. It is likely that other explorers had probably traded with the natives through the last 300 years or so. During that time, tuberculosis had been spread among the native people, right along with the trade-goods.

Same old sad story . . . .

Archeologists have been working all across the top of the continent from the early digs; at Thule in Greenland, the Eskimo culture has been carried back 8 to 10 thousand years. Strangely, their flint artifacts date pretty much the same as those of the American Southwest, with spear and arrow points at Akaktuvak Pass roughly paralleling the Folsom and Clovis points of New Mexico, 10,000 years ago.

Palisade II Points from Krusenstern are thought to be 8,000 years old, with the Denbigh artifacts found all across the top of the continent to Thule, dating back some 4,000 to 6,000 years. At Krusenstern, Denbigh, Palidades II and Norton, thought to date back 3,000 to 3,500 years and several of the points were identified. The Old Whalers dated about 1,800 years B.C. and were discovered on Beach Ridge 53, and since their artifacts were for whale hunting, their culture seems to have been isolated from the usual Eskimo way of life, as they lived at the Drusenstern beaches both winter and summer.

Phyllis and I got the most interested in the archeology of the area when we met Doug Anderson and his wife Wanni; Doug was on sabbatical from Princeton and they were working the Onion Portage dig and the Andersons were just a fun couple. I would fly him up to the site and then back and he would give me like a whole season's archeology lessons during the flights. He took both of us to a lot of different active sites and many, many more which had yet to be opened and examined. We learned that what we thought were just 'bumps' on the ground were probably sites; he believed that the surface of Eskimo archeology had hardly been scratched. He pointed out where many Mastodon tusks had been discovered. Alaska has so many yet-to-be-answered questions, it would take a lifetime to learn the answers, even if there were answers could be found at all.

The Andersons and others fired up our imaginations about the people whose midst we were living in. It made understanding the present day customs and mannerisms much more meaningful and understandable. The Eskimos appeared to us not as just indigenous to the region we happen to be living in at the time, but as a culture of many centuries, with refinement and with traditions and customs of meaning and worth. Learning these facts broadened and deepened our interest in the people we worked with and came to know and we enjoyed them even more for it.

"SOD HUT ON THE EAST END OF KOTZEBUE SOUND"

"DOC HOOK ON BANK OF KOBUK RIVER WITH MASTODON TUSK"

CHAPTER 5

"SAY AHHHHHH" AND MOBY DICK

My fledgling co-career as a dentist began in one of the little villages around Anchorage. Dentistry was always in heavy demand; the larger hospitals had a Dentist on staff, but there was no way one person could treat an area of 30-odd villages with their 48,000 odd-teeth once a year. I'd learned enough during my internship to perform basic nerve blocks and do extractions, and I had collected . . . by methods that I choose not to discuss . . . 2 sets of dental instruments, and usually carried them with me every time I went out to see patients for any reason.

Prior to any dental work, numbing is done on the facial nerves and that necessitates going in the mouth and back at an angle to reach where the mandible nerve comes out. It's important that the initial nerve-blocking injection 'take' as it's pretty tough to go back in and shoot around each tooth, protected as they are by the jawbones. Eskimo folks are a pretty stoic bunch and that is a matter of fact; I've pulled as many as 10 teeth at a time from the same patient. Thankfully for the patient, I could usually get the nerve block to take on the first try so it didn't bother them too much. I especially hated to have to hurt little kids, even though some pain is inevitable regardless of the skill of the doctor. The young ones with big brown eyes looking up at me, all filled with trust was always touching and they seemed to understand I was helping and they really appreciated someone trying to stop their teeth from hurting.

The little town of Sleetmute had a good turnout for our scheduled T.B. clinic visit. We spent one day doing appointments in the clinic facilities, but the rest of our patient care had to be house calls and the weather necessitated it be by boat. We started out early on a beautiful spring day; the nearby river was running high with ice floes which made our boat trip rather more interesting than I would have preferred.

The boat was a fine and hardy vessel, assembled, as it appeared to be of gum, duct-tape and unfailing optimism. Although it would have been pleasant to sit back and enjoy myself, marveling at the grandeur of the surroundings, I was kept busy staying alive by manning the oars and hoping to avoid colliding with ice floes that spun around us like cubes in a blender. We approached our first dwelling on this round of house calls and were greeted by the daughter of our patient, and by the pandemonium from the dozen or so hopefully well-tethered sled dogs. The home was typical of the locale with beds surrounding the walls on three sides, leaving the middle area as living space.

The interior was dark as there was only one south-facing window, it being high and near the ceiling. So, drawing on the marginal hours of training during my internship, I uttered my first "say ahhhh" to an old native elder under the inadequate glare of a bare-bulb lamp. He was seated on a folding chair while I loomed above, grinning with what I meant to be a comforting and confidence-building smile and brandishing my non-orthodox-ly procured and outdated instruments.

It's well known that whenever indigent native peoples become 'civilized', they acquire a taste for homogenized-sanitized-artificially flavored and refined food and drink, which causes their dental health to suffer right along with general health conditions. The dental situation of the Eskimo people I treated was almost universally abysmal. It was common in adults at the time that when faced with extractions of several teeth to request that I, 'pull 'em all'. Such was the case of my first patient. He had six teeth that were beyond saving and the rest were already missing or needed large fillings and he was tired of the whole oral care business.

As an aside here, an older lady told me that she and the other women in her generation felt like they had no further use for their teeth now that the men bought their clothing in stores, rather than the traditional method which entailed the woman's-work of chewing skins to prepare and soften for use in making shoes and outerwear for their families. Now that store-bought clothing was so readily available, the women, as she said . . . . "didn't need teeth anymore".

That was touching and poignant to me. At the very least, it was common to see women of a certain generation and older with teeth so worn down from chewing that their teeth were even with the gum-line. So, back to my first patient . . . it seemed he was in need a combination of extractions and fillings in addition to medication for his raging case of *ascites* which is extreme fluid retention in the abdomen and is secondary to cancer. He had been hospitalized until the week before but he insisted that he wanted to be brought home to die. There was really nothing more that could be done other than make him comfortable, which is just what I was doing by removing the teeth that were causing all his pain.

As I finished and packed up my instruments, planning to sterilize them when I got back to the clinic, the old man and the daughter both stood up, faced me and thanked me graciously with a lot of head-nodding and smiling. Even the patient grinned, showing his mouth full of gauze, and bestowed on me what I interpreted as a happy smile and I didn't need an interpreter to tell me that! I repeated the information to them about post-extraction care of the mouth: keep a firm grip on the gauze for a while, then, simple rinsing with sterile salt water every hour or so and nothing to eat that isn't already chewed. The ascites would either run its course and go away on its own or be present when he finally died from the cancer, neither of which I could do anything about. At least, the unrelenting dental pain and the build-up of poison in the body that extremely severe dental caries create would be relieved with the extraction and the antibiotics I left with him. For this, I felt positive that I had provided some aid. It is not *too* heartwarming, though, to realize your proffered dental care is only one step up from the use of pliers, the foremost common treatment utilized.

Looking back now and remembering the great trepidation I suffered over that first extraction, it sure was a long and winding road to the, shall we say, "more efficient" methods I was using towards the end of my medical practices in Alaska . . . doing dental work, Hooker-style, with the demand of high numbers of patients in the least amount of time, it went something like this:

* Patient A would shine a bright flashlight, or whatever was on hand for illumination, into Patient B's open mouth.
* The Aide, who was assisting me, would be standing on the other side of Patient B, handing me the sterilized instruments.
* I would reach in, tap on the intended tooth and wait for the patient's nod of approval that designated we had the right one zero-ed in on.
* I would then extract the tooth, whereupon the Aide would pack the open socket with gauze. This exercise would repeat with however many teeth the patient wished for me to extract at one sitting. The record was 10.
* Patient A, then, would relinquish the flashlight to Patient B, who would, while gripping his gauze in his mouth firmly, shine the light into Patient A's mouth and would then be joined by
* The Aide and I, both having washed up and sterilized as best we could, and then it was time for the little operettas to repeat . . .
* This would continue until one of two things happened. 1) we ran out of patients, or, 2) my arm got too tired.

There were many other dental stories I wish I could recall that didn't get put into my journals, but one I recall with clarity was while I was working on a particularly difficult extraction, it seemed to be taking forever. I would get a good grip on the rotten thing and it would not budge. Finally, I braced myself with one knee resting on the patients chair for leverage and gave one final, determined pull and off popped the crown (the above-gum line part, not the artificial crown of present day dentistry) of the tooth. POP! it shot over to the other side of the room, and went 'ding', right into the metal trashcan 15-feet across the room it hit . . . a billion-to-one-shot for sure and it had sounded like a 22 Rifle went off . . . !!

~~~~~~~~~~~~

Reverend Slowoko lived at Hooper Bay where he tended to his flocks' spiritual needs on Sunday and tended to their dental needs during the week. He felt he had learned enough by observing a dentist at the village clinic pulling teeth. He must have enjoyed it and had a knack for the bloody business. We got to know each other over the first months I held clinics in his town and I enjoyed his company.

He told me his record was 82 teeth pulled in one day. He also confided in me that he always requested permission to keep the teeth as trophies but there was lot of superstition about that sort of thing . . . something similar to some American Indian tribes further south and many other ethnic cultures on other continents . . . that evil spells can be cast with a body part such as an extracted tooth. Can't fight tradition!

That belief sure throws a negative light on the "Tooth Fairy"!

He stopped in once to visit with me while I was playing dentist so I stalled and didn't go back to working the mouth I was in until he left, for fear of embarrassing myself. I did dentistry by numbers and used a chart telling me where to inject and which forceps to use. Reverend Slowoko was certainly better than I was and probably still is . . . assuming he has lived this long. That would make him about 108.

Georgetown was a poor area with a lot care issues. Upriver villages are usually nicer than those on the coast; the homes and businesses are generally built of log and there is a certain element of civic and house-pride evident. Also, inland villages (and inland villagers) smell of wood smoke while coastal dwellers and their dwellings are less . . . . how should I say it? 'gentle on the olfactory senses' and have the lingering smell of seal oil . . . . but that was not the case in Georgetown in 1965. The year I spent there one week is etched on my mind: between TB sputum tests, routine medical care and repairing horrendous mouths, I was kept busy for some extremely long old days while I was there. While the old folks' teeth were worn down and ground nearly to the gums with wear from using them not just for chewing food, but also for making clothes, boat repair, pliers and food processors, the young kids' teeth cried out for total extraction by the time they were 10 or so. I got all revved up about the situation when I was a newbie and first introduced to the little villages and their masticating needs, so the next time I followed up with village visits I took about a zillion toothbrushes and dental health supplies that I'd talked a local dentist-buddy into donating and taught impromptu classes in the use thereof. I thought it went along swimmingly!

So, then, when I went back to the same villages I had bestowed toothbrushes, paste and even dental floss to, I found the tooth decay problem no better! Eventually, I discovered that the kids had taken the brushes home and their dads used them to clean out the jets in the carburetors of their snow machines and the dental floss served as fish line! The solution I came to was to provide the teachers in the school with the brushes, let them personalize them and oversee their usage during school hours. It wasn't perfect but it was a plan nonetheless.

Combining the Chapter on dentistry and the one on whales may seem an odd choice, but other than the obvious commonality of wide-open mouths, there is scant little to link them, I admit, but on we go nonetheless.

There are several kinds of whales that were and are important to the Eskimos, I learned. The Bowhead Whale is one of the largest animals on earth and yet they feed on some of the smallest creatures on earth: plankton. It is sieved through thin louvers of baleen that are laced with 'whiskers' which filter out the plankton from the tons and tons of water the whale sucks in.

In olden days, these sticks of baleen were used, for one thing, as girdle stay but now they are mostly used in the making of fine baskets.

These whales are massive and my mere words cannot to give you the real sense of how large they really are from the words on this page; there is just no way to properly describe the mass!. They weigh about one ton *per foot* in length; when they come up close to the ice and you are standing there watching a pod of them go by, it is impressive, to say the least.

Scheduling my visit to Cape Hope for whale season was no accident on my part, but admit I was awestruck and humbled to be invited and allowed a part in the century-old whale hunt. It literally took a whole village to get a whale, and this event caused them to function in a homogenous, cooperative group, something that was sorely lacking in some villages and the way any small town *should* be, ideally.

The whales swam right past the Cape, so that when the assigned 'watchers' saw one blow they would sound the alarm and the people would all come running out, jump in the special boat, pick a whale and start the hunt. They would first shoot a harpoon into it, which had to hit just the right area in the head. There were many skills involved; the harpoon gun was a fearsome weapon, kind of like a bazooka. The boat had to be in just the right place, too, for if it was too close when the whale 'sounded', or rolled, the boat would capsize and everyone on board would just be dead very quickly and surely as few could swim in the 28 degree water for long.

After the harpoon hit and lodged, the next step was to sincerely hope and pray that the whale would come up in open water and not under the pack ice, for, if it died under the ice, it would most likely wash up on the beach in the spring. The townsfolk would get *really* tired of it before summer was over. The hoards of birds and many creatures that would come to feed on it could not take care of it all, even with the help of larger animals like Polar bears and grizzlies. The beach was just horrible and mortifying for the rest of the year. One time, when I was at Point Hope, a snagged whale did come up under the ice and somehow the villagers found it. They chopped down through the ice, a hole about 60 feet long and ten feet wide . . . and that through probably 2 feet of ice! Determination is not a strong enough word to describe that scene. They got it out and salvaged the meat.

At Point Hope during the hunt I was in, the minute a whale was 'hooked', everyone seemed to know where to put ropes and spears and they were able to tow this massive body over to the pack ice and rig up a very elaborate block and tackle. It would take the biggest part of a whole day and the whole lot of them to accomplish this. Sometimes, the ice bearing the mammoth would crack off and they would dig what is called a 'deadman anchor' further back to fasten ropes to and pull it toward the land.

The gift they made to me of a good-size cut of whale blubber was an honor, and although I found the black skin tasty, the white blubber tastes just like lard. In the case of the village getting a whale, everyone who was able began the butchering process armed with an oolug, a two-bladed knife, and they did it standing up and stooped over, never squatting or sitting. The oolug was razor sharp and they could cut up an incredible amount of meat in a very short time with those knives because they hit and sliced from both directions.

An absolutely amazing thing to watch, and I got to be there beginning to end.

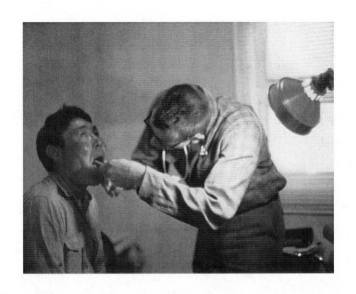

"MY FIRST DENTAL PATIENT, GAZING UP TO HEAVEN
FOR HELP, IT APPEARS!"

"WHALE JAWBONES AT POINT HOPE"

CHAPTER 6

'GREAT WHITE HUNTER', OR 'YOU ALWAYS HUNT BETTER WHEN YOU'RE HUNGRY!'

Now, for a lot of guys, if they had access to hunting and fishing and a love for it, Alaska would be a paradise. I was living every real, red-blooded American man's dream!

Admittedly, as soon as we moved up north and I began hearing people talk about the area, part of the reason Kotzebue always held such a fascination for me is that it's is right in the middle of big game country and excellent fishing waters, too. When we were settled in, after accepting the position as Physician at the Kotzebue hospital, and moving up there was accomplished, then I had a chance to go try it out, it was even more incredible than I could have imagined. I felt like I could never get enough of it!

While there wasn't much extra time with my pressing workload, generally the only hunting was during the summer or in the daylight months, but there were some unforgettable trips. As far as sport hunting goes, I did a little in the beginning but got enough of it 'way early on as the reverence that I observed in the way most of the native people lived among the creatures in their midst and used them wisely without intentional waste was an epiphany, one that's remained with me.

Hunting birds was not too exciting for me . . . more so for the ducks, I suppose. We hunted ducks out in the Kotzebue Sound;

I had a bad experience there once, hunting alone. I was out in the Sound in a small boat, and could *not* seem to find the right channels to bring the boat around and head home. The thought crossed my mind more than once, as it got later and later, that I may not make it back in before it got so dark that I couldn't see at all. The wind was blowing and I was chilled, but eventually, just when I'd had about enough and figured that my last gasp was forthcoming, the Guardian Angel of Fools steered me into a recognizable channel and I was able to get back to my vehicle and back home under my own steam.

Duck season, in the particular area we were in, didn't start until the ducks had migrated south (lucky ducks . . .) so there was precious little time to hunt. I usually went with three or four guys and we hunted in the traditional way: chasing them around using a boat. One guy to run the boat and another two or three got to shoot. We took turns. Because we were hunting for meat, not a trophy, as so many visitors up here were, we went about it in another way and I followed the way locals looked at hunting and fishing as an important part of life and not merely entertainment; killing simply for killings' sake is morally wrong in my mind.

Hunting was, and remains, an expensive hobby. Shotgun shells were 25 cents apiece back then and I was earning, on salary, the equivalent of about $10 an hour so that made it expensive enough for me! The redeeming value was that we always had plenty of meat and we needed it because in that climate, the body burns a lot of energy simply keeping warm and needs fuel in abundance and that makes meat the #1 staple. I recalled a time when I nearly pulled my arms out of their sockets packing 100 lbs. in each hand, carrying reloading equipment onto a commercial plane coming back from Seattle. Even with saving money by reloading, it cost big to hunt. One chap I heard about went out on a field trip by plane and brought his gun, loaded of course; he hit some turbulence and blew a nicely-placed hole right through the side of his plane. Didn't hurt anyone but himself, luckily, but he sure had a hard time living down the story.

One thing we hunted *legally*, I might add, and quite often, despite the fact that it is the Official State Bird, was Ptarmigan; it was kind of a side-bar that we shot them when we saw them, while hunting for something larger. They are delicious little morsels . . . the flavor resembles pigeon . . . they even look a little like a pigeon, like a pregnant pigeon to be specific. They are interesting in that, like several other wildlife varieties, they change color with the seasons from snow white in the winter and a mottled gray in the daylight months. They were numerous around Kalsag and some of the other villages I visited.

They nested on high ground in the spring and the little chicks fed on the grasses, cranberries and blueberries that were still on the bushes from the year before. In the winter they ate willow buds. Mother Nature's pantry. There seemed to be trillions of the prolific little buggers and they flew in veritable swarms, like hugely overgrown gnats. The best goose hunting, or should I say, the area that was most hunted for geese, was at a place called Adrian Lake. The beach grass that grew there happened to be essential for a certain type of basket weaving, so each spring, Eskimos from the village of Hooper Bay raid the eggs from Northern goose nests and those in the nearby lakes, carting them out in baskets woven from the available grasses. They take all the eggs and even the downy nesting material. They also kill all the adults they can.

This is mostly a money-making project for them. They sell the down to companies making down-filled coats and catch the goslings, gut them and boil them whole . . . even the feet . . . for food. I have to admit that for all the wholesale killing and the seemingly negative effect on the environment, at least every bit of the creature is used: feathers and down for pillows and clothing adornment while the softest skin was used to make coat-like clothing items for little children and babies. Even the heads and wing meat get boiled up for soup. If they got to the eggs freshly laid, of course, they ate them as eggs . . . nearer to hatching, the egg-contents were meat. Of course, the likening to the Plains Indians and their use of the buffalo is obvious . . . a lot can and should be learned from them both.

Nunivak Island, when we visited there, was famous for the Musk Ox herds. The government transplanted some on the island a long time ago and they not only survived, but also thrived and now are considered native. The 700 lb full-grown oxen have what the native's call a 'kulik', which translates to 'shawl' ; it's grown by the Musk Ox for winter protection. It is an exquisitely fine fur and the women used it to make beautiful knitted items that sell for a good price. I never did find out if they actually captured the Musk Ox and sheared them, like llamas or alpacas. Perhaps they merely gathered it after it shed off in the spring. Hmmm.

In the later years, big game hunters would pay a thousand bucks or more to be taken out to the Island for a Musk Ox head trophy. The herd was at one time dangerously reduced to feed the greed of the hunters and guides, but Government intervention has cracked down on that so that the women can go back to collecting the kulik-hair for knitting.

One jaunt I recall was when I took an acquaintance of mine, Dr. Sessions, who was an ear-nose-throat guy, up in my plane. We planned an hour flight up the Squirrel River and had planned on it being a quick trip but it turned out to be a great day for spotting game. We got to see a small pack of wolves, around 8-10. I was pretty adept, I thought, at being able to snap pictures and fly the plane at the same time, and got some good shots in. We then saw a grizzly, a few Caribou and even a moose. He just about jumped out of the plane in his excitement, taking picture after picture. After a bit, it got awfully quiet in the back and I turned around and ascertained that the good Doctor Sessions had run low on stomach and had apparently lost it while I was trying to get him the chance to take some really good shots by spiraling down, almost to the ground, and then pulling out quickly . . . too bad!

∿∿∿∿∿∿∿∿∿∿∿∿

Having just finished a quick jaunt down from Point Hope, Kivalina and Noatak . . . a 2-day trip . . . I can report that I successfully and single-handedly examined all the children in Point Hope and then in Kivalina. I picked up Titus Nashukput and took him with, so he could look for caribou on the Tuesday morning I was leaving. He had expressed a need to get some more meat for winter and I had seen a good herd up that way, so offered to take him along. We also picked up my Sanitary Engineer, Pete Ambrose, in Noatak, so he could do some game spotting, too.

As Murphy's Law dictates, it seemed that the only time you see something to shoot is when you don't have a reason, a permit or a gun to do so. It was that way for the three of us. Just when we agreed the whole day was a bust and I began the long, slow turn back the way we had come, Pete spotted a beautiful big Grizzly bear, enjoying his day and strolling along a sandbar, oblivious of the three sets of eyes that were watering up at the sight of him. Titus began bouncing around and pointing and finally choked out something that indicated he wanted me to try to land so he could get a shot. I guess that although caribou was the preferred Meat de' Jour, and that was what we were after, bear meat would suit him just fine, too!

I started looking for a good landing spot on the sandbar and Titus and Pete were clattering around behind me, dropping things and cursing in their haste. Titus let out a moan that began from deep in the recesses of his man-soul and then found voice, as he whimpered, "Hey, Hook, these shells don't fit this gun."

Apparently he had brought a 300 Magnum and 30.06 shells. I was sick about it and I am sure Titus is still in therapy. Although I was not too fond of bear meat myself, Titus and Peter would've shared between them, of course. But, it was not meant to be on that day in that particular bear's life.

Or ours.

Speaking of bear stories, early in my flying career, I ran across an old sow grizzly running across the Tundra. I didn't have a gun with me that time and would have taken the meat back to one of the villages I was visiting that next day where it would have been greatly appreciated. So, out of aggravation, I decided to buzz her a few times before getting back en route. She really got mad, too, as I continued buzzing, flying right over her big, hairy bum. I was trying to get a good picture out of the whole thing, at least, and had trimmed the plane to nearly fly itself, while I held the stick between my knees.

Just as I got ready to shoot the picture, the stick flipped out of control from between my knees and the plane made a noise like . . . sssssSSSKKK! I dropped the camera, grabbed the stick, and pulled out just before I splattered all over that particular patch of tundra . . . and Big Girl grizzly would have had me for lunch instead of the other way around! After that, I learned, when flying alone, to trim it for a nice long climb before taking my mind off of the Numero Uno business of flying to take pictures! It came too close to being my Swan Song . . . and also turning me into instant antipasto for Lady Grizzly.

According to my journal, in May of 1969, one of the BIA teachers took his plane, I took mine, and we each had a passenger riding with us, eager and interested in an adventure. The sun hardly even sets in May so it never gets too dark at that time of year. After my teacher friend was through teaching for the day and I finished my clinics in the evening, we just took off and flew up and down the rivers, reveling in the beauty of the land and just seeing what we could see.

It was very easy to hunt Caribou in that vicinity and I spotted herds of them for the village hunters all the time, noting locations so they could harvest more successfully. Fresh Caribou meat was a much-needed staple for their families. We located a good size herd on that trip and, finding a good spot, landed on a nearby sandbar and *went hunting*. There was no posted limit on Caribou so I felt good knowing everything that would be taken out that trip in the two planes would be appreciated and eaten. The weather was favorable and we weren't in any hurry. The herd was large enough to choose a choice young doe or buck; absolutely perfect conditions for hunting.

Caribou hair is hollow, like deer hair, and skinning them and using their skins was especially useful for insulation for outerwear. The hide on their legs is perfect for mukluks; they are lighter in weight than the oogruk seal mukluks and they don't smell as bad as the seal does when wet, nor are they slippery like the seal skin.

They winter mainly on the vast tundra where they paw down through the snow and eat the lichen. Once, a professional guide in the area and I were hunting together and he bet me he could clean a Caribou in five minutes. I mulled that over and decided to take him up on it. Well, we bagged one that I'd spotted and he took the shot. After that, I just sat back and watched: now, Dear Reader, if you are a big-game hunter, listen up: this tip alone is worth the price of this book!

First things first, he had a very sharp knife to use and the beast was lying on the ground rather than hanging up; already that was not the norm. He reached over the large middle of it and split the belly, making a perfect cut near the top of the neck. He then dived up and into the rib cage with both hands and brought down everything from up there, after the surgically-correct cutting had loosed it at the top of the neck. It seemed to come out quite easily: notice, I did not say 'neatly', but it sure looked like it was done easily, despite the blood and gore he ended up wearing as a coat and hat. Fact of the matter, he resembled me after a tough night in the ER.

Then he pulled the entrails out and piled them on the ground. A well-executed cut around the rectum followed and in even less than five minutes we (or, I should say 'he') had all the guts out and the meat was steaming . . . cooling and cleaned. Voila—a $5 lesson for me and a very good investment at that!

Another time, two guys whose names are gone from my mind, decided to fly up to a cabin owned by a mutual friend, Bill T. He joined us for the expedition. His cabin was on the Noatak River, in a remote and beautiful part of the country. As we were getting close to the location, we spotted a grizzly sow on a sandbar, near a small herd of Caribou. By the time we got to a place to land, she'd disappeared into the woods; it had also begun to snow. Not willing to risk danger in inclement weather and explore anymore, I turned the plane back around towards the sandbar, bearing down on the caribou herd again so while in the air, Bill bagged a young Caribou that had gotten separated from the herd. We landed nearby, gutted it and trekked up to the cabin, lugging it along with our minimal supplies.

Picture it: just below freezing, crisp clean evergreen-scented air, the promised warmth of a good fire, a snug cabin and fresh meat for dinner. It just does not get any better than that!

We dropped our gear and finished cleaning the caribou quickly, leaving it hanging on a high limb of a nearby tree. It probably weighed in, cleaned, at about 200 pounds or so. The cabin turned out to be a pleasant surprise: being as it was in Grizzly country, it had been wisely put together with a double door . . . the outside door swung out and was made of heavy planks. The inner door pulled in and was barred with iron and thick cross-boards of what appeared to be oak.

Outside on the porch, you could see the claw marks that had scored it high up, even tearing bits off of the outer door . . . a jaw-dropping sight, but satisfying too, even if rather grim. We had cut off enough Caribou steaks for the evening meal, which, fresh as it was and eaten around a crackling fire and surround by good company, provided a memorable experience in and of itself. We bunked up early.

Sometime during the night, I was awakened by the unmistakable sounds of a bear . . . the deep growling and whuffling sounds that told me a bear had probably found our caribou and must have considered it an offering: the equivalent of a midnight snack from Mother Natures' refrigerated pantry. Rex sat up, too, and he and I peered out of the small barred window, staring out until our eyes adjusted and the moonlight brought the details in clearly. We could just make out the beast, standing up and dining on the hanging carcass; it was erect and had to be over 7 feet tall! The caribou carcass was tied up as high as we could reach into the tree, so the bear's height could be determined. It was big! We looked at each other and both spoke at the same time: "It's a grizzly! Let's get it!"

Hurrying back to our bunks, we donned pants and coats and slid into boots; I don't know about Rex but I was shaking like a leaf. Our actions woke up the other two guys, who were shuused, and then they learned from our hoarse whispers what was heck was going on!

Rex and I turned in the direction of the sturdy double-barred door. Reaching out for the heavy crossbar that secured it, we also seemed to simultaneously realize that we would have to open BOTH of the doors, and, once they were both open, it was all over for us if the Grizzly decided to change tactics and it's main dish of caribou and come on into the cabin. I knew it could move very quickly and easily outrun us for short distances and there would be precious-little time to shut and bolt both doors behind us.

My 300 Magnum was in the gun rack next to the door and I had it all ready. It was a profound moment . . . .

Well, you guessed it . . . neither of us had the guts to open those doors. Clear thinking and avarice had won the match and the next morning, when we all went out to the butchering tree and saw that both hind quarters were gone, we couldn't have cared less! I'd have offered the danged old bear the whole caribou if it had become an issue, rather than argue with him about it. He won. Hands down. We stayed one more night but the bear didn't show up. Probably still stuffed from the night before. We reckoned he had to have eaten around 80 pounds in one meal. We salvaged what was left of the untouched meat further up on the body and headed for home with a great story to tell!

~~~~~~~~~~~~~

When you think of hunting and Alaska, the Polar Bear comes to mind and that particular hunting issue has always made me angry, for when the "Big Game Hunters" came in to bag one for the head or hide or even just a picture of themselves with the carcass, it was not hunting at all in my opinion. This is why: the bear is spotted from a plane in its white, featureless surroundings and from then on, it doesn't usually stand a chance. You see, two planes are normally used; one of them stays in the air and sort of herds the bear in the direction they want it to go. The other plane lands and the hunters give chase. With no place to hide on the pack ice, the bear is a fairly easy target that cannot escape.

There's little danger for the hunters . . . once they have landed safely, most of the danger is over. The only chance of disaster is maybe dinking up the plane when it lands because, depending on the time of day and the absence of shadows, it's hard to read the surface of the pack ice—there are no shadows to judge unevenness so the only way is to drag it as best you can, but you still come down and landing not knowing just what you are getting yourself into.

Polar bears are not considered aggressive like the Grizzlies sometimes are. Grizzlies can move over the land at the speed of a racehorse, granted only for a short distance, but very fast, and an unschooled hunter could easily underestimate it's pace.

The front legs of a Grizzly bear are shorter than the back legs so they can come UP a hill at great speed, while descending is awkward for them. They have tremendously strong legs and they are MEAN . . . they seem like they would rather fight than run. My limited opinion, only, you see, and what I'd been told since living in Alaska. That is all I have to go on.

Now, I know some would disagree: I watched "Grizzly Man," the incredibly interesting documentary . . . the photography is unreal and should not be missed. The shots Timothy Treadwell takes of the bears is *not* from a spot of safety with a long-distance camera lens . . . he is right there with them, within touching range, sometimes! I know it's his opinion that Grizzlies are gentle, unassuming creatures who are mild-mannered unless provoked, and that human beings have cruelly and heartlessly hunted the poor, misunderstood and noble . . . the noble . . . . what? . . . . oh . . . . OH . . . that's right! . . . Timothy was EATEN by a Grizzly . . .

Hail, the magnificent Polar bear: the quintessential symbol of Alaska in my minds eye.

Our little family's chosen food animals were Caribou and Moose; Caribou were much more plentiful and easier to bag, but Phyllis and I preferred the taste of Moose, and some of the friends we had shared wild game with agreed, so we always had a good supply. One of those friends was Jim Keane and a certain trip we went on together is etched on my mind.

Jim was the hospital Pharmacist and he and I had planned a moose hunt, the details of which we thought we had down pat. We reveled in the planning of the Crusade and had plenty of time to anticipate the Big Adventure for some time. For part of the transportation into moose country, we were going to use a boat we'd bought together. We loaded it down with six 5-gallon cans of gas for the 20HP engine, as well as food, guns, bug spray, TP . . . . all that stuff.

After carefully choosing a weekend with a fair weather forecast, we set out in our Titanic early one morning. After rounding Pipe's Spit in our trusty boat, 15 or so miles around the peninsula that Kotzebue is located on, we caught a bad wind and had to hug the shore. We shoved it on down to an old fish camp and got directions to the other side where the mainland was. According to the map, we expected to find Riley's Channel at the mouth of the Kobuk River but we didn't find it, crossed over, and went aground about 200 yards out.

It was unusually cold for August and the wind was blowing off the Bering Sea, which is always cold. We finally made it down to John Nelson's camp where they welcomed us, let us warm up and fed us boiled dried fish. We recouped our energy a bit then he walked outside with us, pointed out proper directions, and even showed us a shortcut on our map.

We borrowed an anchor from John, having lost ours, and set out on the choppy sea with the sight of a far mountain as a landmark to guide us. It was a long boat ride. After landing, we lodged that first night in a sod hut that marked the entrance to the lake we planned to transverse that next day. We slept well in our luxury accommodations. Arising bright and early, we found a channel through the slough but it was clogged with weeds and that made the going rough but we finally got to the Melbourne Channel. There were ducks galore . . . and also mosquitoes galore . . . but we camped 2 miles from Kiana, the village we were aiming for, and after shooting a duck apiece, tied up and made camp, planning to stay the night.

A couple of boatloads of people, spotting our fire, and in true 'bush' style, stopped by just to see who we were. Warren and Rodney Koffin of Noorvik were in one of the boats and they had a camp near. The weather had settled down, the fire was soothing and the dinner of spit-roasted duck was fit for a king. It was what we were hoping it would be. We had to sleep under tarps because of the mosquitoes, but awoke refreshed and continued up the coast. We reckoned we had traveled about 120 miles and were able to buy gas as we went along. The trouble that we had not anticipated was that, however easy it was to spot Moose from the air, they stayed in the sloughs over by the riverbanks and unless we used mental telepathy and stopped in just the right spot and were able to climb up on the bank and take a look, we couldn't see them.

Which we didn't so we didn't . . . ever . . . and came home without Moose meat.

It was a nice camping trip but a poor hunt.

That fall, I took 2 Moose over by the Squirrel River when I was hunting with John Worland. I often located moose for people that I knew, usually asking for 'payment' of a drum of gasoline, which at that time cost about $25. If we didn't have to fly far, I made out pretty good, usually coming home with moose meat to share and maybe even some gas leftover. The day John and I were going along, we spotted 5 of them, all feeding in the same slough. We circled around and landed the plane on a sandbar about half a mile from where we had seen the herd of moose; we snuck over the sandbar and up over the edge of the slough, hopped over the riverbank and bagged one each!

We couldn't pack all of the wonderful meat in the plane so we just took the four hindquarters and covered the rest of it up with a couple of space blankets and came back to get it later.

Another year, a Moose hunt netted a big bull, the biggest I have ever shot; two of us had gone out, heading for the Interior and stopping near a lake. The other guy didn't have a game gun and had just brought his 22 along while I brought my 30.06; I also had a hunting license and he didn't. He just wanted to come along on a hunt and I was always glad to have some help in case I bagged something. We had hiked a couple of hours, circling around and not straying too far from the sandbar and my plane. He climbed a tree to reconnoiter while I soaked my tootsies in a stream as we had walked a good ways and they hurt like heck.

I heard sort of a Ppppfffffhhhht sound and I looked around to where it had come from and this moose walked right between the tree and where I was sitting. There I was, my bootless feet in a stream and unable to reach my gun and my hunting buddy, just spotting the thing, got over-eager and banged at it with his little 22, which was just like shooting it with a pea-shooter and it ricocheted off into the woods! Believe it! Pea-shooter or not, I was glad that bullet hit the moose and not *my* tender hide! It would have done a lot more damage to me than it did to the moose. The moose just shook his head and looked a bit confused and stood still long enough for me to grab my 30.06 as it started to move off. I aimed and fired and made a terribly accurate shot at an astounding distance of 20 feet. Any closer and I could have hit the poor bugger over the head with the gun stock.

My shot took him right down; he was very large . . . there was over 40 lbs of tender meat in his neck alone! The total weight of the meat was over 1000 pounds. I cut the head off and skinned it and later had the hide tanned, then I cut the torso in 4 parts, tossing the guts in the brush for the lucky varmints to clean up. We had the choice of either floating all the meat across the Lake or carrying it around the Lake in about 4 trips. We chose to use the raft.

We must have made an unusual sight: rather like George Washington crossing the Delaware. We each had a paddle and were sitting on this monstrous pile of moose meat, just about 2 inches away from shipping water. We paddled vvvvvvery careful-like and slowly to the other side of the lake and the plane, where I was never so glad to touch shore in all my life. The fear of capsizing and drowning was one thing, but losing all that meat and the trophy head too? Unthinkable!

~~~~~~~~~~~~

'HUNTING CABIN NORTH OF KOTZEBUE'

'CARIBOU HEAD WE ARE GOING TO TIE TO THE WING
STRUTS; 150 MILES NORTH OF KOTZEBUE'

'BILL REMBER, GARY HERBERT AND I WITH HIDE OF BLACK BEAR WE SHOT'

'HAULING THE BOAT OUT ON THE PACK ICE, GOING TO HUNT WALRUS'

CHAPTER 7

"A DREAM VACATION OF A LIFETIME . . . ALL INCLUSIVE!"

It was coming up to the last six months of the end of my two-year assignment in Alaska, and at this point in time, Phyllis and I were discussing where to live. I had been offered a good position in the city of Kotzebue, further north of Anchorage. The lease on the house we were in was running out and there were decisions to be made, whether to re-up the lease and stay in the Anchorage area, or give notice and get out.

She didn't like one little town about 40-miles north of Anchorage that we had once considering buying and starting private practice in, and although we had discussed it seriously for a time, and I wasn't enthusiastic, either. The only home there we could find that was suitable cost $30K and in that time, that was a huge wad of money and not much house. After a lot of prayer, we decided to take the Kotzebue assignment that had been offered me: a doctor in the Kotzebue Hospital. Looking back, perhaps we weren't confident enough to face the big wide world on our own. Ah, hindsight.

Since whatever the decisions would be, we would be in-between assignments soon, we decided a vacation would be a Good Thing; we chose the Admiralty area because, for one thing, I heard the fishing down there was fantastic. Admiralty is 18 miles by float plane from Juneau and the beauty and diversity of the area was raved about by several of the Hospital and clinic folks we got to know who told us that for spectacular scenery and absolutely awesome outdoor experiences that area was not to be missed. Sold!

We planned for this two-week vacation well in advance and with much care. It took quite a while to pack and unpack and re-pack and sort out all the paraphernalia it takes for the sustenance of 2 Bigs and 3 Smalls for 2 weeks. The Hooker Caravan and Mobile Survival Vehicle left Anchorage at 2 PM on a Friday afternoon with our best friends Larry and Dru and their 3 kids in their Volkswagen beetle and Phyllis, Kyle, Kit, Kelly and me in ours . . . . both vehicles loaded to the gills.

It was a beautiful day and just the knowledge that we had 2 weeks of FREEDOM was exhilarating and very nearly vacation enough. We sang on the way, the kids alternately snoozed, snacked, and screeched, but even that did not dampen our enthusiasm for the trip ahead. We made it to Tok Junction before we had to stop because of the rain that soon became very heavy and made even driving difficult, so we stopped and pitched our tents for the night.

Yes. That is what I said: Tents. Night. Rain. Words cannot describe . . . .

The next day, regardless of the fist-shaking and oath-making that the impromptu entertainment the night before had spawned, the sun DID come up, all 3 AM bets to the contrary. We wrung out all the rainwater that we could, saddled-up and crossed the border into Canada and covered miles and miles of dirt roads; again, words cannot express the bone-rattling, dust-breathing, kid-screaming, butt-breaking, chassis-banging, tire-eating stretch of hell that was the Canadian Highway System on that particular length of road in 1968.

Finally at about 10 PM, we passed through Customs.

Oh, did I say 'passed through?"

My mistake. They were closed. Thankfully, a man was just leaving the office, but upon seeing our pathetic caravan, he re-opened and let us through the gate! We could have pitched our tents on the highway itself out of sheer frustration, I suppose . . . .

Something mysterious and almost other-worldly happened between the time we stopped and turned off the car for a spell for a stretch-and-potty-break, and the time we crawled back in. Getting into the cockpit of the VW, the lights would not go on. It's impossible to guess just what transpired in the inner-workings of whatever passed as the mind of the little car: perhaps it felt frustration, too, and exhibited its dissatisfaction in the only way it could . . . by simultaneously blowing all of its fuses . . . perhaps that is the Car Version of a Primal Scream.

No one can say.

So, with no other choice, we continued on without lights because, from that moment and without warning, the battery could only turn the engine over and power the car, OR power the lights.

But not both.

We let Larry and Dru and company go in front and we followed closely behind them. There was precious little chance that we would be rear-ended by a speeding motorist as the top speed possible was barely 25 MPH . . . . no worries!

We got into the town of Haines after 14 hours on the road; we located the phone number and address and woke up Stan and Pat Jones, whom I had met earlier in the Spring of 1963 at a Medical Convention and kept in touch with. Cordially and Good Samaritan-like, they accepted our motley crew into their home at 11:30 at night. Hot showers and hot chocolate and snug, dry beds were never more appreciated.

I feel strongly and without a shadow of a doubt that Stan and Pat Jones will be waiting in Heaven, and when (if) I make it to some degree of Exaltation, I will crank my head and gaze upward and there they will be, enjoying blessings in the Celestial Kingdom, due to the Hugely Benevolent Acts they performed that very miserable, wet night in 1968.

No kidding.

Phyllis seemed to be handling everything well at that point, as she always did, but I personally was ready to turn around and go back home, put the kids up for adoption and become a monk. The way I saw it, the trip up to that time had obviously been cursed already and we had 12 more days of misery ahead of us!

However, the next morning, with a new battery and fuses installed on our trusty V-Dub, and, I am glad to report, a better outlook on life for the King of the Road, we gathered up the passel of kids, (we discussed leaving a few of them behind but Stan would have none of it) fed and dressed them and ourselves and headed for the Ferry Dock.

Impeccable planning and timing got us there 5 minutes before it left. We must have had 400 pounds of luggage and we had to run down the gangplank, dragging it with us. Some people already on the ferry were pointing and laughing at the sight of our little boy Kit who had misplaced his belt and was trying with all his 5-year-old might to hold up his pants with one hand and carry his sleeping bag with the other! It was a beautiful day; the ferry took 4 hours to Juneau and then there was a long wait for the cars to unload, while foot passengers could just walk off. We were 10 miles out of town and there was nothing for the kids to do but wait in the car or fall off the ferry and we, given that choice, in true Good Parent mode, tried to entertain them in the one-square-foot area that was not packed solid in the car. They were very bored and restless and unhappy until it was time to go. We made the Coastal Ellis Airport in Juneau at noon for our 4:30 flight and that left us with some time to kill.

We were able to find a nearby store and we purchased a myriad of other little things that traveling with kids necessitate. Still having a bit of extra time, I looked up and called a Dr. Reeder who I'd known during my internship; we'd kept in touch. He and I chatted about old times until time came for boarding the plane. The conversation with him made Phyllis and I realize that we had not completely made up our minds about Kotzebue after all; Juneau would have been a nice place to live, the little we had seen of it. Dr. Reeder had confided that he needed help and would have taken me into his practice right then and there.

It certainly made for some interesting conversation between my Companion and me while we planned our future. Well, on to the vacation . . . .

We hadn't bought our airline tickets in advance (pre-PC-days), but had merely called and got the prices, after being assured there would be space a-plenty. Since that fact-finding phone call a week before, the Alaska Coast Airlines, (long shall they wave), brightly informed us upon arrival, that we owed them $39 per person apiece more than they had quoted 6 days previously. Apiece. More.

Translate that from 1968's dollar to 2009's dollar and multiply it out and that is as if we had to come up with around $1,000 additional! I caused a big scene but finally gave in when Larry reasoned with me and pointed out we really had no choice and that hijacking the plane would not be in our best interests! Then, after *all* of that, the airport crew held the take-off an hour and a half later than scheduled so the pilot could get back from a fishing trip . . . . Grrr . . . .

Finally in the air, Baby Kit fell asleep in the Grumman Goose, but the rest of the smalls squealed all the way across the inlet to the island. I was hoping the racket wrecked some revenge on the pilot, but I doubt it. He wisely kept his headphones on.

After a pleasant and breathtaking 30-minute flight, the pilot circled our camping spot and the plane taxied right up to the shore. Larry and I jumped out and started unloading while Dru and Phyllis rounded up the kids and the gear . . . no mean feat. Admiralty Island was the spot we had chosen to vacation on was very remote, 18 miles out in the ocean, so there was no way to get back to 'civilization', per se, until we were picked up again the next week.

We had arranged to rent a large double cabin from the Forest Service for $2 a night for each family; they were neat little places with two beds in the one big room, two beds in an offset room, kind of a basic kitchen, a water pump, one old boat with oars, a garbage dump and an outhouse. Situated as it was on the Hasselberg lakeshore, there was a view from the front porch that was improbably beautiful and impossible to describe. The air was achingly pristine and pure and carried the odor of pine on a gentle breeze. Couldn't ask for more! What a relief to finally *be* there and not just going there.

Sunday, Monday and Tuesday we had sunny weather . . . we were initially concerned about it being warm enough in July but it actually was a little too warm and the adults slept in open sleeping bags in the main room and the kids got the beds. During the day, the weather was perfect for sitting in lounge chairs and forgetting all about medicine.

Fishing was OK but not superb; we caught lake trout, cutthroat and coconee which is a land-locked salmon and really good eating. A fellow named Londstrom from the Old Reliable Transportation Company in Juneau showed up by boat on Sunday evening while we were relaxing by the shore. Larry and I expressed our mild disappointment with the fishing, so he told us where the best places were to go and we listened to every word. It turned out that about three miles down from our camp, where the river emptied into another small lake, was the Ultimo, Number One, Especial', Mongo, Big Kahuna Fish Mecca of North America. Three miles away!

NIRVANA!

Whereas Londstrom had showed up in an outboard and we only had oars, the next morning as soon as we could guiltlessly leave camp, Larry and I had to row which meant an hour and a half to get there with sore hands and sore bums. But, we were fueled by enthusiasm and anticipation, and, as any devoted angler will tell you, it was finally worth it when we caught 26 large fish in two hours . . . . two *blissful* hours!

We then rowed the 90 minutes back, but those fish tasted indescribably delicious cooked over an open fire in bacon grease with sourdough biscuits and fresh local tomatoes the girls' marketing at the dock had produced. Millionaires didn't eat any better than we did that night!

All was not harmonious in the camp, however, and it's not the whole story unless all the details are brought up: the fish were super vacation additions but some unexpected and uninvited guests posed a real problem: M.I.C.E. We should have gotten a clue that first day while we were all unpacking and Dru opened a drawer in the kitchen and found a dozen or so USED mouse traps . . . the real, old-fashioned, spring-loaded jobbers. That discovery should have sparked at least a head-scratch, a furrowed brow and a deep-throated 'Hmmmmmm," especially taking into consideration that the traps were obviously well-used: bloody, rusty and almost sprung-out. Turns out, we could have used another dozen in any kind of condition.

The first night, the Leader of the Rat-Pack ran across Phyllis's face. When she sat up and screeched, shouting the name of her husband and protector, he (the mouse) disappeared and her trembling account was simply sloughed off as a bad dream. The second night, though, one got tangled in Dru's hair and she screamed everyone awake and Larry grabbed it and managed to get it out of her hair and out of the cabin as well. About that time, we heard two of the 12 traps we'd prepared go off like rifle shots. Larry and I took care of the traps and their gruesome, pop-eyed occupants and silence reigned once more, but since it was 4AM and nearly light outside, Larry and I decided to go fishing while the wives and kids lay back and snoozed on.

Apparently, after we left, more mice ran across the beds; Dru had enough and got up, wrapped herself up in her sleeping bag and sat on the table in the middle of the kitchen, armed with a broom. She said that from her vantage point she saw two mice fighting over a piece of bread right in front of her on the floor; it was later discovered they also gnawed on the rolls of toilet paper, which, consequently neither Phyllis nor Dru would consider using. This was pre-Hanta-virus, but they were fastidious ladies and would not be swayed; lucky that we had ample supplies of the un-chew-ed sort.

Later that day, Dru gathered up her things and her kids and moved to another cabin down the lane a bit, hoping to get away from the creatures. Phyllis, while not a mouse lover by any means, did not have a real phobia about them like Dru had, so Phyllis did all she could do to help and aide her fellow-sufferer and stayed put.

Meanwhile, as soon as the intrepid fishermen arrived at *The Spot*, our spot, the Spot of all Spots on the river, it started raining, but we set off down the slope to the fishing hole anyway.

Well, yeah!

Decked out in waders, we slogged along in the water, which seemed to level out at about knee-deep, looking for a good place. We splashed away, inhaling the beauty and fragrance of our surroundings; I was lost in thought, a bit in front, and, glancing to my left, I saw Larry's hat bobbing along in the water to the side of me.

I found that odd.

Turned out he had stepped into a hole that was over his head. I grabbed at his hat, and just then, he surfaced a little bit downstream and pulled himself ashore, righted himself, dumped 100 gallons of river water out of his waders and continued fishing from the bank. My pal Larry! What a trooper!

It continued to rain but the fishing was good enough to take our minds off of our physical misery. Apparently, this is a concept lost on the female gender. After we ate our damp sack lunches later that day, I went off downstream, armed with my trusty Mepps spinner, and managed to snag a 18" cutthroat. I was really soaking up my self-manufactured glory and was anticipating showing the fish off later at camp and then on my very next cast, I hit a *really* big one. It was so huge, I was afraid I wouldn't be able to reel it in, but after about 32 hours, (minutes?) of fighting, I finally got him landed! He measured 24 inches and was so thick and fat, the small hand-held fish scale couldn't weigh him. We ended up digging a pit to roast him in when we got home! A pit! For a fish! Big! Big fish!!!

Wish I had pictures, but you know how pictures deduct 10 lbs from fish . . . while every telling of the story adds 10 . . . . a pit! We had to dig a PIT!

Strangely, the wives didn't seem to be having as good a time as Larry and I were having, so he and I thought it over, and we went into action. I grouped all the kids and organized an expedition to pick blueberries while Larry worked on a little 'hut' built out of branches for the kids to play in, close to the cabin and far enough from the water for the mom's comfort levels.

The girls napped in the hammocks.

The more the kids and I walked, the more bountiful the berries were. Larry found us an joined in, for there seemed to be *tons* of the succulent little beauties and we all brought back sacks full, as much as we could carry. The kids were covered head to toe and resembled little Smerf's, sporting bright blue hands, arms and faces but it was a happy group.

Now, I happen to really LOVE blueberries with sugar and milk: not just like, mind you, I use the word *love* here, so after a *superb* fish dinner, I poured some canned milk over a big mixer-size bowl of berries, sprinkled on some sugar and dug in. I left the cabin and went outside to a front-porch settee and was contentedly engrossed in reading a book and scooping berries into my mouth. After a bit, I glanced down at my bowl and noticed there were two tiny white-ish worms floating on the top.

"Hmmm," I thought. I flipped them out with my spoon and just kept reading and eating. Then, I saw some more worms floating on the surface of the milk. I was suspicious by this time and closed the book and took a spoonful of berries to the outdoor table near where I was eating and popped a few open with my knife: almost every fifth berry was nearly empty . . . . except for worms.

My supper was finished before anyone else, so I had gotten to dessert first. When I made my toothsome discovery public, everyone else stopped short and quit spooning them up. No one else had dug in as of yet, I don't think. The kids were keenly disappointed when their mommies went around and collected all their little bowls of fruit and my suggestion that we just let them eat the darn berries they had picked, worms and all, was not met with much enthusiasm from the maternal section, even after I pointed out they had been eating them all afternoon anyway.

Being a true-blue (no pun intended) carnivore-omnivorous of the nth degree, I just kept on eating and even finished off the abandoned bowls everyone else had left. I jeered at the nicey-nice non-eaters and they made ugly, gagging faces at me.

All in all, the gals had a tough time with the swarm of kids and the rodent plague but after the mice problem was solved and Dru's terror was assuaged, she didn't feel too badly and enjoyed the outdoors very much. We all did a lot of fishing, taking turns babysitting so everyone had a chance at the boat; Phyllis would fish but not clean and Dru didn't care for fishing but cleaning fish was challenging and she said she didn't mind. Serendipitous!

The weather stayed stable and the lake was jewel-bright and placid; the sharp, clean air that was heavy with the aroma of evergreen and the musky odor of sphagnum moss and ferns was exhilarating to breathe. Deer and moose were frequent visitors, and although on the way OUT of the area, while we were on the ferry, Phyllis got a hold of some literature that described our idyllic Island campsite as, quote, "the most heavily-populated area for brown bear in the United States", unquote . . . an extraordinary one bear per square mile! Phyllis turned green and was ill on the ferry ride back . . .

Guess it wasn't a vacation story that would be touted in the tourist informational pamphlets as a perfect family holiday. Not perfect but certainly typical: the guys have all the fun and the wives end up with most of the work and the kids only remember the worms . . . .

THE BOYS, HOLDING SMALL POLAR BEAR SKULLS THAT I
GOT FROM A GUIDE, WHEN THE ZOOLOGY DEPARTMENT
OF BYU WANTED SOME

PHYLLIS CARRYING KELLY. 1968 IN KOTZEBUE.

"OH, BOY, LOOKIT THE HORNS ON THIS ONE!"

PHYLLIS SNOW-SHOING NEAR KOTZEBUE.

CHAPTER 8

"ONE-EYED MEN" AND "VILLAGES"

"In the Kingdom of the Blind, the One-Eyed man is King"

At the time we were there, Georgetown was a poor area with many health care issues. The town was inland and inland villages are usually nicer than those on the coast; the homes and businesses are generally built of logs, or at least wood, and there is a certain element of civic and house-pride evident. Also, inland villages (and inland villagers) smell of wood smoke while coastal dwellers and their dwellings are less . . . how shall I say it . . . gentle on the olfactory senses . . . . but that was not the case in Georgetown in 1968.

The year I spent there one week is ever-etched on my mind: between all-day TB sputum testing and a few hours' sleep on the provided cot which I fondly called 'The Rack', things could certainly have been better, but, I did get my first dogsled ride and that was cool! I really enjoyed the thrill of being pulled along at a brisk pace in silence, just the 'whoofling' of the dogs as they ran and the crunch of the snow beneath the sled runners. A fellow named McGee was a teacher there and a great guy and Phyllis and I enjoyed his company as well as his wife's. She taught also, but they did not live in Georgetown, and were residing in the town of Lower Kalskag.

It's an interesting fact that teachers in these small Alaskan villages are often unofficially put in the position of Judge, Officers of the Law, Idea-source and God-substitute to the native people.

It can make or break a town's future success and growth, even its ambience, so to speak. Unfortunately, as everywhere you go, there are bad teacher or teachers who used their occupation to hone their skills at being 'little Napoleon's' and treating the villagers as their subordinates and as lesser people—their unpleasant demeanors seemed to negatively affect the very people they were sent there and supposed to aid.

Granted, I have expressed my opinion on this issue before, but it is one of my pet peeves for sure! If I am ever elected King of the World, I shall travel about, in disguise, rewarding kind, good people and cutting the heads off of all the officious, rude, arrogant and dastardly ones, bury 'em, dig 'em up and kill 'em again . . . . my wife says that point of view shows just a tad of repressed hostility . . . .

Luckily for Lower Kalskag, the McGee's were fun-loving and seemed to be dedicated to the town and its people. It was a pleasure to work with them. I have to share, though, Mrs. McGee had dependence on something that I never considered to have such an addictive nature: every week, the supply plane would come in and bring her a case of Coca Cola . . . remember now, this was well after real, honest-to-goodness cocaine was *removed* from the brew in the early years after it's first initiation. As expensive as airlifting was at that time, it must have run her a buck a bottle and that's when earning a dollar an hour was big money! Not to mention hard on the teeth!! I'd be surprised if today she still has any of her original teeth—or her liver!

∾∾∾∾∾∾∾∾∾∾∾∾∾

Upper Kalsag was a place that could always be counted on NOT to be dull! I recall one weekend I was working on a patient, a forty-year old fellow with an 80-year-old body full of problems. It took him 20 minutes simply to relate all of his ills; it was enough to make me give up practice and go into research.

The citizens here are generally half Eskimo and half Indian; they are a pleasant-looking people who are polite and happy for the most part. I had some extra time, so I taught a bunch of third graders practical anatomy. Also pulled a LOT of teeth! On this particular day, my journal relates that I pulled 39 teeth, took 78 x-rays, started 20 individuals out on INH, a prophylaxis TB medication designed for converters and their families, and lastly gave an impromptu lesson on radio use and etiquette, which they seemed pleased to learn. All in all, a good 2 days and I left Upper and Lower Kalsag with a warm and satisfying feeling that I had aided the population of those hardscrabble hamlets and left them much better off than I had found them.

In the four years we were in Alaska, I made at least a dozen trips to this area; it was a prime example of the core facts I'd learned, and that was that one or two individuals can make a huge difference on a large number of people . . . an influence that passes down through generations, even. As I have mentioned before, it was fascinating for me to observe how even trifling events or attitudes can have such profound effects on the lives of countless, even un-met future individuals.

We came in contact with so many people in Alaska: some unforgettable for pleasant memories and some unforgettable for the damage they caused. I have forgotten many, many things over time and not everything made it into the journal. It's been over 40 years since we left the lower 48-states for our time-warp in Alaska. I am grateful for heeding the counsel of a Prophet to keep a journal, so these people and events were not forgotten by me, as I am sure they'd be without that record. In fact, while reading these first draft pages, it is almost like reading something new and not about me at all. My wife tells me I'm losing it and that if I didn't have so much of 'it' to begin with, I'd be a drooling idiot. Not sure what exactly what that means but I am taking it as a compliment!

Another couple that stands out in my mind is Bob and Carol Clark . . . they were teachers by the simple definition but oh! so much more. They were a great couple and assets to the 4-teacher school. The Principal of the school there and his wife, on the other hand, rarely spoke to me except when they needed something . . . I was kept at arms' length until the arm reached out to grab . . . in many cases, a prescription or some other medical 'favor' they needed from me! Then I was treated as their new best friend . . . but only temporarily! I had private little code/pet names for the people who were less than nice . . . not just to me but to others, too. It was probably a petty affect on my part but it certainly satisfied me and was a better way of coping with willful ignorance and pettiness that out and out confrontation would have been. I've never been a confrontational-personality type . . . it's been a learned response over the years but I've found that the older I get, the less crap I'm willing to take from people.

My 'revenge method' went as follows: I would shop at the PX every chance I could and load up on fresh produce. Fresh fruit and vegetables were very desirable items, as you can imagine, in a land of almost perpetual cold and as far away from local stores as to be unimaginable. Carrots, celery, lettuce and any assorted soft fruit that was available were my 'thank you' notes to whomever I was staying with while on I was on rounds and the calculation was simple: if they were nice, they got to enjoy fresh goodies, BUT if not, they were in my mind, big Zeros. If I was working in a place and the teachers or other personnel I worked with were pleasant and helpful, they got fruited.

No nice-y, no fruit-y.

The stuff just stayed wrapped up in my baggage to be taken to the next stop . . . almost like Santa's axiom. 'He knows if you've been bad or good!'

~~~~~~~~~~~~

One lady I will never forget was half of a couple in Hooper Bay; they had been missionaries in the Congo or somewhere else rather secluded, prior to serving as teachers for the BIA. There was a standing joke about her and I got the scoop early in my stay and so I was watching for her when the first freeze-up came in September. I really do appreciate her as I am sure she positively affected my health and added years to my life with the amusement she unwittingly afforded me. Every time she left her house to walk to school, it cracked me up to see her. She would get dressed for the trip to school by donning face mask, goggles, flight pants, extra-long parka, knee high boots, crampons and an ice pick!

Me: 'Hi, have you been out on your Skidoo this morning, or mountain climbing, perhaps?"

Her: "No, I just came from my house", she would answer, a bit huffily I always thought. Her house was probably 20 yards away . . .

She wasn't very likable and about the best you could say about her was that she was entertaining to watch. Her husband was a rather mild-mannered and indistinct man (isn't that the way it goes?) and the two of them kind of balanced each other out. I gathered they didn't like the couple that lived next door to them in the duplex. The building was long with two apartments built on each end into it for the teachers. The two apartments had *adjoining* kitchens, which was the problem as far as the other couple was concerned. Since the other couple used to fight a lot and fight loudly, these old folks kept their years' supply of food, cases and cases of canned goods, stacked up against the wall in the kitchen to keep the noise down from the ruckus next door. I had breakfast with them one morning and when the husband took down a case of canned milk for cereal, it left a hole in the sound barrier. The old wife really got on to him about leaving a space for the sound to travel through.

~~~~~~~~~~~~~

The villages that I traveled to were as diverse as the huge state of Alaska. As I have expressed often, with 'civilization', the villages adapted in their own ways, and there were so many factors in play. One factor that was interesting to me was the BIA teachers and their individualities and how it affected the villages.

~~~~Chevak~~~~

Chevak was the first village where the people came up to me and offered crafts for sale; I felt guilty if I refused because I was afraid I would offend them. Later, I found out that was not the case at all . . . regardless of the outcome they went away with a smile and good feelings. It was still hard for me to say no, even after years of getting used to the hawking of wares. Chevak was really poor and the villagers sold baskets and mukluks and about anything marketable just to have a little money; even the hunting and fishing in that area was poor.

The local and only store carried a lot of credit and got paid back slowly if at all. It seemed to me to be an area-wide pocket of depression, perhaps because of their poor location and the lack of anything really productive to do to earn money; they all seemed demoralized and really had to pull themselves up by their bootstraps to get anywhere.

The BIA teacher told me about one man who had an order for six of these masks at $50 each; apparently, he was quite an artist but he just never got around to making them. Some of the men worked at the cannery during the summer and when they got paid, spent their whole checks on things they really didn't need and didn't put anything away for the winter.

Frustrating stories like that abound in all cultures, it seems, and there is little anyone can do about it: you can't change an attitude of non-concern or instill an urge for personal betterment if there is no desire on the part of the people you are dealing with.

So, when I was approached and was offered an item to buy, I would ask 'how much?' and I would usually get a shoulder-shrug and, "Oh, any-much," as a reply, so I would state a price I thought was fair to both of us and they either accepted it or not. One woman made a pair of mukluks for Kyle after I had seen her work and provided his size; she heard me mention that I had another little boy, too, so I asked her how much they were going to be as I didn't have a lot of money to spend on that . . . and would she make two pairs for $15?

She answered, "E-e-e!" which is Eskimo for 'yes'. She went home, worked all night on them and brought the second pair to me at the clinic the next day to take home. The little guys were thrilled with their 'big ha-wryy boots.'

Another lady brought in a pretty basket that I liked the looks of and I asked her how much. "Oh, five dollar, or four dollar." I knew she probably needed the money and I didn't want to be a hard-nose about it, so I just said "How about $4.50?" and she placed the basket in my hands with a big smile. I could have stocked a small souvenir store; a lot of these things I bought were given as gifts or just given away to whoever expressed an interest. Kinda wish I had brought more of them back with us now. They would be worth a lot, as ethnic crafts are in big demand, especially 50-year-old craft items. Would have been a much better investment than most of my stocks . . . .

My time in Chevak went quickly that trip; the temperature was around 10-degrees above that day which wasn't too bad except for the addition of wind. I started out with the Health Aide to go around to the individual homes and collect sputum cans that had not been returned, as they should have been. Got numb hands and face very quickly and the idea of continuing around to every house became a daunting endeavor, especially when I went to each home, everyone had something for me to "look at."

Of the first ten people I looked at, one had a bad case of glaucoma in one eye that I couldn't fix of course, another had an umbilical hernia that needed surgery and another little boy had a bad heart murmur which necessitated taking him into the hospital.

That was about it for town of Chevak . . . still a memory after all these years.

~~~~Bethel~~~~

The area that Bethel Hospital served was the largest and poorest in the state, if you believed the census reports and the bureaucrats that complied them. There were 44 small villages around it that depended on the Hospital for service. Bethel itself was a town of about 300 with a 60-bed facility. As was the custom, I put up in transient quarters when I flew in and worked there; the hospital paid for overnight rooms for different visitors like x-ray techs and doctors and anybody else that had business of more than just one day.

One night that I spent there was a real experience. It sounded like the exceptionally popular female in the room next door had tied one on and according to the traffic patterns in and out of her room, each complete with one-door-slam-going-in-one-door-slam-going-out. This went on all night, it seemed and during her quest to entertain every guy in town, I was obliged to listen, unwillingly, to giggles, groans and grunts all accompanied by the cacophonous Song of the Bedsprings.

After a reasonably long length of quiet, someone began banging on MY door and I heard a female voice entreating me to "open up."

I had to call the Hospital security guard before she broke down the flimsy door. When he got there, I opened the door and between us and we tried to quiet her down, but she was not ready to call it a night. Back in separate rooms, she turned on her radio really loud, as if to get me back for my in-hospitability and when I tried to call up the guard again, he was not to be found . . . . hmmmm.

Because our work there was complete, we tried to fly out the next morning but it was much too cloudy to try and get to our next destination on that round. I recall this trip well because I had an x-ray tech with me who appeared to be alcoholic. I worked with him on several occasions; one night after we had finished, he went out but later came back to the quarters and I honestly thought he was going to lose it and try to kill me.

His raging dislike for me seemed to center on the fact that I wouldn't drink with him, it turned out. Well, that couldn't be helped. The threats and actions did not get physical, or I would have turned him in, but when he did his work, he was valuable. I just let the animosity fly over my head and out the window.

On this particular trip, he had a roaring hangover from the night before but had scraped himself together enough to get on the plane, and then he fell asleep in the back seat of the Cessna 180.

We were really crammed in tight; the weather went from bad to worse, so the pilot made a wide, sweeping turn and headed back to Bethel.

We landed and I said, "Come on, Ron . . . wake up . . . we're here."

He popped up, holding his head and shielding his eyes from the daylights glare and staggered out of the plane. Looked around and said, "This ain't Chevak! We're back in Bethel!" His nightmare had followed him and now we were both stranded in a dump with lousy weather, stray dogs, drunks and garbage everywhere and the generally inhospitable bunch at the Hospital who only barely tolerated when we Medical personnel came through, treating us like a nuisance instead of looking at us as aid and help with the staggering workload. Never could understand that . . . .

Ron just started in drinking again, as there was little else to do, I guess. I read four books that I brought along. We were there three miserable days before the weather cleared enough to take off.

The first trips 'a-field', so to speak, were wonderful in that they were not routine: there were places to go and things to see that were new and different and I have always liked new and different. I got back on the plane after this first visit much lighter than I was when I arrived: there were so sick people in need that I had gone through all the supplies I had brought . . . it was a light and fast ride home.

~~~~St. Mary's~~~~~

This was a Catholic village, it turned out (no! really? what gave it away?) and a certain Father N. was head of the local Church, and in reality, the whole town. One of the reasons that these villages were so poor, in my humble opinion, seemed to be that the Catholics are fanatical about birth control; that meant the women of childbearing age had about one baby a year if they were 'good Catholics.' The only birth control allowed was 'rhythm' aided by breastfeeding, which does give a mother a bit of protection against getting pregnant again, as long as the hormones that control milk production are active. I saw kids come home from school at noon to get breastfed. I'm not kidding. Whatever works, I guess. Father N asked me to give a talk to the village on rhythm the last night I was there. That was a real experience for me since, there being absolutely nothing else to do, there was a big crowd, and, teaching the Rhythm Method to a bunch of nice Eskimo ladies through an interpreter was a bit out of my line of work.

How he filled up the room, I don't know, but there they were . . . 40 or so eager faces, waiting to be enlightened. Now Father N was a great guy, about fifty and very pleasant to be around and he seemed dedicated to the people he was stewarding. Formerly, he had been a professor of physics at some Catholic university. Being the Spiritual leader of the Catholic community, he was in fact an absolute Czar over what the people did. I don't know whether HE did this or not, but I had heard of Priests going into homes and looking for birth control pills and throwing them away.

About this time, the best way NOT to get pregnant, other than the obvious or the permanent, was a little devise known as Lippes Loop, as we called them. So many of the really young girls had more looks than brains, this not being unusual at all in circumstances such as these and with this age-group. Dumb is dumb everywhere; but, illegitimacy numbers ran unusually above average here, though, and there seemed to be an inordinately-high number of retarded young women who were also promiscuous, and would get pregnant over and over and give birth, mostly, to retarded babies. Even if the baby was born normal, simply being raised without any of the necessary mental and intellectual stimulation that babies and toddlers need, turned out just like their parent. There is another entry in my journal about Kalsag, Upper and Lower . . . the town and it's people really must have made an impression on me, as I recorded my visits there more than once. Well, here is more about this neat area: Kalsag is upriver from Bethel and there are a lot of trees and lots of good fishing. The houses are built of logs with outhouses next to them . . . NO HONEYBUCKETS!!!!

Ralph and Lou had been teachers in the Philippines the year before where they got married. They were then assigned to this village and the kids in the town just loved them and they loved the kids right back! That is one reason I enjoyed traveling back deeper into in the bush so well . . . the people seemed to like me and I liked them—it sure makes life easier when you have mutual respect with the people you work with. When I would go into a village like this one that was clean and well-kempt and the people had pride in ownership and ambition and the icing on the cake was having a great school for the kids to learn from where the teachers were good examples and really loved the children and parents, too . . . I always got a lift out of playing a part in all of that: my little trumpet solo in that orchestra.

The villagers were open and friendly; they are Athabascan Indians, for the most part, and although there is a moderate amount of drinking here, it's not like a lot of villages I visited where it is extensive and that is all the people did. This is a heavily wooded area and the log homes are in direct contradistinction to the tin and plywood shanties that have been thrown together in the area out toward the Bearing Sea.

People came out in force to the clinic and I completed my TB workups in about three hours, x-rays and all. I spent the rest of the evening pulling teeth . . . one was impacted and I had to dig out the root. Sweaty and bloody . . . for Doctor and patient alike!

The school building there is built of wood, too, and is very old with two large classrooms and the Siedels living quarters on one end and storage and whatnot on the other end. I conducted my clinic and did my x-rays in a sunny, west-facing room on the by the classrooms; since I was traveling alone this trip, I did all the x-rays, sputum collections and kept all the records. This actually gave me more freedom in that I didn't have to ride herd on a bunch of technicians and it relieved the teachers from the inconvenience of putting up with a bunch of medical people stumping around in the house. The other folks in town seemed organized and were applying themselves to making their lives better, too, and I thoroughly enjoyed my visit.

~~~~Lower Kalsag~~~~

The McG's were the teachers in Lower Kalsag; they were from the deep south, and were very formal, and seemed more unhappy with their lives than Sam Magee . . . because they took themselves very seriously and managed every last little detail of the lives of the villagers, and in a most efficient way. They had an intercom system between the school and their home and they talked to each other, and only each other, on this intercom, using "10-4, Roger—Roger . . ." all very efficient. It appeared from what they said in our visits that they considered their jobs as teachers included also being judge, prosecuting attorney, marriage and family counselors, social directors and arbiters—in their own words, 'to brighten up the homes in the village.'

Because they acted so exacting and joyless, the villagers with their totally different set of values, found them intolerable; no one came around them enough to find out that they were dedicated and sincere . . . just lacking in social graces, somewhat. I enjoyed them quite a bit and I had stayed with them for 4 days once, waiting for a plane.

In this particular town, I set up the clinic in a quasi-storage room in the back. A lot of the stuff had been cleared out for me but a lot still remained. There was barely space for a mushy mattress in a corner of the room and the x-ray machine area in another about. This was the large Catholic Church and School mentioned in Chapter 7 and was run by the Jesuits. They showed me the kindest hospitality that had yet been afforded me. I had a 16X16 room all to myself with a very comfortable and warm straw tick in one corner. I set the x-ray machine up in another corner and enlisted a couple of the school boys to drive and we started down the river. Very soon, we were So, despite all the hubbub, I ended up making it back to Anchorage and home the next day; I was escorting a fellow with a hypoglossal duct cyst that needed to be removed at the larger hospital. I had picked him up in St. Mary's to travel along with me. I also had a kid on a stretcher with a skull fracture that I thought might require surgery if it turned sour. Besides all the stuff I requisitioned to take back and restore the coffers of my clinic, I added to the fray with a huge box of spare x-ray tubes and tiny coffin with a stillborn baby that I was taking back to be buried with the fathers family in Anchorage. I felt more like a macabre delivery guy than a Doc . . . .

~~~~~~~~~~~~~~

Sundays were rarely ever the same for me and although I really believed in honoring the Sabbath and keeping it Holy, it wasn't always do-able. On this particular Sunday, I was away from my family and marooned by inclement weather in a village, the name of I didn't even record in the journal, only the event. Anyway, it was really looking like a quiet day of rest, so I decided to walk the few blocks from my makeshift clinic and quarters into town early in the morning with my camera. The sign on the structure read 'Covenant Sunday School' which I learned later was a sort-of branch of the Pentecostal faith. Services were to begin at 10 a.m. and it was a little early, so I thought I would go in, get a seat in back and leave whenever I wanted to without disturbing the congregation, so I opened the unlocked door, went in and sat down. There wasn't a soul there, no pun intended; I checked my watch and it was about 10 minutes before the hour. I stayed sat on the long back bench that was built into the walls and surrounded the small, straggly bunch of 10 chairs in the middle, and I waited to see what would happen. It must have been about 20-degrees below . . . I learned to tell the temperature by gauging how far the streamers of steam went out in front of me from my breathing; I could see it swell out to about 5' that day. Cold.

Five minutes before the services were due to start, a warmly-suited guy walked in, nodded in my direction and quickly started a pre-set fire in the wood stove by opening the cast iron door and tossing a cup of gasoline on top of the waiting wood, backed up and threw in three lit wooden kitchen matches. It was rip-roaring in no time.

The building was about fifteen feet across and maybe 25 feet long and that was it . . . one big room. The gaggle of folding chairs was all of such a differing style and color that it could have been a pretty good diorama representation of every type of folding chair ever made. A veritable Museum of Folding Chairs Through The Decades. Apparently, in lieu of a steeple and bell, the sight of smoke coming out of the chimney meant that services were imminent, and the errant yet religion-hungry congregation came running in from all directions.

Soon, the majority of chairs were filled but not with the congregations' bums: everyone seemed to have a place staked out with room for their family members and the chairs were used to lean against or draw lines of distinction between the family groups. Most people preferred, it seemed, to throw down thick fur skins on the floor and sit on them rather than the chairs.

The children and younger people seemed to like the chairs better so there were little clumps and clots of people, waiting patiently, their breath fogging the air along with the acrid smell of the gasoline-fired heater. Soon, a short, heavily built man entered by a side door close to the front and stood behind a small platform in front.

The service was given in half Eskimo and half in English and the man that was presiding over the service was someone I must have met before as he looked familiar to me and when he looked in my direction and caught my eye, he gave me a solemn nod and then began to speak. Some of the words I knew and I got a little of it all and it sounded like he was reading a litany of people in the town who needed our prayers for one reason or another. Then, he gave an opening prayer that must have lasted 10 minutes.

After the invocation, he motioned to the crowd and 8 little children gathered in from the audience and lined up and started to sing but when they caught sight of me, they were so bashful to see a stranger that they ducked their heads down and pretty much quit singing. That caused the rest of the congregation to look back, also, to see what was so entrancing. When I realized that I was unwittingly causing the problem, beings as how I was unfamiliar and that all I had to do was glance in their direction and they would blush, rather than leaving which I thought would be rude, I scrunched down in my chair and just listened.

Then it was time for Pastor Slowoko, the aforementioned dentist that I had finally recognized after the information portion of my heavily-taxed memory clicked into recall-mode, to offer his directives for living a good life. He took over his position at the pulpit with obvious pride and a self-satisfied look on his face. He began his verbal epistle and was giving a very dramatic sermon with much arm waving and quoting of Isaiah. He held a large battered Bible which he occasionally opened and read from, and its dramatic effect as a prop was most useful.

As he seemed to come to the climax of his talk, and his audience was still and staring, his voice had gotten progressively louder and higher in pitch and then he took a deep breath and fastened a steely eye on the whole congregation, taking in all 30 or so of us with direct eye-contact, one after another. Then, in a dreadfully modulated voice, embellished with much gusto and bass vibrato, he reported that we were all sinners and dreadful in the eyes of God and that God thought we were pretty worthless . . . he repeated the last statement both in an Indian dialect I had heard before, then Alaskan, and even came through at the end with the statement in English, probably for my benefit:

"We are awful. We are rotten!" . . . . a pause for dramatic effect, "We stink!"

It was probably holding at 10 below outside when the service neared its end. I was certainly feeling uplifted and full of the milk of human kindness after that rousing speech. The temperature outside would be a relief after the fire-and-brimstone that had just been showered on our heads. By this time, the stove had warmed the room up to maybe 20 degrees *above* zero inside. I had noticed the fact when I had entered the room that there were no coat racks provided so now, as the sermon ended, I could see that none were needed as everybody had kept most all of their clothing on, taking off only hats and heavy parkas.

Suddenly, in the middle of what I took to be the Reverends closing remarks and prayer, the door opened and a boy burst in and shouted something and I heard a few words I knew. It seemed his mother was having some kind of attack. He was talking so fast, I only caught a word or two that I could understand, but apparently she was at the family home, only a few doors down. All eyes were on the boy and, as one, the roomful rose and charged for the door. I joined in, keeping up as best as I could.

Following the running lad, we raced to her and when I say "we", I mean the entire stinking, rotten, seeped-in-evil congregation, including their Prophet Isaiah. I was hard-pressed to maintain my position right behind the boy.

Reaching the house well ahead of me, the Reverend said something to the crowd that made the throng fall back and open a path, and all eyes were on me as I approached.

As I entered the home and my eyes adjusted to the dim light, I could see her. She was sitting up in bed, gasping and groaning and was in a high state of distress; her pulse was irregular at about 30, her wrist told me. My little interpreter related that she was on digitalis and he had retrieved the bottle from a cupboard near her bed. Her lungs were rattling with each labored breath when all of a sudden she moaned loudly and fell over backwards, absolutely unresponsive and limp, with her eyes rolled in the back of her head and her mouth wide-open . . . I thought she had died; I could feel no pulse then, at any point I tried to take it.

We've all witnessed a scene like this on stage or in the movies: everyone just turns into pillars of stone and time seems to stand still. The classic wide-eyed, open-mouthed, immovable and suspended-in-time crowd was almost too atypical and would have been funny to witness if the situation had not been so serious. My training held me in good stead, however, and I was just leaning forward to position her and position myself to start CPR, when suddenly, the woman sat up, leaned over and vomited . . .

Now, I will inject a teaching moment here, if you don't mind: if one is vomiting, it is a Good Thing to be sitting up rather than lying down . . . my objection was not the actual vomit-ing, per se, but my unwilling compliance in being vomited-upon. I pulled back just in time and shook off the worst of it, then turned back to my patient. My guardian Angel must have acted in my favor upon the circumstances so that I wasn't actively giving her mouth-to-mouth when she spewed . . . there is just no getting used to that . . .

Her pulse rate came back strong as I listened with my stethoscope. I never went anywhere without generous pockets full of emergency medical items and once again I was thankful. She seemed much better, but just in case, I gave her fifty mg of Phenagran, an anti-nausea. I was ready for a dose of tranquilizer myself. I surmised that she had an attack of paroxysmal arterial tachycardia which is an important-sounding name for fast, irregular heartbeat, and then when she passed out her reflexive vomiting sort of slowed things down to normal. The wonder of the human body!

The crowd dispersed, sure that the drama had passed. Between the unique Sunday Services and the melodrama that followed, it remains in my memory as one of the most unusual Sabbaths of my life.

~~~~~~~~~~~~~

On one of many trips to Nome, where I had been detailed to travel to, my carriage arrived in the shape of an old DC3, a workhorse of a plane that was outfitted to fly between the islands and such. Usually, it crewed the same pilot who had been sent over by Weins Airlines to St. Lawrence Island and back every day. He was a nice-enough guy and it was easy to get to know him; he always helped me load the many boxes of equipment that went with me where 'ere I traveled, and I appreciated that very much. This particular time, almost immediately after take-off, with me in the co-pilots seat, he began to relate his medical woes . . . heck, it goes with the badge: all Doc's know that it's almost inevitable that people want to talk about their ills whenever a Doc is handy and I didn't mind.

From what I could make out in his descriptions of his ailments, he probably caught something by being in the wrong bed and although he had gotten medical help before, it didn't seem to be doing the job. He told me he'd had a bad reaction to the penicillin that was first proffered and so he had to forego that. His biggest concern was that when his detail was over, he would return to his happy home and his loving wife and that would NOT be the kind of thing she would appreciate him bringing her back as a souvenir.

Since he'd always been helpful to me when I was in this part of the state, I decided to see what I could do, unofficially of course. After I wrote the orders myself, I sent him for more lab work and selective tests and finding the exact result that I had suspected, I began to treat his gonorrhea. I must have gone through four courses of different drugs, and each one had such bad side effects for him that he had to stop taking them. He was actually too sick to be a good pilot when the pills had him breaking out in hives or vomiting.

I had used just about all the cards up my sleeve, but on each trip as we village-hopped through western Alaska, he would greet me with, "Still got the drip, Doc," and I knew I had to try something else, trying to hit the jackpot. I didn't have a lot of confidence in the Nome lab so was even doing some lab-work myself. His Nome assignment was ending soon, as would his marriage, and I was running out of options.

Different medicines in different strengths were all I had to fight it with and I really got concerned for his stability as failure after failure kept piling up. One trip with me in the cockpit and him sobbing and pounding his fist on his thigh to accentuate every word, he said, "You (thump) just (thump) have (thump) to do (thump) something!" (Thump, thump and thump.) I was genuinely concerned that he might freak out and it crossed my mind that I might have to fly the plane in if he totally lost it!

Well, drug approach #5 seemed to do the job, as on my return flight 3 days later, he seemed to be in better spirits. The correct meds are truly miracle drugs, especially in cases like this that have such straightforward symptoms. I advised him strongly not to quit taking the pills until they ran their course and were all gone and he assured me he would comply, and promised me a final culture before returning to the waiting arms of his wife.

The words, "Serves you right!" were very close to coming out of my mouth. In fact, I think I may have mentioned that to him . . . . never heard from him again, so I would like to think all ended well.

He had seemed very contrite and vowed to the Heavens that he would never stray again.

Catching an STD should be mandatory with any extra-marital sexual activity.
My opinion. Probably won't catch on . . .

~~~~~~~~~~~~~

AS THE GRAPE TURN-ETH.

On a quick trip to Nunapitchuk and Kosigwan I stopped in to visit the Fergusons and to see old John C. a real legend in the Bush. He was capable, knowledgeable and active in about everything that went on up there. It so happened that around Christmas time, each BIA teacher would make up an order for supplies to be brought in by boat the following summer. Impulse purchases were not feasible. Neither was window-shopping. John was a long-time teacher in Nunapitchuk, and a pretty cagey old fellow; when it was his turn to order, he really went all out requesting large amounts of things like raisins and dates and prunes: anything that he could ferment. It seems that he had rigged up a still in the basement of the school where he kept his supplies.

Once, when I was listening to the chatter on the BIA radio system, I heard the unmistakable voice of old John C. come on and say he would trade anybody anything . . . . cases of cookies or crackers or whatever he had, for six cases of raisins. Apparently, somebody at Headquarters in Juneau had figured out why he wanted all that dried fruit and wouldn't ship them to him anymore and he had to trade everything he owned for raisins because his very profitable business was going belly-up without the fruit to produce the raisin wine he sold around town.

My impression when I first met him was that he was a gregarious and smiling guy about fifty-five with a real Ernie Bilko persona. He always had a deal and a trade and you knew he was going to come out ahead and sock it to you, but he was so fun to be around that you didn't care. I almost wished I HAD a case or two of raisins for the crafty rascal.

MEANDERINGS.

People in the area around Upper Yukon spoke an Indian dialect and not the usual Eskimo I was used to hearing. Many other things were different too, for instance the Mukluks made here were made of moose and caribou hides and I liked them better because they didn't smell like the ones made from seal hide. I ordered a face mask and snow shoes and a big fur zipper-pull. The zipper-pull tied to the mittens so one could zip and unzip without taking off mittens. Very important sometimes . . . think it over. I had an interesting experience in Fairbanks: a group of folks were brought in to the Hospital from a village called Anaktuvik Pass, 'way up North of Fairbanks.

This is the pass that the Caribou migrate through Spring and Fall and the name 'Anaktuvik' means 'where the caribou lay their dung'. Enchanting. It is one of the most primitive areas in all of Alaska. What an expansive statement that is! . . . . but it was certainly the truth in 1968 . . . I would be interested to know how it is there now and if it has gotten all civilized-up. That would be a shame.

~~~~~~~~~~~~~

A man named Savage was the village president in Anaktuvik. This type of leadership was just catching on up there and seemed to be well-accepted and practical. The State Troopers had trained two of the locals, Moses and Alexi, to be the town marshals. So far, I was informed, they had arrested a fellow and sentenced him to 6 months in jail for boozing and causing a ruckus. What an improvement! There seemed to be a lot of civic pride there and the Health Aides were getting paid on time and correctly, resulting in good humor all around. The more I heard about it, the more I thought it looked like it was going to be a successful experiment in local government.

In the past, there had been so much trouble in the village; it seemed to be full of bad sorts that beat their kids and their wives, drank or drugged it up, and raised hell in general. In a village like this, a majority of the people live out all of their lives in one place; add that to the fact that they are not only living in the same place but in most cases, in the same way that their parents and their parents before did and so forth, on back no one knows how far.

It seemed to be that there were a very few of each generation who were a little more energetic than the others; they didn't drink all the time and seemed to want to better themselves and their families, as well as their village. Some chose to go out and get training and come back and be Troopers or Councilmen with some authority over the town. They could arrest people and they had the backing of most of the population, except the ones whose toes got trampled on, of course.

The more I observed the Eskimo and Inuit people, I came to be of the opinion they seem to be a generally passive people by nature. It was very difficult for me, when I was at the Hospital in Kotzebue, to hire a good supervisor because they simply did not discipline one another. They just weren't 'wired' to be aggressive and critical. That's a good thing, but can be negative, too, I suppose.

THE UGLY AMERICAN.

Once in a while, a specialist would come up from Anchorage and go on my outbound trips to the villages with me and with whoever else I got to take with me, whether it was the local Health Aide or a Nurse. We enjoyed taking these fellows out for a village trip because in most cases, they had just been sitting in the cities and had no idea what a real Alaskan village was. Generally, they were interesting to be around, they cut our work-load down and I definitely learned a lot from each of them.

One fellow I recall was Dr. Herschfeldt, and he was a really great guy; we always made time to go hunting or fishing on these village missions or, after I got my plane, I could take him sightseeing and I enjoyed seeing the magnificence of Alaska through other eyes. Some Doctors, who I wrote about often in my journals named Pearson, Koyle and Carlyle, came up often and they were fun, too. They got in a lot of work, but were good to team up with. Once, all three were with me and I damaged my Snow Sport trying to take them all fishing in a remote and rough area. They were OK hikers, too, I found out. Good thing. We had a ways to walk!

One of these unforgettable persons was unforgettable in a negative way. He was an eye specialist and although I have a record of his unusual name as well as the memory etched in my mind, I, for legal reasons, shall call him Doctor Z. On a bastard scale from 1 to 10, he was, as the old joke goes, at least an 11. His idea of fun seemed to be putting other people down to show off what a great and witty guy he was.

The trouble being, he was a pretty superior specimen: highly intelligent and with a large vocabulary that he was pleased to showcase; physically he was just a moose! He liked nothing better than to go hiking or hunting and just purposely run his companions into the ground, saying all the time "Oh, come on now, you gotta keep up!" Nearly in-exhaustible, he often talked about that fact that he had grown up on the south of Chicago where competition was the name of the game and he brought that blood-in-the-eyes manner with him. There's nothing wrong with friendly competition and I will be the first to admit it if I'm bested in any area, but this guy could *not* be taken down.

One time, we were holding a clinic together and as the day wore on, I was getting to the point that I could not tolerate being in the same room with the guy. His bedside manner was very condescending toward his patients, too, and although I would not have let him, or anyone for that matter, get away with out and out *cruelty* towards someone else, he came darn close to crossing the line.

Anyway, it had been a long day and after it was over, I suggested that we both go for a ride together and get in some fishing as the sun was still bright and I had a pretty good snow-machine those days back then. I told him I'd show him a good time. My snowmobile would go about 45 MPH and in was 'way good; we had 2 other guys with us. They were sharing a machine but since the passenger seat on my machine was packed up with fishing gear, I had 'Z' sit on the back; he was being pulled along on the platform like a water-skier. I took off, hell-bent-for-leather and just floor-boarded the snow machine with him barely hanging on there on the back. Snow that was kicked up by the machine was getting thrown up around six feet and settling back down on "Z" and, knowing this, I did not turn around once. See no evil . . . hear no evil. After about an hour of this, I figured he must have totally frozen his bum and turned into a snowman by that time, so I stopped and yet, he did not complain! Not a PEEP!

When we got to the fishing area our guide had directed us to, I jumped off the machine, all warm and comfy from being behind the windshield and having the warmth of the engine, too. He just kinda creaked off the back of the thing, dropping great avalanches of drifted snow. His trademark mustache was frozen solid and he was moving slowly, but forced a smile nonetheless. I asked him how he liked the ride and he said, "Oh, yeah, it was great fun!" I had hit every bump in the pack ice I could on the way there and only wished I could have planned an even more bumpy return, but other than push him off in front of a Polar bear, I could only do so much. With witnesses. His time in the area ran out before I could come up with anything dastardly enough. Guess I'm just not an evil genius type but sure wish he had gone down hard! Enough to knock off some of that arrogance.

~~~~AS THOU SOWETH~~~~

On one of my trips out and about, I needed the services of a snow machine, so I went to Koyuk and visited with a Robert James, a former Health Aide that I had struck up a friendship with. From there, I traveled to a burg called Shaktoolik where I had the absolute worst experience of my entire Alaska career.

The BIA teachers assigned there were just flat-out the most awful that can be imagined, and, considering some of the mixed nuts I had met up to that time, that was a grandiose statement, but they were just awful. They both had ignorant attitudes and acted as if they didn't like anyone or anything: pure negatively flowed out of them in a gusher. They met me, unsmiling and grim, and sort of pointed to where I could set up the medical equipment I had come with and stood by, arms crossed, offering no welcome or help at all, while I toted it all in.

The Health Aide in the village filled me in as soon as she got to the schoolhouse that would serve as my clinic while there. She told me, among other things, that they would not let her use the radio at all . . . even though it was a vital part of her job to use it and report any cases she needed advice on. They kept it locked in a spare bedroom, along with ALL of the First Aid supplies, and they would not let her have a key.

If she needed to get anything, even a Band-Aid, she had to go all the way around the building and ring the bell at their house, then wait while they took their sweet time coming around to let her in. Sometimes, she related, they just didn't come to the door at all, although she knew they were in there. She was intimidated by them, as was everyone in the village, she said. They held the whole little town literally in their control and that was the way they wanted it.

It was about nine in the morning when I arrived that day on my first visit, and I probably had not taken time to eat breakfast; usually, I would eat with the school kids at lunch and I always enjoyed that. Well, they charged me $4 for the food they got for free and the Aide told me that they always ate the supplies that were ear-marked for the children, in addition to the items they were entitled to, and on top of it all they charged the other teachers.

Well, I had missed breakfast and was in the middle of setting up some x-ray equipment over lunch period and so missed that, too. By dinner, I expected the customary invitation to eat with the BIA teachers . . . it was just a part of my visits, but all was silent. They had not come over to see me, nor spoken one word and the general feeling I got was that they were watching me only to make sure I didn't steal the silver or something!

The only place to buy food of any kind in town was a bit of a hike away, but I walked it gladly and bought a box of crackers for $3 and that was all the food I was to have for my 26 hour adventure in lovely Skaktoolik. The clinic ran right along, despite the chilly atmosphere, although they both showed up at the door at 4 o'clock sharp, announcing that the clinic was over and that school was closed. I had not had enough time to see all of the children and when I pointed this out to them, the old man made a muttered comment about my speed and skill and we got into a rather heated argument. My journal notes do not elaborate on the details, only that after our little chat, I told the Health Aide that I was going to go to the next village on my route, Koyuk, and that I would not spend the night under the same roof with people like that.

In fact, as this was my first visit, they had not even pointed out where I would be sleeping, perhaps that was just as well . . . they may have intended I curl up in a ball and tuck my nose under my tail and sleep in a snow bank like a sled dog.

It was getting dark when I finally got loaded up and ready to go; the Aide had told me that Koyuk was about 30 miles, depending on whether you chose to cross the bay on the pack ice or go around, and I told her to just find me someone, anyone, with a machine to take me out of there! There was no problem getting a 'taxi', as I paid the going rate of $1 a mile. As I departed, I left this absolutely horrid couple with a few of my choicer epitaphs, stressing that if I got any more reports of medical supplies being misappropriated or the Health Aide being kept from doing her assignment, I would report them to the BIA Chief and see where that went. All I got in reply was the grim satisfaction I felt when both of their hairy, puckered old mouths dropped and that was the last thing I ever saw of them.

After my inglorious exit, I had about 4 hours on the back of a snow machine to Koyuk, and then on to Elim and the kindly ministrations of the Frances', who were ever-so gracious to me, but while my dander was up, I composed a letter to the BIA and told them what anti-social, egotistical, barbaric old Nazi's that couple were and that I would not go back there, ever. The next thing I knew, I had a teletype from Anchorage and my Boss was telling me that the BIA had communicated with him, asking what the big, bad doctor was doing, causing trouble. Now, he knew me well enough by then to know that I am just not normally vile to other people.

He said although he felt I was in the right, he had to apologize for me, but I told him I would walk out before I would say 'sorry' for anything I had said or done. An hour phone conversation later, he told me that he had been around them in another village and had heard many distressing stories about the negative atmosphere they seemed to breed and exude everywhere they went. The sad part is that it was the townspeople that suffered . . . they were the ones that got shorted. Even their own bosses knew what they were like but they had been with the BIA for so long, they couldn't get rid of them, so they had put them in the smallest village in the whole state where the least damage could be done.

Ironically, the Health Department and the BIA were all supposed to be there for the same reason: to improve the lives of the citizens of the state. So much for playing the game of politics, for we were dependant upon the BIA for their radios and their buildings to hold clinics in and they were dependant on us for the medical care. Why couldn't we all just get along? The poor Shaktoolik-arians . . . all 203 of them!

~~~~Marshall~~~~

One couple who lived in Marshall remains memorable to me *because* of their *typicality*, really. The name of the village conjures up visions of *them*, rather than any details of the town itself. They were kind of a archetype for lots of the BIA teachers we ran into . . . euphemistically, they would be called 'talkative' which translates, in Alaska-ese to "bushy". They were so hungry for somebody to talk to, or more correctly, a *new* pair of ears to fill, that they would dismiss class . . . just quit teaching school as soon as I got there, and come over to wherever I was and talk *at* me all day long.

As the clinic hours wiled away, I looked forward to finishing my work there, and wanted nothing more than sew it up and get away. As luck would have it, I'll be darned if it didn't happen that *every time* I was in Marshall that the weather would turn sour and I'd be stuck in the urban Mecca that was Marshall three *more* days, (that felt like 30) waiting for a plane! When I finally got out of there, my ears actually hurt and I had a stiff neck from nodding and my smile was permanently plastered on, along with a glazed look to my eyes.

A typical day in one of my 'traveling MD" runs started by seeing patients at 7 AM and I would just keep on straight through until I pooped out at 10PM or so. But, during the trips to Marshall, when I would try to skulk away and drag my tired butt to bed, the old fellow-half of the BIA team would actually follow me into my sleeping room and chat while I got ready for bed! I was relieved to find a lock on the bathroom door or I believe he would have come in and chatted there, too! The last night I was with them, right after dinner, I actually fell asleep sitting up in the middle of one of his marathon stories and when I finally came to, he was gone, to my eternal relief!

Another funny story I heard about him (and I only mildly jest about him here as I know he has been gone a LONG time from this earth and I figure if it upsets him to have this missive his only memorial, I will likely have to answer to it someday) was the 'clean water anecdote'. Seems he would go out along the river during winter and cut out some big blocks of ice with a chain saw and then bring them home and stack them outside his house. These crystal-clear blocks of ice were his treasure for they provided drinking water all year. The fly in this particular ointment was the dogs that came over and relieved themselves on the pristine blocks! He bought himself a shotgun, filled it with birdshot, and took aim at any dogs that dared try to turn his clear ice yellow . . . his stash couldn't be guarded 24/7, however, and that was the part that seemed to make him crazy!

It really was obnoxious of me, but I couldn't resist having a little fun at his expense; when I would visit there, I'd ask for a glass of water and then I would gaze at it and remark that, perhaps, it had a shade of yellow . . . . that would start him off on a tirade about the lousy so-and-so dogs and dog owners. Little light moments like that made life bearable for me, but it probably didn't do too much to enhance his!

On February 8, 1967, my journal relates, I was going to take a run at the trio of villages of Upper Kalskag, St. Mary and Pitka's Point. It was snowing when I caught the plane out of Anchorage into Bethel where I then chartered a Cessna 180. The wind was about thirty miles an hour and I had 400 pounds of baggage with me when I was dropped of by the Charter plane in Upper Kalsag. There I was, standing by the river bank and there was no one there to meet me and take me to town; finally, just when the thoughts of "just how late/cold/windy can it get?" were flying about in my mind, Ralph Siedel, the teacher, showed up to rescue me. It was good to be rescued and especially by Ralph and Lou: they were fellow-teachers and about my age.

They helped me set up in a corner of a nice, sunny room; the x-ray machine area was in another. Somehow, before my arrival in Alaska, all the original survey films from Lower Kalsag had been lost so I had to do a complete survey of the whole village from scratch. I took about 80 chest x-rays.

It was quite a circus doing it alone . . . it consisted of taking two films, running into the tent to change cassettes (those little metal things that hold the films), running back out and then doing the next two people again. My real anxiety about this trip . . . which was the first trip I had done alone . . . was that the films would not turn out or get mixed up and I'd wind up being the laughingstock of the home office. This was because all the x-ray technicians who collected per diem on these little jaunts were hoping that, without them, I would fall on my face! Or fall on something! After quite a few experiences, I felt the job gave them too much free time and that there could be better use for them, thus saving the Service money. You are no fun, Doc Hook!

The weather was bad the next morning and I couldn't get out, so I was sort of glad when I got a call to go out and do a house call on an Eskimo home in the afternoon. When I got there, my patient turned out to be a teenaged boy; he was sitting up in bed, not looking particularly ill and his mother informed me he had a "bad toe", so I took a look. Sure enough, he had a badly infected ingrown toenail, so bad and so deep that the best remedy would be to take the nail completely off. I did the sterilizing prep work and proceeded to give the rather none-too-bright-looking lad a nerve block that would counter the pain, much like a dentist giving a shot prior to an extraction. I turned back around after injecting the boy, holding the needle aloft, and the poor kid just keeled over!

Now, here I was a long dog-sled ride out in the boonies, and it appeared I had just killed a fifteen-year-old future rocket-scientist by giving him cardiac arrest! I had only the barest of essentials with me, but I hurried and gave him a shot of epinephrine anyway and sure enough, his breathing and blood pressure stabilized and it turned out that he must have just fainted when he saw the needle. I should have given *myself* the shot . . .

Once my pulse slowed down and I ascertained that his was still going, I went ahead, while he was out for the count, and ripped loose the offending nail, trimming the dead tissue and cleaning up the mess, leaving a healthy nail bed in its place. That was honestly the scared-est I had ever been, up to that point, thinking he was going to die of an ingrown toenail and I didn't have all the necessary equipment to resuscitate him, nor had I yet succeeded in raising the dead . . . .

~~~~St. Mary's and Pitkas Point~~~~

One of the reasons I was in St. Mary's was to survey Pitkas Point, at that time, a ramshackle fishing settlement of maybe 25 people. The Public Health Nurse had found TB converters there so we knew we had an active case somewhere in the area and it was up to me to find it!

Tuberculosis, beware! HOOKERMAN to the rescue!

It was a little overcast but not bad, so, the Aide and I straddled a Snow machine and the two of us joined the machine's driver and we started down the river. Very soon, trekking along happily, we were overcome by a sudden and totally unexpected blizzard. Then, as we had no choice at that point, we got about a mile downriver and the Snow Traveler went 'ka-put'.

The Aide assured me that it was not far, so we decided we would walk; after all, she said, the wind was at our backs.

By the time we had finished our five-mile death-march, we were a *little* cold (this was early in my stay in Alaska and I didn't, as yet, have all the warm gear I eventually acquired) and I was very very glad that the Aide knew where she was going. Admittedly, there were points along the way when doubt besieged me . . . about the only thing that could've made it worse would have been getting lost.

Or being found . . . . by a Polar bear.

After we thankfully arrived and warmed up at the first house we came to, she went around to the houses in the village, because she knew where they were and who lived in them and they knew and trusted her. The boy that had been driving us on his Traveler warmed up a bit, too, and then headed back by snowmobile with someone to fix his machine. The faithful Aide and I sat tight in the relative warmth of the small house and we were fed some boiled Shee fish by the quiet volunteer-host and it sure tasted good!

As it got later, it seemed apparent that our original driver was not having any luck with the ailing Ski-Doo, so after some downtime, a good Samaritan-type came with *his* Snow Traveler and picked us up, and on the way back, we played taxi and picked up some of the Pitkas Point people who were already starting to walk up the River to the clinic!

This was a touching thing: the people appreciating what we were trying to do and cooperating. It took me four hours to go five miles down and back but every single soul that lived in Pitkas Point came to the clinic, so we could do case work on the converters and their families, trying to ascertain where the active TB case had come from.

A lot of the town's people, as well as those from St, Mary's, had baaaaaaad teeth and needed extractions. I handled that as well, having enough deadening meds to counter the pain. I probably pulled 30 teeth. We were able to do some other exams, too, while we were in the neighborhood. I felt a sense of accomplishment and it came with the knowledge that I was appreciated and that made it all the sweeter. It was the reason I was here in the first place, doing what I did.

The next morning there was a 30mph wind coming across the river from the south. I despaired of getting out but I felt I had to try, so I broke all the equipment down and took the x-ray machine apart and packed it all into the ten little bags it came in and got all the luggage out on the river bank. Then I went back to one house and called around on a short wave radio, trying to rouse someone who would come pick me up.

Finally, I found someone at Marshall who said he would come over, get me, and take me into Bethel. When he got there, it turned out that my driver and Father Kanieke were good friends and he decided that he would sit down and have lunch with his friend and the people in the Mission before we went back. I did not want to wait but had little say in the matter.

Hospitality was always very important in the Alaskan 'Bush' at that time; doors were never locked and anyone and everyone were invited in for a cup of coffee or a meal. This time, it was hard for me to kick back and relax for I wanted to get to Bethel in time to catch the evening plane for Anchorage and get back to my home and family. But, I settled myself down as best I could and enjoyed getting to know Father Kanieke, too. It seems that he had never taken his final vows; he was about my age and it turned out that he was just a fantastic pilot and he taught me several important ways to be a more observant pilot. The knowledge she shared with me that night cannot be bought and it was worth a fortune.

Among the many stories he shared with me that night, one was of particular interest: he said he had landed in a village that wasn't Catholic and, apparently, had some residents who were not only not Catholics but were not very appreciative of Catholics. When he finished his business there and came back out to his plane, somebody had snipped his rudder cables. He did his usual, and in this case, life-saving "anal-retentive" pre-flight check and discovered it before he took off.

In another town, he related, he took off after someone else had gassed his plane and he lost power just after takeoff but he was still so low in altitude that he was able to land safely. Turned out, he had been "gassed" with kerosene. This could have been unintentional but it stuck in my mind and from then on . . . and up through today . . . I always make sure what I am getting in my tanks even at a regular gas pump at an airport—I check the tanks myself.

Great guy. Great tips. Great time.

Going back, we hit a headwind of about thirty knots so were making only about 120 MPH or so and it lengthened our trip home, so just as we landed, the larger F27 airplane that I needed to catch to go home was just taking off so it looked like another delay, this time overnight in Bethel.

There was a little excitement that night, however, and it kept me entertained. Seemed someone had been siphoning gasoline out of the Hospitals tanks . . . the ones that served the ambulances and trucks and things. This made it a Federal offence: no, really, it was a FEDERAL OFFENSE because the Hospital was government property—it upped the ante somewhat for the guilty person or persons unknown.

Apparently, the FBI had been sent out and they put in some kind of a radioactive marker in the gasoline in the Hospital's tanks and, after an appropriate amount of time had passed, they were now going around with an Official FBI-Type Super-Duper Grade A

Geiger Counter, checking everyone's snow machines. There was a veritable *parade* of Snow-Bees headed out of town to hide on the tundra until things cooled off . . .

Even some of the Docs at the Hospital Complex were nervous about the presence of G-men, too; seems they had appropriated hospital plywood that was left over from some project, and they used it to build a little hut on the tundra for sort of a club house, get-away, overlooking the Kuskokwim River. They were really sweating the plywood. There was a quick 'sanding party' organized to remove all the identifying marks from the plywood that night . . . .

∿∿∿∿∿∿∿∿∿∿∿∿

There will be other villages and settlements and little snow-bumps-on-the-map as we continue . . . each one had a flavor all it's own, as did the people living there . . . these descriptions were in the beginning of the journals I kept.

∿∿∿∿∿∿∿∿∿∿∿∿

THE GOOD, THE BAD AND THE UGLY.

Aniak was a village I visited quite often over the years. On the first visit, I was doing an X-ray Survey; I had found out that, barring the fact that the village had a full-time Health Aide, I radioed ahead several days prior to the visit and informed the BIA teacher or whomever was in charge that I was looking to hire an assistant for the 2 days I would be in the village. Then, I did some quickie interviewing first thing upon arriving; the helper, then, had the privilege of running all the tests I did not like to do and acted as my "go-fer", in essence. In return, the individual chosen had the dubious honor of being a Big Fish in a Little Pond, while assisting me and earning a bit of money as well.

In the early days of getting a village organized and scheduled for regular well-documented visits, the lowest-rung job seemed to be running the sputum inducer. This is a gadget that was charged with glycerin and salt water and made a little vapor that irritated the heck out of the patients lungs when breathed in and he would cough and hack and spit up . . . which was the whole idea as we needed half a one-ounce bottle of sputum for TB testing purposes.

It wasn't too thrilling for me, having gone to school to get my highfalutin' education for all those years, just to run a little machine that pumped out stuff in order to fill spit bottles. It had gotten *real* old in a *real* hurry, so from one of my first trips there and for all trips forward, I hired someone and paid them myself. The first candidate for this honor in the village of Aniak was a young man whose name I did not record in my journal and I have forgotten over the decades, so, I'll call him 'Chappy'.

He was a likable enough young fella and he had filled out the simple application I'd prepared and given to him with deep diligence and care, leaning far over his writing as if to shield the tender words from sight. There were only 5 individuals who had signed up for consideration; Chappy's talents included a mastery of English and enough common-Eskimo-Inuit words and assorted basic knowledge of other Alaskan languages to cover most occasions in the village.

Chappy looked to be about 14: smooth-cheeked with no sign of needing a razor and a plump face the color of caramel, with the typical high cheekbones of the persons on his family tree.

The application that I had glanced at said he was 23 and he wore his jet black hair a little long for my taste, but it was clean as was he. His affect seemed pleasant enough, although all during my interview of him, he did not smile. He was slim and taller than the average height of the indigents at that time of around 5'3"-5'6"; his clothing was neat and clean and he didn't smell offensive: now go right ahead and laugh at that, for that wasn't always the case in some areas and with some folks! We would be working closely and the odor of putrefying gum diseases, unwashed-until-Spring private areas and the overpowering odor of fish, fish, fish was just not going to be acceptable to me, if I had a choice. In Aniak, I had a choice.

After quickly interviewing the 5 hopefuls, I settled on Chappy, and I announced it; the other applicants stood and left the room without another word or look in my direction, although I came to learn that this wasn't an insult, it was just that we had ended our necessary time with each other and now it was time to go our separate ways. I held out my hand to shake with Chappy and to seal the deal.

Then I got the full-ear-to-ear-grin and it brightened the room . . . . even with the vacancy caused by the loss of his four front teeth! So, Chappy's initial in-depth training went thus: "OK, here's is a list of names of the people who have registered and will be in the waiting room. You call a name and then have the patient sit here; you take this little machine and have the people suck the air into their lungs, like 'uuuuuuh'." I would then demonstrate, pulling forth all of my latent theatrical talents. "and then have them spit enough into these to fill the three little bottles for each one and each bottle has to be at least half full. Write the patients' name three times, label the bottles and on you go. Now, here, you go ahead and do it."

On we went.

Very in-depth, that.

I hope you weren't confused by the technical verbiage . . . .

There were about 300 bottles of sputum collected after a Long Day in Aniak . . . wow that sounds like a good name for a Fellinni film! Anyway, all the little bottles of dubious treasure were labeled and packed in a box to be taken back to the hospital for testing. The workday was officially over.

Came a good nights' sleep and in the morning I was packed up and ready to take off back to base and then home when Trig Olsen finally picked me up in his plane, running really late that day. We had not flown far when we were forced down by a 100' ceiling.

It was little scenarios like this that convinced me to eventually buy the plane, for, if we had left when Trig was supposed to have arrived, the ensuing adventures would not have been as harrowing . . . . and the frustrating chain of events that followed would have never been. It looked grim for a while, but we finally landed somewhere on the Kuskukwin, and I am glad to report we were equipped with snow skis. Makes landing ever-so-much-more-comfortable. We both looked at each other when the plane stopped and without saying a word, we knew were just going to have to wait there until the weather cleared to finish the trip. It was about noon.

Four hours later, it was still storming. The plane had grown much too small hours ago, so I got out to stretch . . . we had landed really close to shore and the ground was covered with knee-deep fresh snow but with four inches of ice water underneath. The wind was whipping in at about 30 and the earlier snow had turned to freezing rain. I was drenched before I got back to the plane.

If I may report delicately, spit is not the only thing that can freeze mid-air . . . .

Being prepared for any emergency, I broke out my survival food that I always carried in a small hook-to-the-waist-pack, which I suppose in today's vernacular, would be called, appropriately enough, a fanny pack. I carried with me some power bars, which were kinda hard to find back in the 60's but Phyllis could sometimes get them at the health food stores whenever she had access to one, about a half-pound of jerky, and hard candies. I shared this bounty with Trig. He was impressed. And grateful. We were both used to unscheduled stop-over's and had learned to just try to get comfortable and sleep, but as it got later and later, we resigned ourselves to the fact that we were going to spend a long, cold night right there and we were not going to be comfortable, not by a long shot.

We tossed gear we did not need outside of the plane to make enough room to stretch out, because with all the gear I had and given the size of the cabin, it would have been impossible to sleep as it was with our knees practically around our ears. Out went a lot of supplies, deflated raft, tools and extra gas cans. Out went the boxes with the sputum samples, too.

Now, I always had full body-gear either on me or near me whenever I traveled like that as I was not and am not a fan of shivering. Trig had nothing with him to stay warm but his parka, so I gave him my extra outerwear and then curled up in the back seat in dry socks (VIP!), mukluks, down underwear and parka to wait out the storm. Trig's luminous wristwatch told us it was about 8PM.

Sometime later, we heard something outside the plane: I thought I was dreaming when I heard snow machines and saw headlights bearing down on us. It was the teachers from Tuluksak and one of the local natives; they had come up the river, driving side by side and it looked like a car or truck tooling up the middle of the lake! It was around 2 a.m. and awakening to that sight was surreal.

They pulled up and had brought us hot coffee, which I didn't drink, but they also offered a ride back to the village. The pilot did not want to leave his plane, understandably, and I had too much gear to move, so I decided I'd just stay on, too. It didn't make much sense to leave and just have to turn around and come back. I felt badly that the good Samaritans had snow-machined 30 miles in that kind of weather, all the way from Tuluksak, to provide a cup of coffee!

The sun came up about 5 AM and it was still drizzling but Trig decided he could safely see to fly out, and so we left but not before I checked on the 'spit boxes' and of course, they were soaked and the labels had all slipped off and the box they were in was toast . . . . Really, we had no choice because even if they had stayed in the frigid airplane cabin, they would have frozen and split.

Trig and I almost froze and split.

When all was said and done, I tried some self-talk to convince myself there was a bright side: 'we could have been killed' was about all I could come up with . . . I was so disgusted and discouraged that I just left the whole 3 cases right there on the ice, where, I am sure they sunk to the bottom of the Kuskokuim River and will remain until one day, some archeologist will discover them and speculate just what they must have been! The thought of that made me smile, finally.

Speaking of freezing, that reminded me, while going over the notes for this book of a story I did not put in for whatever reason . . . perhaps because it is on the in-delicate side, but it sure epitomizes the unusual conditions that are the heart and soul of medical care in the Arctic. You see, along with the focus I had on TB, it remained that I did a lot of routine medical care along with my TB duties. On of these was examining and giving pap smears to screen for cancer, to local women patients. I have related how my 'examining rooms' and the space allotted me as I set up shop all over the state, were seldom even adequate at the best.

Another feature would be heat, or rather, the lack of heat in the rooms I had to use. It was not uncommon, then for an attending Aide, if I had one, to instruct the female patient as to her clothing removal, then have her hop upon an examining table and place her legs in the proper position for me to examine what was there for me to check out.

Boy, I just took two whole paragraphs dancing around the point I am trying to make here, which is, when I would perform a vaginal exam, I would take the COLD metal speculum and insert it in to the WARM, moist female cavity, and more often that not, steam would rise and fog up my glasses until the surrounding temperatures of the patient and the cold air got closer together. It's just a mental picture that has been difficult to erase from my mind over the years . . . . and now, yours too.

Spit, Samaritans, sleet-and-snow, scary weather, and steam . . . all in one day and only in Alaska!

"A GLIMPSE AT HOOPER BAY, WITH MAN CUTTING
WOOD, CLOTHES FREEZING DRY ON THE LINE, AND
THE ARMORY BUILDINGS IN THE BACKGROUND"

'HOOPER BAY CHILDREN PLAY ON A SLED'

'LITTLE GIRLS OF UPPER KALSAG'

CHAPTER 9

KOTZEBUE HOSPITAL STORIES

Since I spent so much of my 'Alaska time' in the hospital, I thought it only fitting to devote a chapter to it. Granted, most of my most memorable adventures were had away from town, but it was an integral part of my life there.

After my two years in Anchorage, I was given my choice of working at any hospital in Alaska: Barrow, Dillingham, Tanana or Kotzebue, or, I could have stayed where I was in Anchorage. I had occasion to visit them all from time to time and I felt Kotzebue was the most interesting of the lot. I liked the flavor of the inhabitants of the area: there were good, conscientious doctors and the native population was on the positive side of the scale, attitude-wise. I enjoyed the heck out of the outdoors and everything connected to it; never was, nor did I ever want to be, a Big Deal trophy hunter, but I liked what I had experienced in Alaska and Kotzebue was a good area for that, too.

Getting ready to move to Kotzebue was a little like an old Keystone Cops comedy short: frantic packing and repacking and housecleaning in Anchorage, with help from friends Terry and Nancy Salustro, who finally did the last big favor of driving us to the airport, after feeding us breakfast on that final day in Anchorage.

Alaska Airlines was nicknamed "Elastic Airlines" because of their loose and stretchy scheduling, but having no other options, I took a deep breath and loaded up Phyllis and the kids. The flight, once in the air, would take about an hour on the Boeing 727; Kotzebue was around 500 miles north and a tidbit west of Anchorage.

As we boarded, we waved to the pilot, who was Brother Pettyjohn our neighbor and member of our Church ward; and he already knew we were leaving that day. As is customary when the plane was in the air, the pilot got on the inboard intercom system to welcome the passengers aboard. This time, it took a little different turn . . .

"Ladies and gentlemen, Brothers and Sisters, this is your Captain, welcome to flight 1898. We will be flying at an altitude of 10,000 feet. The weather is clear and we are on our way to Kotzebue Airport today, and, en route', we will be passing over the uttermost boundaries of the Everlasting Hills . . ."

Baby Kelly was just a few months old and she was screaming her head off as we climbed in but the two boys, Kit and Kelly, were excited about traveling. We had 500 pounds of excess baggage and the rest of our stuff went into big container boxes on the freighter which got there some weeks later, and consequently caused us to survive in a rather primitive fashion for a while.

The day of arrival, we wiled away the hours unpacking our lives and setting out the pieces thereof; I had caught cold and had a raspy voice so all the people who heard me talking on the radio or met me in person that first day or so must have thought they really had a winner for a new Doc . . . an impression I'm not sure they changed!

I dived right into the work as that same day, as it turned out I needed to fly to a village called Selewik where an Aide had called with what sounded like a case of botulism . . . food poisoning. The population up here often suffered from this as it was easy to ignore proper handling of canned food, which was left out far longer than it should have been. I flew in hastily but although the patient was having seizures, she was better when I arrived; perhaps the Aide had over-reacted, as did I. Better safe than sorry, however, and the important thing was that the patient didn't die.

The first week at the Hospital really felt overwhelming to me. I'd been taken away from regular routine medicine after only 12 months of Internship in California and even though I had a lot of academic stuff fresh in my young mind, I didn't always transform knowledge to action fast enough to suit myself and to get a patient feeling right in a timely manner.

Sometimes, too often, it seemed to me, professors or visiting Doctors came through and they always wanted to see what the hospital looked like and we had to stop whatever we were doing and give them a tour, which was a pain in my opinion. That was not the only place and time I had to Make-Nice, for Phyllis and I also had to act like a good host and hostess and give them a meal, too. It seemed a big time-waster to me with too much time spent playing politics.

During that first week also, there was a scheduled ENT, which is Ear, Nose and Throat Clinic and even though I wasn't real sure of how they were done there. We had just huge numbers of kids that had chronically-draining ears; we made little headway (no pun) with this problem while I was there. Kids with draining ears were thought to just be normal because their folks had always had that malady growing up; it seemed to be just a common childhood complaint, like runny noses, and was pretty much ignored. Because of that, around 250 of the kids I examined in that first ENT Clinic had holes in their eardrums and compromised hearing. For life.

It was a sobering situation for me.

Why it escalated to that point was due to a combination of lack of knowledge about proper hygiene and lack of medical care, for when the kids would get a cold, the bacteria would travel up into the ear canals and settle there and do the damage. Also, the kids weren't taught way of blowing their noses and disposing the germy tissue, there was usually no tissue to be had, so people came in to the clinics with their kids and they had pus just draining out of the ears and down their cheeks and the parents would just reach over and wipe it off with a sleeve or a mitten or just a bare hand. Then, back the germ-laden bomb went to spread zillions of germs even further. This is why I tried to fit in routine cleanliness training and encouraged the Health Aids in following up.

The treatment for the badly-infected ears was to place a small polyethylene tube in the kids' ears and let them drain out, kind of like lancing a boil. Followed by an antibiotic course, the problem was easily cleared up, generally speaking. The Hospital staff or clinic staff would prepare the necessities, then line up the kids . . .

often 50 and occasionally as many a 100; then, assembly-line fashion, we would put them to sleep, zap the little tubes into their ear drums and they would wake up and go home the same day.

We would spend almost a week at this sometimes; it was a tremendous logistic situation, with kids coming in from villages all over to get tubes put in. We'd sort of schedule these things regularly, setting up a clinic or hospital event with a specialist and a couple of anesthesiologists. I am sure it saved hundreds of kids' hearing and bought them some much-needed time until they outgrew the problem.

During this first week we moved to Kotzebue from Anchorage, there was an electrical storm; everyone who could get away went up on the Hospital roof and watched the show. Thunderstorms are very rare up North as the air is uniformly cold and doesn't have the up and down air currents that cause electrical storms. People were amazed, and a little scared, too, and that seemed odd to me because I didn't know it was so rare. A lot of the people that were up there that night had never seen a lightening display before. The North Star was directly above us and the Big Dipper surrounded us, so using them for guidance was not much help. The Eskimos had many superstitions and cultural mores about the Aurora Borealis . . . one tradition taught that if a person went out and played in and among the Borealis beams, he would die within 6 weeks. Odd. One wonders where this unusual bit of logic came from and why. The native people who told me these tales were very serious about this belief.

Occasionally, when the Northern Lights would stream down to the ground and you could actually have a feeling of really being within the lights. I often wondered what kind of electrical power was in them; they were a sight for the uninitiated to wonder over, especially at 30,000 feet in a jet. I experienced it once in a small plane and the sensation intensified and became ethereal . . . . other-worldly . . . and it felt like my spirit soared to meet them in the air . . . and it has been over 6 weeks . . . and I'm still alive.

In the town of Kotzebue, the population was either white or Eskimo, generally speaking; the whites were either at the DEW line (Distant Early Warning) radar site or with the FFA, which had about a dozen people running the control tower and airport, and the BIA offices had about 30 people. The Public Health Service Hospital accounted for around another 25 or so. Some whites were in the town as traders or big game guides and Weins Airline also had staff there.

There was always an Alaska State Trooper or two assigned to the area and with that position came some animosity, I found out, with the whites as well as the indigent, so the Troopers were transferred every few years or so, avoiding the problem of getting too friendly with either side. There was certainly plenty to do . . . and it sure wasn't a matter of putting in your eight hours and heading home: you stayed until the work was done. There was always plenty of patients to see and I ran them through . . . I hope NOT like cattle . . . but I would try to see as many as I could and get them diagnosed, treated and on their way.

In my profession, you just can't spend a lot of time with each person; I have found that with patients universally, and with Physicians everywhere, ALL want more time to be invested, but there were always others waiting who want the same involvement in their care, too, so it's a Catch-22. People naturally get impatient when made to wait but if I hustle them through once they get to me, to go on to the next impatient patient, well . . . you see the problem. Multi-tasking is the answer.

That is a phrase that was not heard or used in the 1960's vernacular, but it's certainly applicable to what I was trying to do. I'd take all the history I could *verbally* while I was doing the actual physical examination and I would be writing out a prescription while I gave explanations and directions. All the while, I would be entering the ever-important history in my cryptic scribbles. I got so I could see a hundred people a day in the clinics and still fit others for glasses at the end of the day . . . that still left me with a bit of time to go hunting. Now, we are talking about some days with twenty-two hours of bright daylight and only a couple of hours of dusk, you know!

Granted, it was a frenetic life but the long days didn't bother me. If I didn't get enough sleep in all of this hustle and bustle, my otherwise cheerful attitude and gracious bedside manner would suffer. (ha ha)

When at the Hospital sponsored by the Methodists, one of us on Staff went out on a field trip, or down to assist in Nome, the one left behind had to be on-duty 24 hours a day. Then later, of course, the guy that dragged in from the field trip was in no mood to go out on rounds or take calls as he would be just as exhausted and burnt out as the little piggy that stayed home. Also, we seemed to have a lot of guests visiting the Hospital, as I mentioned, and as Service Unit Director, it sort of landed on me, and in turn, on Phyllis, to entertain, so we had plenty of so-called 'social life'. Too Plenty, sometimes.

We really met some fascinating people, though. I recall one fellow who had just cleaned out all of the gold in his mining operation and was passing through on his way back to the States. He must have had fifty pounds of gold—in pickle jars!—We managed to put it all into the hospital safe because we sure did not want it kept in the house overnight! I don't recall any dirty, thieving or awfully disagreeable people in those days of Forced Hosting; I'm sure there were plenty of ding-a-lings in the bunch as that's just the odds, but memory has thankfully faded over the years. We didn't drink liquor but a lot of the people we associated with sure did; distilled spirits were cheap on the Air Force Base. Being around all that didn't affect me nor make me want to join in because I much preferred to get in my plane and fly somewhere and be with friends that enjoyed hunting and fishing and escapism as much as I did. No artificially-induced euphoria was needed.

Phyllis was shorted, I feel, and the kids too, maybe, to some extent. The regular Coffee-Klatch-Gossip-Fest did not appeal to Phyllis at all; it seemed as though social leadership had shifted to us when I took on the role of Service Unit Director. We were considered the Father and Mother of the Hospital, even at our young ages. Phyllis was pregnant at the time and was having a tough go of it. Looking back, I am surprised that she just didn't throw up her hands and leave, but that was not her style. When I was off-duty, I wanted to just get in the air and go and do fun stuff, but she was held in place by our little Rug Rats and getting a babysitter was only an occasional splurge and not because of the monetary outlay . . . she just didn't want anyone tending her children but her.

In pictures of the Kotzebue hospital, the most noticeable thing is the water tank, which looms up and monopolizes the view; it was a big round affair, holding tens of thousand—gallons of water.

Inside the metal shell was three feet of foam insulation, but even with that it would freeze up in the winter and water had to be pulled from the center as the ice around the outside insulated it to some degree but eventually we had to turn to using distilled water, which cost three cents a gallon.

The main hospital consisted of dentist offices on the left and to the right was the clinic with access to the Hospital itself. It cost a million dollars a year to run in 1968. It had cost $3 million to build in 1959. I would estimate it was around 100,000 square feet and have 30 beds, about 5 clinic rooms plus an x-ray department and one surgical suite.

Going back to the beginning when it was designed and built, there was the difficult chore of constructing a building on permafrost. One way is to sink pilings down to bedrock, then build four feet from the top of the ground on these supports. Most commercial buildings are built this way, but the Hospital was "floated". In this method, the foundation would go up on top of the ground and then, melt the ice of the permafrost and sink down to a level grade . . . not a great plan.

The engineers from the company based in Albuquerque apparently had no idea of how to build in the conditions of Alaska; we had cracks in the foundation that you could literally crawl through! By the time I got there in 1968, most of the hospital personnel were used to it, so we just patched it together often and made do: there was no way a new one could be funded. It stood as another shining example of poor government planning.

When we were there, Kotzebue had a population of about 2,000, of which a couple of hundred were white and the rest Eskimos, and some of them had ancestors who'd lived there for centuries before. There were 2 other doctors assigned to the hospital when I showed up; our staff was also responsible to man the clinic at Nome, as well. The last part of my 2 years up there as the Director of the program reeeaaaallllly had its benefits: I can't think of what benefits exactly, but I know there must have been some . . . . Oh, yeah! I remember: Free aspirin!

Anyway, preparing the schedules was difficult as we tried to keep two docs at the hospital and have one in the field all the time. We tried to visit every village twice a year for a formal excursion, which meant that a doctor either tested or treated almost everyone in the village once a year.

At the time I was there, we oversaw villages with populations of 50 to 500. We held clinics every day in the hospital where we would see fifty people or so, as well as tend to the patients who were in-patients there. I did surgery, deliveries, autopsies and Public Health. A Sanitary Engineer worked out of the hospital, teaching the natives, whose entire way of life was undergoing drastic change, to drink clean water, dispose of wastes properly and upgrade their living conditions. Old customs and habits were not sufficient for the modern day world that was steadily encroaching on them.

Another indispensable part of the whole Health Picture in Kotzebue was the Aides. They were chosen to act as medical go-betweens, sort of like permanent triage in each community. In order to hire for these vital individuals, the positions were advertised for and interviews conducted before a small number were chosen by the village Health council, some were good, some not so much. They then went through weeks of training in the hospital. At first, these aides were paid by the village but the checks were erratic at best, so by the time I got there, they were paid by the Hospital. If I recall, the pay scale was around $150-$200 a month which was pretty good money for someone living in that area and at that time. We did get to pick and choose a bit when hiring and retaining good Aides.

Every morning at 10 and each afternoon at 5, we'd have what we laughingly referred to as 'The Agony Hour' when these aides radioed in, via shortwave, to report on medical situations in the far-flung towns and villages. To protect the privacy of the patients from the listening ears of anyone who happened to tune in that frequency on the radio, we gave the Aides a coded option of four basic things. That way, we could reassure them that each concern was either not serious . . . . kind of a 'take-an-aspirin-and-call in-the-morning' thing, or not; if it seemed more serious, we'd prescribe something from the local clinic pharmacies which were really just big cupboards. They were kept locked and stocked with medicine consisting of four kinds of antibiotics and most of the necessary first-aid type of medicine . . . some simple things that were within the Aides expertise. The Aides could handle 90% of the assorted villagers' accidents and sicknesses, much in the same way modern Emergency Room personnel treat, for the most part, rather up-front and normal, situations or common get-well-on-your-own's . . . .

There was a US Mail airplane that made scheduled trips to the villages; patients with more serious afflictions could catch a ride on that to fly into Kotzebue but we had to pay their way and there was a very limited travel budget provided for this. In the real emergencies, we would fly out and get a patient and fly back with them to the Hospital, but this cost so much that a doctor wouldn't elect to do it unless he was new or just gung-ho.

Charters were $50 an in-air hour so it had to be a really critical case to warrant that method and get it approved. A board who answered to another board, where it came down, then, from Anchorage, supervised the budget.

Then we took our turns and went out to the clinics for the regularly scheduled visits, in an average-sized village of four or five hundred we'd usually spend around 4 days. We'd start by doing general exams on all the school children, beginning with TB tests. We did heart exams and pap smears on every woman who would come in and we'd check everyone, beginning with the kids, for glasses and we might write up 50 or more scripts for eye corrective wear over the course of the visit.

When working the eye exams with the kids, we did what we called "open-mouth refraction." Normally, you tell a kid, "OK, look at the chart on the wall over there and read me the top line" . . . and the kid would go, 'uuuuuhhhhhh". The Eskimo kids didn't articulate the sound "uh" rather, they just opened their mouths and looked. When you had patients like this who didn't understand English, or little kids who didn't read, you could use a retina scope and by looking at their eyes at a distance through lenses in a trial pair of glasses of different strengths in this thing in front of their eyes, you could come pretty close.

With people who couldn't respond at all and you couldn't make them understand what you wanted them to do, all you had to do was use this gadget and when they got fitted, put the lenses in and let them look through it: it was incredible to see the wonder on their faces when they could see clearly! Sometimes I couldn't hide an ear-to-ear grin and I got goose bumps all over just watching this . . . it made everything well worth it!

One of the guys that taught me how to do the refractions joked, and said that some of the kids ended up with 20/20 eyes but were still stuck with their 20/70 brains. When he said this, I thought it sounded kind of harsh, but I came to find out what he meant, for when we tested each kid, sent the prescriptions out and then got the glasses back on the kids head and got them all fitted, all that took a lot of time . . . over several hours or more per patient . . . and then we would find out that the next day, most of the little nose-pickers had either lost them, stepped on them or given them away. It was frustrating, to say the least. The budgets were limited, of course, and it was disheartening to see what limited funds there were wasted through neglect and carelessness. Kids are kids all over!

We appreciated the responsible teachers who went the extra mile and collected and labeled the glasses from their students each night before the kids left for home and then passed them out the next morning; this was a good practice, at least until the kids learned a little responsibility!

Once I got smart and into the swing of things, I was sometimes able to schedule my trips to the villages when there was something going on there; Point Hope had whaling in the spring, right around the middle of June, and then walrus would always come by in some of the villages that were in the Bering Strait and I'd try to take half a day off and join in the hunts. It was an honor to be asked, and NOT a common occurrence, I might add. To invite an outsider was a journey out of the norm. What an excellent adventure it was, though, to be allowed to participate in centuries-old tradition, shoulder to shoulder with the sons of the unbelievably resilient indigenous Inuit-Eskimos as they made memories that were passed down, then, to the young ones. There was a turning-away from these customs for several decades but I am happy to report that much as the minds and hearts of the children have turned to their Elders and want to learn of their heritage and customs of their people, much the same way as the American Indians in the lower 48 have witnessed. Regrettably, a lot of history has vanished for good, but it's sure satisfying to see that the yearning to know one's forebears is seeing becoming widespread among Mormons and non-Mormons both, as "The hearts of the children shall be turned to their fathers."

If there were two or three villages in fairly close proximity, to save on transportation costs we would go by dog sled, or, more commonly, by snow machines, because back then in the 1960's, dogs were getting phased out. Now, the 'romance' of the dog sleds is being kept alive for traditions' sake and events such as the Iditarod Race and others remind Alaskan's of the way it was, not too long ago, but also back even further in history. Then, dog and man served one another's' needs for centuries, although not in the Hollywood representations. Some archeologists believe the sled dog was being used in the area we now call Siberia 4,000 years ago, and there are several places I would visit in Alaska that you could toss a rock and it would land in Siberia!

Most generally, sled dogs were considered a piece of machinery that the owner kept alive and in adequate health because the dogs performed a necessary function; they were not pets. I have vested a Chapter in this book on the subject, but there are some horror stories that I have not included in this work that illustrate the factual accounts of the human-dog relationships . . . things witnessed that are better left untold.

~~~~~~~~~~~~~~

Many times in the last 10 years, especially, when I travel around and give lecture/slide show presentations on my years in Alaska, I am asked if I learned anything about native herbs or doctoring. I'm sure that the Eskimo and Inuit people had a lot of this, as certainly was the case with any civilization, but what I was exposed to went right over my head. I had so much going on in my brain, there was precious little room left for anything else, so the Energizer Bunny in me worked hard just remembering the practice of conventional medicine and that was taxing enough the first few years.

I had no idea what to expect when I first began my travels to the villages; I'd set up shop and just wait until the people showed up and told me what they wanted me to know; I respected the knowledge that was shared by medicine men/women. As I learned, I'd see where a healer had treated some illness, for weeks sometimes, with incantations or spells or herb remedies. They just didn't say much about it because they thought nobody would believe them or they'd mock them . . . and they were no different from anyone else where that's concerned.

Some times, people in the Emergency Rooms I work in Utah, Idaho and Colorado and other places where I practice, that use herbs and 'Holistic' practices and once in a while someone will say, "I don't want any medicine . . . we have herbs at home." I respect their beliefs now, as I did then, so I just tell them now like I told them then: "if you need any more help, let me know."

While there, I constantly marveled at the resiliency of the children. They seemed to have constant runny noses, impetigo, bug bites, infected ears . . . some were just too small or weak to fight off the hostile natural environment of the Arctic. It is a challenging place for anyone to live. The infant death rates were high in the under-3-year old range. If a child could make it until about 6 or 7 years, the chances of survival increased dramatically.

It's always sad when someone has to leave their home and go into a hospital for an indefinite period; in the smaller and more remote villages, this was especially profound. The native people impressed me from the very beginning: I believed they were really good and solid and strong and I had admired the history of Alaska and read about it over the years, beginning in high school or even prior to that. That is why I truly enjoyed staying in the villages with the same people I was treating, if I could. Sociologically speaking, it seemed the citizens who couldn't 'make it' in the small villages, for whatever reason, would come to the bigger towns like Kotzebue or Nome.

The ones who migrated for that reason often turned out to have alcohol or drug problems and the habits that formed from there led them even further into the even larger cities where the atmosphere was congenial to even more addictions. The illegal substances they craved and the drugs-of-choice were certainly more readily available in the larger cities of Anchorage, Juneau and Fairbanks.

If older people came into the hospital, it was really hard for them to cope with a hospital stay unless they had relatives that lived in the town or at least lived nearby, that could come with them or visit and give their support. If they were brought to a strange town, uprooted from the place they had lived all their lives, they were just too lonely to stay and too lonely to heal.

One old fellow comes to mind . . . I sent him in to the Kotzebue hospital from one of the far-flung villages; his daughter pulled me aside and told me to be sure he got plenty of seal liver at the hospital because he loved it so much. I related the story to Phyllis and, well . . . . you can guess . . . he got his seal liver.

Another elderly woman was really vocal about the fact that she did NOT want to stay hospitalized anymore! She was a long-term TB patient and she spoke some English. She had been allowed to bring some of her belongings from home so the transition to that inevitable long-term care in the hospital would be less traumatizing. She had been a resident in the hospital for some time as well as a Frequent Flier at the clinics, each time we came to town, and she seemed to like and trust me.

Making my rounds one morning, I peeked in and came over to look at her chart and asked, "How are you today? Are you feeling better?" and she said, "Well, the Doctor Hooker, I be sick of me being here and I stay along here just enough to see you before now, and I go home now for I gonna get going now."

It must have been winter because I recall that although it was mid-morning, it was dark outside; she went on to say, "I smile for what you do for me but I not gonna stay no more and this is that!"

Then she made a great show of picking up her cuspuk, which is a long pullover affair, and tugging it on and picked up her bag with her boots and heavy clothing and, head held high and proud, she marched out the door. The dignity of her exit was lessened somewhat due to the fact she had gone through the wrong door and went into a bathroom which was right outside her door and down the hall a bit.

I followed, quietly.

She didn't know to turn on the light in there, I guessed, as the space around the doorframe stayed dark. She stayed in there, not making a sound for a bit and I waited outside, equally silent: I wanted to see what she'd do. After a good five minutes, she opened the door a crack and peeked out. The light in the bathroom was still off. She said, "I think it too dark out to leave but I leave when suns up"

Helping the old gal back up into bed, I pulled her cuspuk off over her head and folded it at the foot of her cot, then re-packed her bag into the closet along with her mukluks. She seemed content once more, for she had made the decision to stay, not I. I realized that she was essentially a bed-ridden patient who could only walk a few feet and she had probably never even been in the hallway, let alone the bathroom, then having used a honeybucket all her life at home and a bedpan after she was admitted, it was clear why she was confused. She was back in her bed, now, with the familiarity of her blanket and cuspuk, and she would smile for the doctor Hooker and stay until suns up . . . .

~~~~~~~~~~~~~~

Sanitary Engineers in Alaska haven't received much notice and few people even know there are such individuals . . . I am assuming here that there still are such officials and they are just as important to the Alaskan people now as they were then. They were trained to set up water systems and sewage disposal units, but they educated the Eskimo/Inuit people about proper sanitation and health education, too. The first ones were assigned to Kotzebue about 10 years before I came; they found that the people were collecting their water out of the rivers and using it without boiling it and didn't realize that it was dangerously polluted from the villages upstream; winters' honeypots got dumped into it: out of sight, out of mind. So many babies died of dysentery because it so quickly led to severe dehydration and death and all without the people understanding why it had happened. While I was there, we would see a couple dysentery cases every day in the summer; we had a fulltime Sanitarian on staff and our water was piped from three miles away and it was always freezing up over the long winters.

So, I remember one of the Engineers that came out to work from back east, bringing his doll of an Italian wife. He was Irish and they were newly married and just as cute as can be; Phyllis and I got to know them quite well. Even his expertise was not enough to solve the water purity problems, but he certainly made inroads into the sorry state of affairs. We hired as many men as it took to work at the problems in the hospital, but we had a great need for a Sanitation Helper full time. We had one fellow named LG who had a drinking problem; we kept him year 'round, though, only part-time because he knew all there was to know about this particular hospital's weird systems and the way they worked. Twice before in the summer months, he apparently decided that the wage we were paying him was not enough so he walked off the job and decided to be a fire fighter instead. He came back to town each time when with a bag of money, I heard, and then when that was all spent, he just showed up, back on the job at the hospital as if he had never been gone!

Peter, the acting Administrator, met with me and we talked, both agreeing that LG just had to go as his drinking and absences couldn't be tolerated. He told me that he just didn't feel comfortable firing him, so the buck seemed to pass to my desk. We called LG in and the two of us explained to him that we were firing him because of all the documented times when he had been drunk on the job and a list of other rules he had broken. He had apparently sobered up somewhat, but not entirely, when we gave him the news. His wife also worked at the hospital, which could have lead to complications, but we had no choice, really.

One day, I was driving along, just outside of town and there he was, walking along, staggeringly drunk and thumbing for a ride; he got in when I stopped, before I began thinking that perhaps I'd acted a bit too quickly.

"Doc,", he began, shutting the truck door after adjusting his clothes and brushing the fallen snow off from his coat and all over my seat, "you are a real hard-nose-son-of-a-gun for firing me when nobody else would, but that's exactly what you shoulda done! You shoulda done it long, long ago!" One person in life that will tell you exactly what they think of you . . . the whole truth and nothing but the truth . . . is a drunk.

~~~~~~~~~~~~~~

The only word that can describe this next story is macabre.

We got an emergency call one night; apparently, in a small village outside of Nome, a seven-months pregnant young woman had collapsed. From the scant details the two Health Aides could give me, it sounded like she had probably ruptured a blood vessel in her brain, for she had gone down very suddenly and very hard with no apparent symptoms.

The Health Nurses in the Mountain Village Clinic were very diligent and after this situation was all was over, I commended them for that, because they started mouth to mouth as soon as they got to her. The area in the patient's brain that the aneurysm occurred was the area that controlled her breathing. Her heart was fine and kept pumping and they kept her alive by constant ventilation for the three hours it took for a plane to go out and pick them up and return them to the Hospital. Above and beyond! My normal procedure on cardio-pulmonary resuscitation is, I start pumping on the chest and whoever is accompanying me has no choice than to start on the rather less desirable chore of mouth-to-mouth. This time, however, the on-duty ER nurse beat me to it, which wasn't really necessary anyway because her heart was just fine, so I had no choice but to take over the mouth-to-mouth when we put her in the ambulance.

The road from the airport in Nome to the Hospital was fantastically rough and the newbie-driver was understandably anxious to get our patient to the ER and possibly save her life, so my ride in the back of the ambulance proved to be almost deadly itself. As I as was doing the mouth to mouth, we hit this humongous bump and I hit my front tooth cap (a tooth I had lost in high school that was replaced with a crown) and knocked it hard, against one of the patients teeth and it knocked my cap right off, unbeknownst to me. With my next deep breath, I must have blown the cap right down into her lung; when I came up for the next breath, I had a big gaping hole where one of my two front teeth had been.

When we pulled into the ER door at the Hospital and got the patient stabilized, it was decision-time: as the clock ticked, it was apparent that the young woman was just not going to recover . . . despite the diligent and immediate care, the damage to her brain was too severe. We could not get the permission of the patient, of course, and no next-of-kin could be reached at that juncture, so the staff made the decision to try and save the baby at least, so I performed a C-section as fast as we could but the little guy was so tiny, he followed his mom in death in mere minutes. Later, when things had quieted a bit, I retrieved my tooth. There was a new dentist close by but I had to stay and finish the backlog of patients first, so I carried my cap around in my pocket and tried not to smile for a while . . . . it wasn't that hard.

~~~~~~~~~~~~~

Generalizations are usually unfair, but I have nothing but good and positive things to say in this next example of generalization so here goes: Eskimos girls are usually pretty. A few of them are fantastically beautiful, especially, it seems, when there is a few drops of another race included in the mix. One of these stunning young women had a white father and a Native mother; the mom brought her comely 16-year-old high school student in to the clinic one fine day, reporting that the girl had complained of abdominal pain.

I began my job of poking around and discovered rather quickly that she was not only pregnant but 'way pregnant and was in late labor. She had simply worn her parka all winter . . . a long, Alaskan winter . . . and no one had noticed! Strange, but true! She had kept it under wraps, literally!

We took her right into the delivery room and rather rapidly got a beautiful, healthy baby boy. The young mother's teary reaction was not tears of joy and the new Grandma was especially glum but then she shakily explained to me why there was an elephant in the room. It seems that the unaware, soon-to-be-Proud Grandpa had a famously violent temper and the mother related that when he was told, it was feared, all hell would break loose and heaven help anyone who was in his way! Turns out, once I looked at the admitting chart a bit closer, I recognized the name realized that he and I had flown together often and I even considered him a friend, so after relating this news flash, they prevailed on me to break the news to him and I agreed to do just that. On my lunch break, I decided to leave the Hospital and see if I could rustle him up. Turned out, the expectant grandpa was out at the airport at the time, so I took a drive and went out. He was doodling around on his plane, so I just stayed in my truck and pulled in close. He looked up and saw me and he waved and then sauntered over, and I invited him to get in.

We chatted a bit about this and that and he concentrated on the oily cloth which he was wiping his greasy hands on. I could tell that he was curious about why I was out his way. In my mind, I figured, "Oh, well . . . what's the worst he can do?" However, I knew that if his immediate reaction was explosive and he exploded, some of the shrapnel might hit me. I pocketed my glasses. I cleared my throat. I leaned a bit further from those big greasy hands.

"I need to talk to you about Angie," He stopped working his rag and looked up, concern knit his heavy brows and his eyes were boring down on me. I hurriedly went on, "Oh, no, she's fine, but she was pregnant but she's not pregnant now and the baby and Angie are both fine and beautiful and you should see . . . . " The look on his face rendered me speechless.

You could have heard a pin drop. But only for a minute.

Well, then all Hell DID break loose and he hammered on my dashboard and flung his fists around while he swore and stormed, finally swinging the door open, he took his rage outside. After stomping around and detailing the atrocities he was going to perform on the unfortunate baby-daddy, he finally calmed a bit and asked for details about Angie, whom he obviously loved very much. He rode back to the hospital with me, then, and of course, took one look at the beautiful grandson he now had and thankfully, the anger was replaced with pride and adoration. He probably could have gone through with his threats and shot any one of a dozen likely guys . . . that was just the way it was up there. The young folks weren't considered sinful or immoral . . . . they were just more casual about life functions than I was used to.

Another story that I found memorable was when a young woman who had been one of my Clinic Aides came in for her first delivery. She looked well and healthy and happy to be having her baby at the hospital. He husband came along but only as far as the desk: this was all women's' business, he said, and he had different business, elsewhere.

The women patients I worked with while I was in Alaska, for the most part, were super patients: their pain threshold's seemed high and they didn't usually complain and holler and scream, for the most part. I see that down in the southern 48, now, too, among the people of American Indian lineage. Now, when I trained in California and worked with high numbers of Hispanic women, the reverse is true: they seem to have very low pain tolerance and begin yipping it up right from the git-go.

Interesting, that. May I add here, for the benefit of women everywhere, and for my own protection, that if childbirth were the lot of men, we would certainly have a population problem and I do mean *problem* . . . not explosion. Our species would die out really fast if men took over the labor-pain route, and that goes for me, especially.

Working with the Eskimo people, we were able to do all kinds of procedures using minimal anesthesia and not because we would withhold it, of course, but that it's always safer to use as little anesthesia as possible for safety's sake, especially in childbirth. Little or no meds is and has always been the best route for the sake of the baby.

My little ex-Aide was really being a trooper: she was cheerful, and, when I got in to see her, the baby had come down partially but then we had a mid-plane-arrest, as it's called. What that means is that the baby was sideways; the mom-to-be appeared to be in minimal pain as I had done a caudal, which is a lighter version of a spinal when I had ascertained that the baby was transverse and there would be unavoidable and stronger-than-normal pain. The problem was that her muscles weren't contracting enough to turn the baby completely around the right way.

During my training, this had come up several times and I was now very glad I had been aggressive about getting in on as many deliveries as I could for the knowledge I gleaned. I had seen a lot for a doc my age, but I did a LOT of praying, too, because I realized I needed the Big Help in a big way!

Although I had *seen* a Kielland forceps and had used them a few times, and I knew that was the tool for the job at hand, but I didn't know exactly how to use them, so I didn't. I tried about everything I could and Nature just wasn't co-operating at all this time and the hours passed and our little mommy was wearing down. I knew I would have to use those forceps which meant that I was going to have to go into the bony pelvis which is dangerous in and of itself. I don't even think they use those forceps anymore, relying on C-sections more, but I hadn't at this time, done a C-sec, either!

So, I finally did what I should have done hours before: I called a colleague in Anchorage and said, "Hey, I got problems here!" He agreed that I needed to use the Kielland Forceps all right and told me to get a pen and paper.

Let me enlighten you on the Cliff Notes for a forceps birth: there are six or possibly eight steps, beginning with the insertion of the right side blade backwards, and then you rotate it around and finagled it around to the top. Then, you put the other one in and get it on the bottom and lock them. Steps three through nine are rather unpleasant to recite, and I would hate the details to be so ghastly that it would frighten a prospective mother, so sufficeth to say, my Cliff notes went over the line from notes to volumes and I took the papers into the delivery room and taped them on the overhead light where my patient couldn't see them. She reported that she was feeling great and was very pleasant as she watched me scrub up again and don mask and gown. We were fast approaching the end of this particular race and she was anxious to pass over the line and hold her baby. Explaining as little as I could to her, I began the process and continued referring to my hastily-written notes, glancing up at them from time to time.

"What do you keep doing that for?" She inquired finally, brows knit. "Oh, a have a little angel that perches on the lampshade to help me with my special patients," I murmured and warmed up the fib with a sincere smile. "You have been so great today, Katie, and I'm going to get this over with as soon as I can so you can hold your beautiful little baby in your arms."

She smiled beatifically and I leaned in once more with another blade. Well, I followed the instructions and by golly, they worked and as the kid rotated around, just like he was supposed to, I got so excited to see it work that I almost forgot to take the forceps out, but remembered and just dragged him out into the light . . . healthy and unmarked . . . in spite of his ordeal. Trouble was, I had an awful laceration to patch up and that took about an hour to do. For THIS, I used a liberal local pain killer! And plenty of it!

She showed up about a year later with baby number 2, so I guess the delivery wasn't TOO traumatic for her. These folks seemed to leave birth control up to the Lord; I'm not so sure they were even that organized about it, mostly. Many, many of them have babies before they are married—and that's not considered a problem. In their culture, a girl is even more marriageable if she has proved her fertility. Note: what a change in 40 years . . . I am pretty sure that the illegitimacy rates are probably about even with every other area in America . . . . take what I say here, then, with a grain of salt and try to remember the time-frame!

When we talk about premarital sex and immorality and all that, the concepts just don't apply 100% because it isn't considered sinful. Up north, there is no such thing as the expression "illegitimate child" in the Eskimo or Inuit language. A baby is generally always welcome in a family at least, when I wrote this entry in 1968 and that was the case. A birth is welcomed, in part because for time immemorial, group survival was dependent on a high birthrate and with high infant mortality taking the bite out of the total; the whole picture was different somehow.

Another thing is that you just didn't see the really huge families of 10, 11, 12 children that are common in some underdeveloped nations in a more southern perimeter. I don't fully understand why this is so, it just is. Of course, I did see that there were births that were badly timed, it seemed, and for some reason or another, the family just couldn't handle another child, but these instances were rare . . . certainly NOT the norm.

In the prospective bridegroom's eyes, a woman who had 'proven herself' by having a healthy child or two was more desirable than, perhaps, even a virgin. So many cultures take great store in virginity and purity and it is just not looked at it that way in some places up there. If a man was looking for a wife to be a companion and helpmeet for the rest of their lives, it was less of a gamble that she may or may not be barren, which, in their minds, is the real tragedy. Same went for a man, I guess.

Morals and customs that were different from mine didn't rub me the wrong way or make me think less of people when their beliefs ran counter to mine. Unlike some of the Great White Ones who felt it was their Christian Duty to cleanse these savages of their evil ways and groom, succor them, and make them as white as possible, I did NOT feel that way. I really had some soul-searing epiphanies while there and it has made me more compassionate, I can assure you!

This social more' was what it was up there and that had been true for centuries, I learned. Missionaries came in, beginning in the 1800's and 'saved' the people and taught them that their ways were evil and that they must change. This is a really sore spot for me. The Eskimo people believed that sex was a good thing, a fun thing and that is was natural . . . an enjoyable pastime . . . and they just didn't get uptight about it like the cross-wearing Holy Brethren preached they should. Grrr. Sorry . . . got sided-tracked.

To lighten the mood, I will share this story; it was related to me by a trustworthy source, and so I guess it's true. Around five years before we moved up there, a couple of prostitutes from the Seattle area decided that with the DEW line military base close in proximity to our location and government employees numerous, that there would be ample fruit, ripe for the picking. They bought airline tickets cheaply enough and flew in and set themselves up in one of the sleazier local motels in Kotzebue, put the word out and just waited for the guys to line up.

Come to find out, after hanging around the local bars for a few weeks and really eating into their seed money, the girls came to understand that the local men weren't too anxious to spend money to get what all the pretty Eskimo girls were handing out for free!

Ah, mankind!

Finally, some of the guys in town felt sorry for the trixies and took up a collection to send them on to Anchorage where they could make a living off the Air Force base there.

Every once in a while we would transfer a patient to Anchorage, which was about a 3-hour flight counting layovers, where they had more complete facilities and lots of specialists. There were three or four options available: one, if the patient was not ill at the time but going to Anchorage for, say, a difficult surgery that we were just not comfortable with in Kotzebue, the patient could bring an escort and the Hospital would send an ambulance for them.

Another way, if a patient was really ill, we could send a nurse or even a doctor with the patient. It wasn't always our decision as medical staff at the Hospital—it was based on the patient. Whenever it came up that I was the one to go, it sure wasn't a bad gig . . . getting out of town for a day or two plus the ability to bring back fresh fruit and vegetables for my family and for friends was a real treat.

Having in my possession one very large suitcase plus an army-surplus duffle bag that could hold 20 pair of complete Army uniforms or a small walrus, and with the generous airline weight allowance of the day, I could feasibly purchase and bring back a hundred pounds of fresh produce that I bought at the base PX for local stateside prices. It was a worthwhile trip for all included.

On this particular trip, I was escorting a little gal named Mary M. She shows up again in this book and is really one of my fondest memories. Anyway, Mary was trying NOT to go into premature labor at six months because my humble little Hospital could not handle a baby that small and it would surely die. Now, Mary didn't drink and neither did I, but back in those days, even a teetotaler Doc knew enough to prescribe hard liquor, diluted and taken intravenously, would certainly slow down the labor drastically or stop it completely and that was the goal: if I could get her labor slowed or stopped and get her to Anchorage, she could be hospitalized for the time it would take for her baby to grow enough to be viable.

Mary was on a stretcher and it took my expertise, learned the hard way on these flights, of taking out the little arm thingy's off of the set of three seats and the stretcher fit pretty well. I had to buy 4 seats but it was the only way to keep Mary and her tiny, internal cargo, immobilized.

The 747 we were on was a tourist flight; they stopped in Kotzebue and let the folks out to browse around for 3 hours; then, it was back in the plane for the next stop, which was Anchorage and the hospital. The whole tour for the tourists included going to Nome for a few hours, then on and out over the Bering Sea. All in all, it made for a nice day for the visitors to the state that is packed with breath-taking scenery so abundant in Alaska, even if was only a short and minute glimpse.

There was a bunch of sweet little old lady tourist-types, one of whom seemed overly interested in Mary and me. I couldn't help but wonder if it improved their day or ruined it, what with Mary, drunker than a skunk on intravenous hooch and singing (badly and off-key) and whooping and hollering then alternately crying and praying in her dialect, right out there for everyone to see. Her labor, however, had succumbed to the level I had hoped for: it was stopped in its tracks, knocked out colder than an Arctic night.

Oh, I forgot to mention that Mary's three little nephews were flying with us, going to their grandmother, temporarily, in Anchorage. Mary had custody of them, Heaven help us all, as her sister, the mother of the kids, was deemed unfit. Well, Granny would watch over them while Mary was in the hospital. It sounded easy as pie, didn't it? I was such a push-over . . .

Mid-flight, the most inquisitive one of the sweet little ladies came up to me and tugged on my sleeve and asked very kindly if I needed any help with 'your young lady and the precious little ones.' "I am a nurse, you see," she confided and in her hand she was holding a battered and yellowing card, proclaiming her to be a Certified Health Provider from somewhere in one the Lower 48 states . . . can't recall where . . . one of the States that start with a vowel, I believe. I told her I was a Doctor and was taking Mary to the big hospital in Anchorage. Thank goodness we wore our uniforms at that time and that certainly helped me look respectable to some degree, to the curious onlookers. The lady seemed satisfied, although I realize I did appear very young at that time in my career, and had not established the serene, confident and unapproachable veneer of a real Doctor.

We debarked in Nome and changed planes. During the 3-hour layover, with Mary being lugged into the waiting area by two husky porters, I was left in charge of the three little angels who, methodically and in unison, cried, pooped, hollered, sucked on a bottle . . . never their own, and threw up. Two of the little beggars were in diapers and there didn't look to be a bare 9 months between any of them.

What a sight we must have made in that terminal: me, a 6'4" fresh-faced, gangly farm boy-type, escorting a drunken, overly-endowed, sexily-dressed, beautiful hare-lipped Eskimo girl who was hugely pregnant, and dragging three snot-nosed, screaming miniature Eskimos along, packing a huge suitcase and duffle bags, almost empty, with the idea of bringing back a load of produce. Perhaps if I had used them to tote the kids . . . probably not.

The glances and downright stares my posse and I got that night really embarrassed me at the time, but looking back now, I can chuckle and I'll bet you those tourist-types never forgot *that* bucolic little scene that played out in the Nome airport. When I told Phyllis all about it, she was disappointed that she didn't get to be in on the fun . . . . of course, in addition to the 3-hour layover, the plane was delayed . . . certainly par for the course at 'Elastic Airlines'

Came a point when I would have given back all my PX produce, traded Mary and all of the miniature Eskimos, singly or in the set, to slave traders or anyone who was interested. "Here, you take this whole mess . . . I'm outta here!" But there wasn't anyone to dump it on . . . there you have it. Well, we finally were up in the air, only to be told the pilot found out that Kotzebue was snowed in so we had to turn and land at Fairbanks. Fairbanks. Alaska. USA. Just for the record here, that is *the worst* terminal I have ever been in all my days of traveling* . . . have not been back to see if it got any better . . . hope so.

Still, it was the custom for anyone on staff, when they traveled out of Kotzebue and had access to fresh food, the traveler was obligated to bring back produce for the others left behind and that made up for the increased workload that fell to the others when one member of staff is absent.Without benefit of a TV, radio or newspaper, I scarcely knew what was going on in the rest of the world. We were on our own up there. Phyllis was always busy making bread, giving art classes, and, oh, yeah . . . raising the kids! I still look back in amazement at the life she unknowingly took on when she married me. A Doctor's wife is made out to be something other than it really is on TV and in the movies. A Doc's wife does NOT live the lush life at all, except of course, the ones married to specialists in Private Practice.

That's a different story than what Phyllis' was. There was scarce little glamour in her life after her marriage to me, anyway, and I admired her then and still for what she put up with.

* **NOTE: 40 years and over million air-miles later, I still hold to my statement about the airlines. We sat there another 3 hours. All in all, a one-hour journey had taken 9 hours. I really earned that produce and could have kicked myself a hundred times for my bright ideas. Mary and Crew, however, thrived and that made it worth it . . . .**

~~~~~~~~~~~~~~~

We were the only LDS in Kotzebue, as far as we knew, anyway, so honoring the Sabbath once a week was an experiment in creative adventure. When we went down to Anchorage to Church, we were in a true oddity. There was even an article in the Church News about it being the northernmost Branch of the LDS Church in the USA.

When we held our own family Sunday services, we kind of played it by ear: we'd listen to tape recording of the Tabernacle Choir singing hymns to get ourselves into a Church-y mood. Then we'd coach the boys through giving little lessons; they were old enough at four and five to present talks that were tailored to them that helped them understand the Mormon way of life. At one point, towards the end of our tour of duty, we experimented with providing some more interactions with children their own ages and enrolled them in Father Geary's Bible School where they met a lot of other little guys, played and sang songs about Jesus and learned that God is a spirit and baptism is accomplished by sprinkling.

Took us a while to change some of those ideas around more to our preferred line of thinking when they came home . . . . but it was all good.

~~~~~~~~~~~~~~~

Really, being a doctor was what I had always wanted to be for a long time. As I've said, when I was in internship in Riverside, I had the reputation as the "go-to guy" who would take over someone's shift if needed. I was all over the hospital, in every department, a sponge for learning anything medical. Most interns had fifteen or twenty patients and I always had twice that many. Yeah, a sponge alright, all wet and full of holes . . .

If someone sick or injured showed up in the ER and they looked out of the ordinary, I checked them into the Hospital myself so that I could observe and learn while I was providing the help they needed. It was a charity hospital and the majority of the patients were charity patients . . . indigents, mostly, plus a lot of illegal aliens . . . . although that was not the terminology we used then . . . . I suppose that makes me sound just terribly Politically Incorrect . . . but those who know me know I am not a bigot and those facts are just the facts. If the clientele had been Russian immigrants, I would refer to them as Russian immigrants and if they had been little green men from Mars, that's what I would have called them in my mind and in my journal notes.

Anyhow, I took Dental surgery and facial surgery when I had the chance as well as learning OBGYN and obstetrics. Now, when I say, 'learned' I mean, instead of four or five years of specialized training, I just had a smattering of everything: kind of like a smorgasbord meal at Chuck-a-Rama compared to fine dining. Believe me, I knew my limitations and whenever I came up against the Real Thing . . . something complicated and beyond my kiln, and there was no other option, I would pray and sweat in equal proportions . . . .

Anesthesiologists have three-years' training and I was putting people to sleep and learning to do those things on a rotating internship which is only supposed to broaden a Doc's education and change the medical school academic atmosphere into a transition from seeing and learning into doing. Being really, really motivated, I was kept very, very busy: after my regular shifts, I'd usually step in as a scrub nurse in surgery or as a special-duty nurse taking care of extremely ill patients.

One night, I got to deliver twins which interns seldom did, but the regular on-duty came down with kidney stones and I had no choice. Made me glad for that in later years when it was thrust upon me unexpectedly . . . and quite unexpectedly for the Mom too, I might add. If one multiple birth babies come down the birth canal with the back of its head facing up, it is called a transverse lie and it poses a very difficult situation, or it may be an occipital posterior which takes a special forceps that even some specialists are reluctant to use.

Uncomplicated twin deliveries were usually simple and I had done them before and was just plain lucky . . . or blessed . . . depending on what you believe, as were the mothers more importantly. These experiences sure helped me out later in Kotzebue, because then, when an OB or surgery problem had to be faced because there is nobody there for me to holler at for help, it was sink or swim.

The patients I treated in Kotzebue were so trusting; I don't know if it was because they were inexperienced concerning medical care or just inherently trusting, but it sure made a difference in how I tried to live up to their faith in me. I would guess that of the hundred or so deliveries I attended while at Kotzebue, I'm quite sure that I saved the lives of five mothers and about that many babies. Most babies just naturally come out and most of the time, anyone with even a basic knowledge of child birthing can assist in a healthy birth, but I know in my heart that is was my 'full-court-press' behavior during my internship in California that was responsible for some of the close-calls that turned around and had happy endings.

Ah, but let us not overlook, however, my dedication, my hard-earned knowledge, and my Great Brain . . . coupled with my Noble carriage and All-Knowing aura . . . combined with my incredibly-honed good looks, killer smile and splendid affect . . . all these qualities unite to form an almost ethereal . . . . oh, me oh my . . . how I do go on!*

* NOTE: the above paragraph was composed without the knowledge of the Good Doctor, and since I don't often get away with ribbing him, I took this chance to give him a hard time. Gotcha, Sonny-boy! MDB

~~~~~~~~~~~~~~

Traveling to Anchorage was rather commonplace for whenever a patient was really critical, I would act as escort or have one of the other Doctors on staff do it. It was set up on a rotation basis but since the Hospital had much more of a family feeling rather than a democracy, I was the Dad and called the shots, so to speak.

Getting to know both the people I treated and the people I worked with during the years at Kotzebue was so great, because I liked the town and the general attitude of the citizens there. They seemed to all have a sense of humor and as a rule, were jolly and optimistic. They didn't *know* they were considered 'poor', unless a VISTA volunteer told them . . . . When I was a kid growing up in Iowa and then later in Arizona . . . we didn't live a luxurious life, but it was a happy and contented life.

Since the subject came up in my journal, I want to explain that last statement: when VISTA volunteers came up to Alaska, they started to tell the locals how terribly bad-off they were and how everybody was screwing them; I believe it went a long way toward planting the seeds of dissatisfaction and discord. If there is any negative feel in my story, here, that is the reason. That was the way it appeared to me at that time and in that place, which is all I can relate. It still applies today and there are even more 'Benevolent-Government' programs sprouting up all over, all supported by already-over-burdened taxpayers and although some of them do a great amount of good . . . others don't.

Toward the end of my sojourns there, some of the native young people were going very activist and anti-white-anti-government, much like the Red Power movement in the Lower-48. I heard that the guy that took my place didn't stay long because of real or perceived threats to himself and to his family.

Back then, when it was good, it was very good: the patients trusted their Doctor, plain and simple. I felt I could make proper decisions because of their trust and we both had faith something positive was going to happen, speaking in a spiritual or psychological way. Everything I did for them was free because the government paid me to do it.

In the more isolated villages, the general health of the citizens wasn't really too bad: most of them couldn't afford to smoke or drink in excess and the kids only got candy and the 'junk food' and such on rare occasions. Just these simple things made a huge difference in the allover health.

Phyllis saw her first drunk at Kotzebue. She had been raised in a safe, quiet area of Phoenix in a sheltered environment, and had been protected from the seamier side of life and it followed she didn't know much about this condition. She was taking the kids to a movie one evening while I was at work: they never made it into the show, for, there in the alley was a woman, stretched out and moaning and incoherent. Phyllis held the little boys' hands and rushed out into the street, finally flagging down a tourist bus, and said to the driver, "This woman back there is very sick and you have to take her to the hospital right now!"

The bus driver appeared very reluctant, Phyllis related, but her strong will prevailed and the driver finally drove over to the alley, gathered the woman up, and drove her in. The Doc on duty was a nice, gentle guy and he didn't act condescending toward Phyllis for her over-reaction, but he did tell her what was wrong with the woman. I would like to have been there to see her eyes! Another time, near Christmas, Phyllis went to the door and there was a drunk passed out on the doorstep. It was about 10 a.m. and the sun was just starting to come up in the southwest so it was hard to see clearly; turns out, the drunk was actually passed out and leaning against the door for support, so when she opened it, the poor guy rolled down a full flight of steps.

She ran down, of course, and tried to wake him up when Bob, the State Trooper came along in his truck. He looked him over, and then tried to hoist him into the back of his truck, finally heaving him in and hauling him off . . . it was nothing out of the ordinary for Bob, as part of his job entailed staying up all night scooping up drunks and letting them dry out, making sure in the meantime that they were not allowed to drive or hurt anyone else.

Phyllis learned about drunks in a hurry, as it was so commonplace there. Once she chased an old gal, Daisy Lamb, across the tundra in the pitch black of night; it was in the dead of winter and Phyllis knew if Daisy fell down or lay down and went to sleep, she would freeze to death, so she managed to catch her and coax her back to town. A Mother Hen with a big heart, that's Phyllis . . .

At one time, Kotzebue had one of the most unusual saloons in the world. It was called the 'Flying Martini' and was a DC-8, a four-engine plane, that originally landed at Kotzebue without benefit of lowered landing gear and there it stayed! This had happened about ten years before we got up there, but I talked to some of the guys that were there at the time and saw it all happen. He related that they ran over to the plane and could hear the radio still going in the cockpit, although the whole bottom of the plane was wrecked. No one was seriously hurt and I was told that the first thing the planes crew members did was grab some spray paint and blacked out the name, "Alaska Air Lines", (at least I think that was the name . . . don't hold me to it!) but the name was painted out before anyone could get there and take pictures of it.

The plane, for all purposes, was a total wreck. If it had happened near Anchorage or somewhere close, the airline company, perhaps, could have salvaged it but it was 500 miles from the airport and there wasn't even a major airbase nearby. So, some wise guy got a hold of a bulldozer and drug the wreck outside of the city limits of Kotzebue, pushed it up on a big hump of dirt and made a bar out of it. Kotzebue itself was dry, so this made a handy place for the so-inclined to hunker down right over the city limits and get drunk.

The place soon became such a nuisance that the town authorities extended the city limits, enfolded it again, and shut it down. It was abandoned and stripped down pretty much, while we were there and it was a fun place to go. All of us who had planes salvaged parts from it . . . if we happened to need connections or some wiring, we just went out and got lucky sometimes. No one actually owned the thing anymore—at least, I hope not. It was all done in the spirit of recycling, see? Our kids loved to go out there and while it had been pretty well ransacked, it was fun to sit in and play around as there were little hidey-holes that they loved to explore.

Kotzebue was the Hospital I had chosen from several that I could have gone to; I liked the setup and I liked the 'feel' of the place and of the people. It was a great hospital, in my estimation, and the staff was exceptional. I have never felt so useful and appreciated. During the next 40-or so years since I was serving there in my career, the fond memories remain.

'CHRISTMAS AT HOME . . . ALL IS CALM, ALL IS BRIGHT.'

'THE FLYING MARTINI, THE PLANE THAT LANDED GEARS DOWN AND THEN WAS TURNED INTO A BAR OUTSIDE OF KOTZEBUE.'

CHAPTER 10

"PLANES, PLANES AND MORE PLANES"

Toward the middle of April of 1969 I bought a plane.

This was right after my new assignment from Anchorage to the Kotzebue hospital. A guy named Fred Muhs was introduced to me on one of the first days I spent on the job. We seemed to hit if off right away . . . you know, the kind of friendship that just clicks right from the beginning. He was a great big old social worker from Nome and we met when made one of his frequent trips to Kotzebue, where he had an office. We tried had lunch together often. He was about my height, probably 20 years older and out-weighed me by 40 pounds or so.

One day, he came to the hospital cafeteria while Phyllis had dropped over and was having lunch with me; I was glad to introduce them as she had been hearing his name from me often. He was a fun guy to be around and so I thought he was joking when he just piped up during a lull in the conversation and asked, "Hey, how'd you guys like to buy a plane?"

I opened my mouth, but somehow Phyllis' voice came out and said, "Sure, how much?'

Well, *that* came as a surprise!

"Fred, we can't afford a plane," I put in quickly to try to cut off this wonderful yet impractical line of thinking.

"Ohhh . . . about $2500 bucks," he said with a laconic grin, addressing Phyllis now, as he must have known he had a nibble on the fishing line. I was earning about $1400 a month back then and still making payments on some small debts and stuff like that.

We just didn't have much 'disposable income', as one would phrase it in today's vernacular . . . even with Phyllis' finely-honed gift of frugality. All I knew was, she told me we were broke all the time but we always had everything we needed.

Again, Phyllis' voice sounded unexpectedly, and this time, she looked at both of us with a grin and said, "Well, I'll buy it if you don't want to."

Wow, that sure came out of the clear blue, but with summer coming and being low on supplies and all, it did make good sense: I could be much more mobile and we could accomplish 10 times as much in the same amount of time without having to depend on other pilots, cantankerous sled dogs and equally cantankerous snow machines with their limited cargo abilities and such. It really did make sense and Phyllis admitted she had been thinking about it a lot, sitting home while I was stranded in yet another village instead of being home with my family, and all due to pilot no-show or something like that.

Yes, a plane would be a Good Thing (and also really fun!). It was something I had always wanted. (and also really fun!) Having Phyllis not only amenable but actually positive about it was a wonderful turn of events! It was these occasions that reminded me just how unpredictable marriage was.

Is.

Still. (and also really fun!)

Well, Fred was selling a Piper Cruiser . . . . I'm not sure where he bought it, but it was a 1946 model, old by plane standards; it was a lot like a Super Cub as it had one seat in front and 2 in the back. It didn't have flaps and had a 108 HP engine instead of a 150HP.

It would cruise about 90 MPH; it had heel brakes and if the pilot were tall like him and me, there was no way to have toes on the rubber pedals and heels on the brakes at the same time: long legs simply don't bend at that angle! Therefore, it was stop or go which made for exciting and unpredictable landings, especially if there were crosswinds when you needed both controls simultaneously.

If I remember right, after 40 years or so, we borrowed money from the credit union or something, but I don't remember if I even saw the actual money before we agreed with Fred to buy it from him, at a lower price even, after all was said and done. Whatever, the case, I felt like a rare and lucky guy indeed whose wife 'forced' him into buying such a cool Big Boy Toy, even if she had ulterior motives . . . .

Turns out, it had the original engine in it, with about 1700 hours logged or something . . . . really run out. When you goosed it, you had to wait a minute to see if any power was going to spew forth at all and in what quantity. It was kind of like drag-racing in a Volkswagen.

Now, it had been a few years before coming to Alaska . . . actually while I was still in Internship in Riverside . . . that I learned to fly from this old guy, Flavio Madriago. He was a big, dark, pot-bellied fellow and although he looked like he would be more at home mechanic-ing planes than flying them, he knew his business all right and taught me the basics in his old J3 Cub on a grass strip. He sat in the back of the thing, over grossing the weight limit of the thing, and I took $100 worth of lessons at $12 an hour.

Flavio and I used to fly around over the desert near Riverside and after enough lessons to clean up my $100 investment, Flavio informed me in his thick accent. "OK. You are ready to solo now," He crawled out of the plane, hitched his belt up and over his big belly and flashed a gold-toothed smile as he started back to the parking lot, pocketing my small roll of bills.

"You OK pilot now," he tossed out over his shoulder; he must have thought that nodding briskly and grinning as he walked away was adding to my comfort level.

Uhmmm, "Look, you get back in the plane," I called out. "I'll give you another 100-bucks but there is no way I'm ready to go up in that thing with what I know."

Thus, another $100 and another 4 lessons ended my training with Fearless Flavio.

So, fast-forward ahead: here we are in Alaska and the plane Phyllis and I were contemplating purchasing was worth maybe a thousand bucks in those days. It was probably insurable, but I wasn't insurable *enough* and that made owning and flying it important to me, because my family needed me financially and would suffer if I were to, oh say, do a nose dive on account of not having enough training.

So, when we bought this plane from Fred in Kotzebue, I didn't feel I was quite ready to fly into the wild blue yonder, just right yet. We arranged a slot of time for me to go down to Nome and took a few more hours; I took lessons there from a young Puerto Rican guy who was living close by and who had a license proclaiming that he was legal to teach. He was flying charters to tourists and hunters and giving lessons on the side. He had an accent that you could cut like butter and it was hard for me to understand everything he said. Of course, he would probably go home at night and say the same thing about me: "Oh, yeah, that big, fonny-looking dock-tor! Hees accent iss so theek, I could not only understan' ever' other word!"

Whatever.

We agreed on sky-training in Kotzebue, too, this time for me and Phyllis both, so when I began, she took lessons, too. We drove out to where the 'Training Center' was on my first day off and there it was: an abandoned dirt road led up to one tin building and no radio tower. Grim beginning! The instructions and the fly-time were most helpful, and together, Phyllis and I left the center knowing just enough about flying to be comfortable with the basics and we still retained the child-like thrill and downright ecstasy that personal aerial maneuvering can be.

As we walked off the field after that final lesson, I suppressed the urge to skip and jump for joy.

After some more additional training, we took our 'new' plane up with Fred in it so that we were comfortable and familiar not just with flying but with our very own, personal plane. We just flew around, too, whenever we had a chance, in good weather and in not-so-good, too, with Fred pointing at things and us nodding. This went on for a couple of days and then he cut us loose.

Regardless of all the *intense* training that summer, I practiced landing and taking off on sandbars: they can be very easy or very hard . . . it depends on how solid they are which is hard to gauge from the air. So landing always has an element of surprise! Where we were flying that day, there were big ones that were smooth and I could see the tracks where other planes had landed. I tried to just steer into the wind and then there was no problem. The problems came when I tried to drag the sandbars myself and make a judgment call on them from 20 feet vertically whilst zipping along at 80 MPH horizontally!

I would gaze down at them intently before attempting to land . . . I really didn't know what I was supposed to be looking for as it was really tough determining whether or not they were soft or hard or if there were boulders hiding under the sand or lots of tricky pebbles. Nevertheless, I gazed intently . . . . and I still wound up just going in wondering, "Is this sandbar gonna eat me today?" The only way to learn the particular skill of landing was trial and error; I sure seemed to have more than my share of the 'error' part, but I was so hardheaded, I just kept plugging away.

The landing strip at Kotzebue, however rough it seemed, was almost a mile long and even small private jets came in and landed on it. Now, remember, this was at sea level, too. Then once, one of the big planes used the strip and sucked up some pebbles during takeoff and although it didn't damage the runway, it sure played heck with the plane.

Sometime after that incident, the strip was asphalted. For the longest while, when I'd land on that asphalt strip, the wheels squeaked and I thought I was making a bad landing, which I probably was sometimes, but I was used to the lack of noise like there was when landing on a sandbar . . .

In the town of Kotzebue, population of about 2,000, at least half of the non-Eskimo guys had their own planes. We government-types got stateside reimbursement rates for flying, which at that time was about 10 cents a mile . . . this princely sum was almost enough to pay for my oil, but was a bargain for the Government all in all: it would have cost many more tax dollars to continue buying tickets on commercial flights. We plane-owners all bought our gas in 55-gallon drums, delivered to the dock in Kotzebue. It was ice-free only about 4 months out of the year there and the procedure would go something like this: one or the other of us would get notified when a barge would dock with a load of gas containers. Then, however many of us could get away from what we were doing would just get a truck, run down to the dock with a bunch of our own barrels, then fill them with gas and store them on the airstrip near our planes. Actually, we let simplicity rule and just tied our planes to the barrels, as this seemed to be the most practical plan.

Whether you believed in having a years' supply of necessities as a tenet of your church or not, everyone had to forecast what supplies they would be using over the next 9 months or so, because that was how often the barge came in. We'd get together and start rolling the drums. Now, I saw some guys who could actually pick up a 55-gallon metal drum full of gas, stacking them one upon another, but I tell you what . . . all of the guys I knew, including me, did not go in for that dreary example of machismo! No siree! We just checked to see if the bunghole was tight and rolled the barrels the short distance from dock to the airstrip!

We'd then just hand-pump the gas from into five-gallon cans and stick a large funnel into the planes gas tank; we'd drape a big, clean chamois over the hole before we poured the gas through it. The chamois strained all the debris out, like sand and leaves, misguided bugs or anything else that happened to find its way in, especially water, for, if you have water in the gas, it doesn't do much to aid a combustion engine! We'd wet the chamois and wring it out as dry as possible, then hand-crank the fuel into the wing tanks.

In the summer, we flew more and if we couldn't get enough gas from our regular sources, we could buy it at astronomically-inflated prices (it will hurt you, Dear Reader, to hear this, but by astronomically-inflated, I mean about 35 cents a gallon). It was running at about $25 for a 55-gallon drum!

Ah, progress.

Anyway . . . our entire Band of Brothers, owner-operators took the housekeeping chores that go along with ownership of a plane very seriously. We checked our own oil levels and did minor repairs . . . even some repairs that were not all that minor. I learned a lot from them, too, so I gradually built up a confidence-level that's necessary for a pilot.

. . . and I learned to fly! Good!

I'd come in to land on a sandbar as had learned to do on an airstrip; in the early days of my experience I was afraid of stalling . . . so I bounced. Instead of going back up and coming in at it again from another angle, I pointed the nose down, which built up my speed and I went boing! Boing! BOING! Up in the air and down again, I made at least four good landings for each approach and one time I made four of the nicest ones I ever made on just *one* approach.

Also, I did a lot of sweating.

Pause here for some personal mulling: I have never been able to understand what it is that drives me to do some of the things I did and DO: dangerous things. Things that, in retrospect, make me nervous; rather, that should have made me nervous back then . . . enough not to do them! Things that make wives and mothers cringe and pray. I do get headaches but I've never had an ulcer caused by stress and doubt I will at this juncture, but it wasn't because I avoided stress. I did, and DO hazardous things on purpose . . . I know I do. I recognize where the Danger Markers are and I push them; as long as it's me and I am not putting someone else at risk, I get very pushy. Risk-taking seems to be a part of my personality but I only do it when I am sure I am not hurting other people directly.

There seems to be an inborn feature in my blood that keeps crowding me a little bit all the time, urging me wordlessly to go further, go faster. Thankfully, I suppose, for my loved ones' sake, at least, I have 'mellowed' a bit and exhibit more caution than I did 'way back then.

Life is a series of lessons and it is my belief that important Life Lessons must be achieved before going on the next plane (no pun here) of existence. Now, a person doesn't have to practice going hungry or thirsty or shivering, so I really didn't feel I needed to perfect those skills, but I sure did a lot of them! Gotta love the life lessons!

~~~~~~~~~~~~~~

I got my REAL pilots license, replacing the student license I had been flying on up to that point, late in the summer of 1969. Eight or ten of the guys who were from the hospital and the school, me included, heard that the FAA inspector was coming into town. We were just hanging out, gathered around our tie-downs, when someone suggested I take the test. Because I had been flying people for quite some time illegally, he said. Because I'd been taking people up for quite some time illegally, decorum told me I might as well get myself and my passengers killed *legally* instead . . .

I was probably a good idea and said I would; one fellow said, "You're not gonna take that piece of junk of yours up, are you?" The general consensus agreed with this point of view . . . "Keep that thing out of sight. He'll ground you for sure if he sees it. You fly my plane!"

Everyone got in on the conversation then, giving me tips and pointers and drilled me as to procedure.

"Now, you bear in mind," one of them said, "if you goof—up or he has to take you out of a mess, or has to give you advice on flying at all, you're through . . . you won't get your license from him."

"As long as he doesn't say anything," another said, "you'll be OK, but if he talks, kiss your license goodbye!"

On the scheduled day of my test, I was looking over my buddy's plane; there was a brisk crosswind blowing, but, when wasn't the wind blowing there, one direction or another? So, I refused to be discouraged and put it out of my mind. When the inspector came over, he introduced himself and we exchanged a miserly bit of pleasantries; then he started in on the preflight routine. He asked a few questions, like an oral test, about mapping a route from point A to point B, things like that. Mapping is a very important part of the test, but I felt like I did OK on that. Then the next phase included actual air-time.

At this particular juncture, it's probably a Good Thing to give the reader some basics of flying, and since I love to talk about flying, it is a Double-Good Thing.

Now, if the wind is blowing and it is coming straight at you, that's OK, but, you can't land well if there is a cross-wind: you must keep the plane aimed into the wind. The trick is to act like you are trying to just drive the airplane straight into the ground, then as you cut the speed, you will come in at a nice slant, but if not, you will end up making a 'crabby' landing . . . that does not need an explanation at all, now does it . . . . ?

On this particular day in question, having no choice in managing the weather the day of my test, up we went. This plane of my buddy's was a beaut and I got off the ground in good form. The Instructor had me land after taking only one circle of the field.

That is where the 'beaut' part ran dry. The landing I made was just awful: we bounced all over. I had never flown the plane before, you see and it was a little sawed-off thing with a nose-wheel and handled a lot differently, albeit, better, than my plane.

After landing that first, time, he directed me to go up in the air again and we just flew south a bit; there was a mountain-range of white-knuckles on my hands and I was growing a headache from the tension. Soon he told me to land and, once again, my usual technique of getting close to the ground and chopping back my power with the hope I wouldn't be killed did not produce the effect it did with my plane and the darned cross-wind make it even worse.

My sphincter muscles were so tight I couldn't have passed an electron . . . . and calling my landing 'bumpy', would be a kindness.

When I shut off the engine and we were once again on the ground, he said, "Let me fly it around a little and show you how," I sat back, grimly, fearing I had just lost the whole ballgame.

We went up and made a circle or two and then came back in with that nasty cross-wind still huffing along, but instead of not holding any low wing on the wind, he held too much, and a puff of wind caught us just as we landed. The wing tipped down, almost to the runway and the Pacer spun sideways and had it not been for the loose gravel we skidded in on, we would have surely cart-wheeled, or, 'ground-looped', as pilots say. He got it straightened out just before a nosedive into a snow bank, and then had to take to the air again to land.

By this time, I was just an interested spectator and I was really glad when we were on the ground without too much *more* trouble.

He steered over to the side of the runway; I turned to look at his face, for the first time in quite a spell, and he was a sickly shade of green. Automatically, I grabbed his arm and started to take his pulse but stopped myself just in time. He reached for his clipboard, signed my license and said "Congratulations," rather grimly and without another word, got out of the plane.

~~~~~~~~~~~~

Once, after misjudging the time we had on the way home from a goose hunt on the Noatak River, I got into a fog so thick

I couldn't find Kotzebue or anything else, for that matter. I had a fellow with me . . . can't pull up his name . . . and didn't want to alarm him but the fact was I didn't have any instruments to tell me which way to go and couldn't have read them even if I had them. I didn't dare cross Kotzebue Sound in that fog without the risk of crashing, so I found a friendly-looking sand bar and landed.

So, there we were . . . soaked to the skin in no time; I had a tent which was made out of an old parachute I had unwisely attempted to water-proof and, on this particular test run, failed miserably. We sat under it, shivering, with the two space blankets that comprised my on-board Emergency Preparedness Kit; we wrapped the tin-foil-like covers around us and we huddled over a small fire, keeping it sheltered from the wet stuff and we stayed like that all night and into the next day.

The rain didn't stop until afternoon and there was finally enough visibility to fly out toward home. It was a sobering event, and it all happened because I didn't manage things as well as I should have and got caught by bad weather. It was a hard lesson to learn but it sure could have been worse!

Another time, I came in to the Noatak on the graveled strip that I wasn't used to. There was a strong crosswind, which fouled things up even further; I should have either dropped my left wing into the west wind while coming in, or come in on a crab. Instead, I came barreling in and almost drowned us because the strip ended at the waterline and then became . . . . well, water. Unfortunately, I DO remember who it was with me that time and it was the Director for the whole state of Alaska, John Lee, and I'm sure he was ready to jump out of the plane and take his chances instead of risking the certain death that seemed to be imminent in the plane with me as pilot.

It took a long time to learn to use the prop correctly and to judge sandbars. I can't believe I got by with the things I did . . . . one time I came in to visit some people up by Kiana and I had no choice but to land on a sandbar that was dotted with rocks in every size. I came barreling in at it 4 times without taking the land. Eventually I'd had enough and since I had been over it looking for a smooth spot so many times so I could get it down, I just hit the brakes and nosed over, bending the prop.

But we stopped . . . .

Gee. Most guys have more trouble getting up rather than down . . . .

The skills I needed to fly safely were not easy to come by but nonetheless, fly I did. Flying a plane should not be acquired with solo, on-the-job training. I recall thinking several times that I should give it up before I killed myself but there was something inside of me then that pushed me to my limit; loved ones have said that I must have a Guardian Angel, but that someday even HE would get tired of rescuing me. I hope not. Maybe they travel in pairs. Or they tag-team. Or get to retire early and get replaced . . . .

On my first cross-country flight, I started from Kotzebue and went down to Nome, which was around 200 miles and due south. I was a pretty lousy navigator and it seemed the flight took forever. Of course, due to my attack of nerves, I had the urge to urinate. It's common to carry bottles made just for this contingency and I had grabbed a used IV bottle from the hospital, turned it upside down, then threaded the tubing down and out of the bottom of the plane through a tiny hole in the floor.

Brilliant! By using it two or three times, it proved to worked quite handily. I screwed the cap on tightly and let the contents out through a drain. This was my first time at this, so when I finally did land and saw that the bottom of my place was splattered with long yellow stripes, it was very embarrassing for me, but commonplace, too, I found out.

On the final approach to Nome one time, the engine started to run rough and then I remembered that I forgot (that doesn't sound right!) to pull the carburetor heat on. I called Emergency over the radio and told them was going to have to come in short and that they needed to prepare for a bad landing. Then, at the last minute, I noticed the carburetor heat and pulled it on and the old engine fired up and I landed just fine. I radioed the control tower that I had just made a little mistake. Common for them, maybe but not me.

So, on my first cross-country flight, I flew back home by way of Moses Point so I could get a fellow to do an annual check of my plane. Old Mr.C had a drinking problem and the local saying went that if you needed a little 'help' with the annual inspection/ evaluation, it would be wise to grease him with $100 bill wrapped up with your request. If you did it on Saturday night and he was in the right frame of mind, he'd sign off on your plane and mark it legal to fly.

The only other way is to take it in and have it checked out by a really good mechanic to make sure it is worthy to fly, or, we would have to go to Anchorage and leave it for at least a day for the checkup to be done. While in Nome, had I flown there, I would leave it at the airstrip for the inspection and use the 'down time' to cover the hospital there for a few days.

At that time, I was sure I couldn't get any reputable A&E to sign off on the plane because the engine was run out and was really on its last legs. Really can't imagine how it got its annual OK the year before: it was certainly rickety. Every time I taxied down the strip from my tie down in Kotzebue, some of the other guys razzed me and said they knew it was me because of the coughing and sputtering of my engine. I really had to goose it to get it going, and then kind of stew along, as if an old stretched-out rubber band was turning over the motor; they called it the 'Hooker Hiccup' and would just shake their heads and laugh.

One of the problems I had was a bent prop which I got because of my numbskull landing on the sandbar months before, so it made the prop vibrate all to heck. I was too inexperienced to fix it myself and too broke to pay to get it done. The prop was about an inch and a half out of track: for you who are uninitiated into the Wonderful World of Airplanes, this phrase won't make any sense.

Eventually, some FAA guy in Nome noticed the prang in the prop and put a red tag on the plane which meant, "Don't fly this plane until you get it fixed, and then we'll check it again to make sure." There was no way in hell my skinflint butt was going to sit home while the plane got fixed, or NOT fixed, by some crook that would just take advantage of my situation and soak me for it, so I just pocketed the red tag and hopped into my plane and flew back to Kotzebue, counting on Providence: the young man's ego balm.

So far so good; then, a few days later, this same FAA guy happened to land in Kotzebue and recognized the plane He nailed me good but I plead ignorance and with a face like mine, it isn't too hard to do. My 'innocent farm-boy' countenance saved the day and he didn't give me a citation as he could/should have. Later on, one of my buddies took a sledgehammer and put the prop back in legal shape and I went right on flying.

~~~~~~~~~~~~~

You've got to work pretty hard to get killed in a Super Cub or a Cessna 180. If you're coming in for a landing in one of those, even with a wind and considering the cold sea level and you can get your ground speed down to 20 or 25 miles per hour, you can actually, truly, really just jump right out of a plane at that rate and survive. Jumping out is a preferable alternative to going down with the ship, in some cases.

Nelson Walker, one of the best guides in the business up there, has both a 180 and a Cub, and before we left Alaska he got a Helio Courier, which is a magnificent airplane. It doesn't cruise too fast: maybe 150 MPH, but it will haul about 1500 pounds and the stalling speed is an incredible 28—you can almost run that fast and that can be an advantage.

A common problem remedied by co-operation from the Band of Pilot Brothers was the fact that none of our planes held enough gas to take us as far as we needed sometimes, so we made caches all over, usually on sandbars we customarily were used to landing on. Then we could go out, gas up, fly around as much as we wanted to, then gas up again and come home.

One time I broke the tail wheel when I landed . . . that was unfortunate and you can imagine why it would be next to impossible to take off without one. I had taken some supplies up country for some friends of ours who were at hunting camp and when I got shut of all the passengers and cargo and was ready to leave, I propped the tail of the plane up on boxes until the airplane was almost high enough to touch the sand with its prop. I got in and nabbed a couple of handy guys and told them to grab on tight and hold the plane back.

There was quite an audience of onlookers who were curious enough to make the trek down to the landing strip and stand around, probably making bets as to how many times it would take to get in the air, or, perhaps, whether the crazy Doc would auger in at last.

Giving it all I had and holding the brakes down as hard as I could, I called to the guys to give me a push. Then I released the brakes and the plane leaped forward. The tail dragged down to some degree but I had so much RPM built up that I got airborne. It was right on sea level and the temperature was about 40 degrees. In the air, I was OK and the missing wheel didn't matter a bit, and except for dragging up a considerable cloud of dust when I landed, I got down all right, too.

~~~~~~~~~~~~~

There was some debate about just where to place this next particular story: would it qualify as a hunting story or a plane story? I suppose it doesn't matter as long as it gets in! So, here it goes. One unforgettable adventure happened on my way back from a forgettable village, when I spotted a big spike moose. Now, many families in the areas that I had under my wing and cared for could always use some fresh meat, my family included. Moose meat is well-liked because of its mild flavor and minimum amount of fat. The moose was looking better and better to me and I knew I could down him with one shot if I could land on a sandbar near him.

All was well until the landing when the sandbar turned out to be a mud bar, because in all the excitement, I wasn't paying enough attention to my surroundings . . . the First Commandment of Flying. It was starting to go dark on me; even so, I jumped out of the cockpit with my 30.06 and nailed him clean as he was running up a hill. It took more than an hour to turn his 800-or so pound body around and get it aimed downhill so I could open him up and bleed him out through the neck.

Pretty intent on what I was trying to do, I finally looked up and saw, as if this weren't enough bad luck, that there was a storm coming in and it was getting really dark, really fast. This was quickly turning into a situation over which I had no control. If it had been light enough, I would have just sat in the plane all night, or made myself a tent out of something. But, I got a little panicky, so I gutted the long-departed moose and piled some brush over him and jumped into the plane, thinking wisely (at last) to get out of there before it was too late.

No go.

I was royally stuck in the mud and it must have taken me an hour of propping up with logs and stones under the wheels to get it to where I could take off. The whole thing had become a nightmare, and it wasn't over yet. When I was finally able to lift off, the storm was down within two or three hundred feet of deck. Fortunately, I could just follow the river down, although by this time it was really dark. I had no landing lights in the plane and no interior lights and no real instruments, and worst of all, no experience with this kind of blind flying so I had no choice but to vector down the river with the wings almost touching the banks.

After about twenty minutes (that felt like twenty years) of flying, I got to this village, Kiana. It was very dark by then but I knew if I stuck to this course, I would fly over the village, although I could hardly see the prop turning in front of the plane.

Passing over the village and knowing there was a hill behind it, I made a sharp turn and picked out where I thought the landing strip was. I did recall that the cemetery was on one end of the strip and the river was on the other end. I lined up with the lights of the town and reconnoitered where I thought I ought to be and it sure looked like a runway down there, so I dropped in and then I saw all these little white crosses appearing under me—very discouraging! I just said a prayer, to this effect, "Dear Lord, I'm in Your hands now; I won't quit You . . . I'll just keep flying the plane but without Your help, I am lost. Help me, Lord." After that I did the best I could and knew that it was the only thing to do.

I probably shut my eyes while I landed. I don't recall . . . .
It rolled to a halt and I got out.

Dropping to my knees, I said a fervent prayer of gratitude, wedged a rock under the wheels, and slopped into town through the mud.

Of course, by this time, people were wondering where in the heck I was because they sort of kept track of the only doctor in the only hospital . . . I was NOT expendable in the minds of the majority of the people I knew, including my family. So regardless of the late hour, I went down to the Health Aide's house and we got into the school and managed to raise someone at the Hospital on the radio. I told them I was all right, to please call my wife and that I would fly in tomorrow . . . and then corrected myself as it was tomorrow already . . . . but I needed to go back and pick up my moose first. Priorities, priorities . . . .

Now, just when you think that is the end of that particular tale, let me finish: the morning broke clear and calm and I made it back home fairly early after a very quick nights' sleep of at least 4 hours. I gassed up my trusty mount, and with a hearty, "Hi ho, Silver," we were away. It happened to be Sunday and rather than take a much needed Sabbath, I quoted scripture in my mind . . . something about 'an ox in the mire', and reckoned that a 'moose in the brush' was about the same thing. I took Phyllis with me as she had been suffering from a bit of cabin fever and one of the members of the Church we were friends with was always offering to watch our kids, so Phyllis took them up on it.

Not really wanting to get back in the lousy Airplane of Near-Death again, having almost made a coffin out of it, *and* it was Sunday, we bundled up and took off anyway.

Nearing the spot that had hosted all of the excitement the night before, I set it down on a sand bar a bit further than the original landing place that was mostly sand and not muddy at all. We had gathered up a bunch of gunny sacks and even some heavy plastic yard-type; we departed the plane and Phyllis followed me to where I'd stashed the moose.

Phyllis, once more, earned her points: united, we cut the meat off of the bone, after performing all of the butchering tricks we had learned since moving up North. Quietly, lost in our own thoughts and with little chatter, we slashed at the lovely carcass and removed hundreds of pounds of the healthy, lean meat, filling the gunny sacks and stacking them to the side.

When every last morsel was accounted for, I left the offal for the fortunate scavengers, who had politely refrained from dining on my moose during the 8 or so hours since I had downed it. I did not want Phyllis to carry any meat, so it took a bit of time for me to walk the heavy, squishy and leaking bags to the plane.

Now, the PA12 airplane has a seat in the back that will hold two people but there is only enough room in the front for the pilot . . . it's sort of a triangular cockpit. I helped Phyllis in first after stacking bags in the back behind the seat as tight as possible; when she was comfortable as could be managed, I packed some more bags around her, tucking them in wherever I could. She sat, then, with a hundred-pound bag of meat on either side of her and one at her feet; there was still a lot of meat waiting on the ground outside. I packed another bag up front with me: it was actually stacked up to the ceiling of the little plane and I have no idea how much weight it was going to be asked to carry up and out of there. Between Phyllis and me, there was about 350 pounds . . . I weighed in at that time at about 200 and Phyllis was quite pregnant at the time . . . and add to that at least 400 pounds of moose meat.

Wow, that was a sorry-looking mess. Thinking back on it now, I have to grin at the memory of Phyllis in the back, packed in between sacks of leaky moose meat, which, by now, had sprung small holes, and moose-moisture was oozing out, running down her face and shoulders. She could barely move: it was a sticky mess but it was also winters meat for our family and others we knew who would make good use of it. Her face, however, and the pitiful picture she made that day covered in moose blood can't ever be forgotten: presenting, the talented and graceful Miss Phoenix of 1964 . . .

We kept along the far side of the river while taking off and the plane just would not lift up; we were loaded so far to the back with all that meat-weight and just before we went 'plop' into the water, it managed to lift groggily up, complaining all the way.

The last ten miles across Kotzebue Sound, the gas gauge bounced around less and less as it was hitting bottom, and I was getting an empty, let-down feeling, too! I would have hated to ditch it the water and forced us to swim out so I stayed real high, three or four thousand feet, until we got close to home, which was sea-level. We just barely made it back—the engine was actually sputtering as I taxied over to the tie-down.

Walking into town on shaky legs, after helping Phyllis out and making her comfortable, I went to get the hospital's ambulance to haul the meat in. I'd have had a hard time justifying to my boss that it was a good use for the vehicle. We trundled it all home and with help from a neighbor, we were able to clean up the meat rather quickly and get it all in the freezer, except for 50 lbs or so that I wrapped and took to the Hospital folks. Oh, did I mention that Phyllis happened to be pregnant with Kiana that time, about

8 months gone or so? Picture it . . . . adds a lot to the atmosphere of the saga, no?

A couple of weeks after that, a good friend of mine, Bill Rember, a teacher at Kotzebue School grabbed me on a rare day off and we took to the sky one Saturday in his Pacer plane to take a look around. A friend of mine from Church, Brother Pettyjohn who was an airline pilot, had told me he saw a beached walrus as he was flying over on his way inbound from Anchorage. So we told our wives we were going one way and then we went another direction, thus violating Rule #2 of The Basic Code of Flying, which states that telling people where you are going is a Good Thing. We didn't want to let word get out so that just anyone knew what we were up to and beat us to it. It all sounds pretty juvenile now, but it made sense at the time . . . .

Sure enough, we found the place easily and there was a nice, fat (well, technically, not so fat now) walrus, rotting on the beach. There was grizzly track all around and the bear or bears had pretty much cleaned up all the meat and left. We looked around a bit with no sight of the grizzly so we figured what the heck, it had been a nice day for a flight.

Heading back toward home, we were beach combing . . . flying maybe fifty feet above the ocean and just watching the beach for any activity. Almost 30 miles from home, which was just right down from the Arctic Circle a bit, we saw another dead walrus! Most unusual. We made a couple of low passes, trying to ascertain if it still had tusks. Ivory was selling at about $2.50 a pound but we weren't really looking to cash in, rather we would probably keep the ivory as an Alaskan souvenir.

Most of the beaches up there are littered with tons of driftwood; it comes from the 500-mile-long Yukon River which carries all this wood from the forests of the interior. It's a big river and mega-millions of tons of driftwood float out each high water. The predominate westerly winds blow all this flotsam matter back onto the beaches. The sand is soft on the beach but at this particular place, there's about a 3-foot tide which leaves a firmer and clearer, albeit narrow, little beach to land on. In theory.

We dropped onto this soft sand and sunk in clear up to the hubs.

Well, we had no choice but to get out; we walked over to where Mr. Walrus was disintegrating back from whence he had come; he had apparently floated in the ocean for quite a while, and then was tossed up onto the beach. I reached down to the carcass, trying not to breathe at all, and jerked out what little bit of ivory that was left, as both tusks had been broken off. We took them to the tide line and swooshed and scrubbed using the sand to take off any remaining flesh and reduce that horrendous odor. One tusk for Bill and one for me . . . . stinky souvenirs, but I still have mine with the hatchet-marks I put on it getting them loose.

It was getting sort of late, going on six or seven o'clock, but with sunset coming along about 11 pm. We got ready to take off, hopped in and Bill revved it up. It didn't move an inch. So I jumped out and kept the door open, figuring that I might get it moving, crawl up on the strut when it was moving and then crawl back in. I pushed like mad and then we actually felt forward movement, so I hopped in and . . . crunch . . . we were back right deep in the sand again. Back to the drawing board.

To give it a bit of advantage, we built ourselves a runway out of boards and driftwood and such, maybe 50 feet long. This particular kind of plane has a nose wheel to take into account; we got our little three-lane makeshift runway completed, started fine, and promptly ran off and down into the sand again.

Every time we tried this method, the nose would go down and the tail would go up which really alarmed us for we did not want to nose over and ding up the prop. We got to thinking that our wives would be getting worried about us and we needed to get serious about getting home.

As a last resort, we pushed the plane down close to the waterline; the wind was shipping up about a 20 MPH breeze in a crosswind that was coming in right off of the ocean. This necessitated Bill having to dip a wing toward the ocean in order to take off properly. We pushed the plane in close to the waves, where they had slapped the sand down pretty firm, then we popped back into the cabin and started moving along.

Bill made his dip and aimed toward the ocean . . . . and the then the wind caught the tip of the wing and we made a totally unintentional turn to the left and in the blink of an eye, we were

IN the ocean about 50 feet from shore . . . aimed straight for the coast of Siberia, a scant 50 miles away! Of course, with the wings full of air, we floated and we took that opportunity to reconnoiter our situation . . . and we too shocked to speak, I guess, too.

In a split second, it seemed, I had made up my mind to unfasten my seatbelt with one hand and use the other to launch myself out of the plane and into the ocean, figuring that it was about to sink to the bottom momentarily and there was just no way I wanted to end my life pushing up algae from the bottom of the sea! . . . and the doggoned thing still didn't sink, thankfully!

Upon the taking of a very deep breath and leaping out of the plane and into the chest-deep water, I can state, most unequivocally, that there is no better way to pull down your body temperature really quickly than to leap into the Arctic Ocean when the wind blowing at 20mph!

Having accomplished my watery mission by turning the floating plane around in the opposite direction, I damply hoisted myself back into the still-floating plane where Bill was trying frantically to jerk his brand-new radio out of the dashboard . . . he had told me on the way over that he'd just bought it a few weeks before, and it cost around $600. I guess there was no way he was going to let it sink to the bottom of the sea. He was either going to go down with the thing or wrest it loose. That plan, however good at the moment, wasn't be necessary as we began floating toward the shore, on the wings of a precipitous breeze!

The wind and the waves quickly pushed the plane back towards land and the wheels were in the sand in short order, so we rigged up a sort of Rube Goldberg apparatus for winching the plane the rest of the way out of the ocean front and back onto (relatively) dry land. We had plenty of rope and even parachute cord on board; the thing probably weighed in at around 1500 pounds. We ended up making a quick-do wench to haul it the rest of the way out of the water and out of the tide.

Bill fiddled with the plane, securing it on the shore while I gathered firewood and started a cracking fire . . . I didn't go anywhere without a bottle-full of waterproof matches, kiddies! I had never been so cold in all of my life. Now, had anyone happen chanced to be flying overhead at that particular tabloid in time, they would have witnessed a rare sight: two nearly-naked guys jumping around a fire and flapping their clothes over a hasty fire and hoping to shed enough moisture out of them to put them back on and crawl back into the beached airplane.

After successfully drying out and warming up a bit, we attempted to get the plane in the air by priming the prop and I'll be darned if it didn't start up! We let it run for a while, hopefully getting the water out of it; of course, by this time it was nearly midnight and too dark to take off anyway . . . not that we could have done it as we had already demonstrated our inability to take off, but we kept telling each other that, 'boy! . . . the thing sure could float!'

Bill had packed some space blankets and wrapped in these miracles of modern science over the top of our semi-dried-out clothes, we were prepared to shiver through the night. The situation we found ourselves in was more embarrassing than life-threatening. We were less than 50 miles from where we lived and even with the worst-case scenario, we could feasibly hoof it home. Even then, someone would probably see us and take us in . . . they'd get a lot of free laughs at our expense, but oh, well.

There was plenty of survival equipment onboard, so the night went by and we were even able to sleep a bit, but during the conversations around the fire, a brilliant plan hatched itself in our febrile minds . . . after looking at a map and estimating where we were, we decided to take another approach . . . a better approach . . . a MAN'S approach! Now, it took time to perfect a plan with this sort of bravery, this sort of brute and manly strength, this sort of . . . . well, anyway, it was getting so dark by this time that we pulled together a crude shelter of driftwood to get some rest until daylight. So, when the sun finally came up about 4AM, we were ready to put the Great Plan into motion!

Now, just wait'll you hear this . . . it's great!! A real *man's-man* sort of tale: we *pushed* Bill's ailing plane to the airstrip and got it going! You know, just like when you were a kid and driving daddy's Chevy and it breaks down and your posse would have to push it to the local garage . . . . just like that!

It was about noon when we reached the place we were aiming for and after nearly 8 hours of pushing, were there and we heaved a big sigh of relief . . . ah, but too, too soon.

As the last statement needs explaining, I will give it. About three miles south of where we were stranded was an airstrip that the Air Force built back during WWII. If you recall your high school history, America gave Russia a lot of planes during that war and Russia had military men that . . . . well . . . were willing to fly and die for their Mother Country (or is it 'Father' Country in Russian?) Well, they only were able to give the boys 30 or 40 hours of fly-time before throwing them into the fray; the Russian Military would take delivery of the planes in Fairbanks and then fly the planes to Nome where they'd re-fuel and fly them home to Russia.

Remember, from where we were at, we could *see* Russia. So, this strategically-located airstrip, called Riley's Wreck for some reason I never found out, was right on the Arctic Circle itself, right on 60 degrees North Latitude. I heard that guys from the area went there occasionally for parties or to take picnics. It was a fairly good strip and had been graded off by our omniscient government in 1968; its original purpose had long passed.

So, that's the story.

Once on the level airstrip, Bill started it up . . . hooray . . . but could only rev it up to about 1400 RPM's which is about enough wind to blow out a match. There was no way we were going to get it off the ground with both of us in it, and since we didn't want this to go down in history as a shining example of our stupidity . . . stupidity on SO many levels . . . we did the only thing we could. I got out of the plane and let Bill taxi down to the end of the mile-long runway. I could see him paddling, pushing, peddling and praying and giving it just a bit more gas, just a little tap or two . . . . just enough to get it going, then finally, right as he got to the end of the runway and we were both thinking that we would have to do turn the thing around and do it all over again, he got off and into the air and then he just disappeared over the horizon. A couple of hours later, he came in another plane to pick me up.

Yes, there were to be many 'Adventures with Bill' in the future; I really liked and trusted him . . . he was the kind of guy you could depend on in any situation and he was just good, through and through. And funny! In my mind, I can still see his face as we started to sink in that plane, and when he was pushing the darn thing, joking and smiling all the time . . . one of those rare individuals that affect your life positively through their living of it and leave some of themselves behind. Of the thousands of people I met and became acquainted with in a lifetime, there are just not many who make such a mark . . . who become so engrained in memory that their essence lingers over the years. Bill was one of those.

Bill and I went on quite a number of trips together. His wife, Jo, befriended Phyllis right away and they became quite close, and we had some great times as couples, too. We traded babysitting each other's kids, that sort of thing. The trust and brother-like love we had for each other was reciprocal and he entrusted many of his private feelings and thoughts to me over the time we spent. The memory of his face and the sound of his laugh will remain with me until I die . . . it will have to, for Bill was killed in a take-off accident some time later, after we had left Alaska.

There is another "Bill" story in this book. I don't know where it will end up, but although I introduce you to many folks in these few pages, there is only one 'Bill Rember' . . . .

~~~~~~~~~~~~~

On a lighter note, I will tell a story that I hope will write itself in such a way that Phyllis and I will still be on speaking terms. This one is for the kids . . . . most especially for the third little member who came along on, too, on our jaunt . . . .

One Sunday afternoon, not too many months before we were to leave Alaska, Phyllis and I were getting a little restless; she was almost nine months pregnant and was real tired of being stuck at home with the Three Little Pigs . . . I mean kids. So, on her request, we left the children with a sitter and hopped into our plane; I intended to fly to a gold dredge, which was about 80 miles, to hopefully get some gold nuggets for making jewelry. I had just put a 150 HP engine in the Cruiser and I thought it flew wonderfully.

For a long time after this adventure, I was not allowed, on the pain of death, to repeat this story . . . but I have abridged it to such a degree that I don't believe she will mind.

Much.

Off we went, into the wild blue yonder! Now, this plane had a four-hour tank of gas, but the pilot, me, had about a 2 hour bladder. Phyllis, at very close to a full nine months, was doing great to hang on for 30-minutes, so barely into the one hour trip, I spotted a likely sandbar and aimed for it but it came in a little hot. The sandbar was canted off to one side, which I failed to see upon initial approach. By the time we decided to go around and give it another try, I was right up to the edge of the riverbank, so I really slapped the power to it and popped it off the ground, just as my front tires hit the water. I didn't have enough air speed to clear the oncoming trees, so I pulled it up sharply and stalled, right in the middle of the river.

It is one sickening, tight-sphincter, gut-wrenching feeling when you hit the water. It took a millisecond for the front to splash down in the water, as this plane was a tail-dragger—and of course, the gear hit first. We flipped upside down so fast, I couldn't even follow the action. The mind really plays tricks on you when you are faced with such grossly unusual circumstances as being in a plane wreck: nothing makes any sense at first, as the brain is getting pounded with so much information and to such a degree that it can't process fast enough. That was the predicament we found ourselves in, so the first thing that popped into my mind was that we were back in one of Catalina Island's glass-bottomed boats for there were fishes swimming around right outside the plane's windshield!

The wings were full of air, so we didn't sink, thankfully. The river was only 4 or 5 feet deep at this point, so I wisely ripped off my seatbelt first thing . . . and fell headfirst into the radio speaker, bunging up my head.

Phyllis looked just as confused when I turned to look at her . . . but she had enough presence of mine to unbuckle herself more slowly and didn't have such a thump of a landing. I opened my door and crawled up on the belly of the plane, which looked like a fat grasshopper and was now sinking, slowly. The tail, being heavier, hit river-bottom right about then and the current spun us around. I crawled over and got Phyllis loose, her big-baby-belly poking right out and making her exit successful, if rather ungainly . . . both us were out of the plane, so I put her on my shoulders and carried her to shore.

This was September and it was about three in the afternoon. There were plenty of mosquitoes even though it was still chilly. As we sat together on the bank and watched the plane go aground downstream a bit, we realized we were in the worst of two worlds: a cold night to look forward to and hoards of mosquitoes to fight off.

Being the prepared pilot, I had loads of survival gear . . . . in the plane . . . and it had gone all the way to the bottom by this time, so I would have to do some skin-diving to get anything out. Plus, the river current was so strong that there would be the risk of getting into the cabin, grabbing a few essentials, and then not being able to get back out again.

So, after a short and quiet discussion, followed by a fervent prayer, we started a good fire and hunkered down.

The decision was made to stay put and I made one attempt to go back out and see if getting some survival items safely out of the plane was even a remote possibility. It was not to be, and so on my way back to the fire, I caught a vision of my little wife with her huge, pregnant belly poking out a mile, standing by the roaring fire, drying our clothes . . . .

In the midst of freezing wet conditions and extreme mosquito warfare, Phyllis's biggest worry was about the children and their babysitter: we were going to be really late. I reassured her that as soon as a few extra hours passed with our little ankle-biters and the babysitter would be on the phone, reporting us missing and offering to lead the search party.

And, sure enough, about 6 hours later, a beautiful, beautiful plane passed overhead and radioed the village further down river that there was a funny-looking object in the Squirrel River, so soon after that, the plane returned with another and picked us up. We were flown to the Eskimo village of Kiana where we were fed, and we radioed the Kotzebue Hospital to tell everyone to cancel the casket order and the funeral . . . our kids would not be orphans after all.

The story isn't over. The next day, after an emotional return home to our little family, I found out how much my being part of the Arctic Flying Fraternity really paid off. I'd gladly have helped *them* do what there were about to do for *me*, because it seemed a bigger task when I was on the receiving end, and not the giving end.

In the morning, eight guys and four airplanes from town came to the house and wanted to know where to put the plane after they pulled out of the water. I had honestly written it off as a total loss as we had really hit hard, and I told them that.

Nevertheless, we all headed out to the lucky crash site; I bummed a ride from Bill, I think. When we landed and gathered, they began telling their own stories about flipping it into a river or the ocean or whatever . . . each one could recall their own misfortune. It seemed that a lot of pilots really flew by the seat of their pants up there. They'd land on a sandbar, see a bear and chop power and really bomb on to the ground, jump out and pop him. No one cruised at altitude, and did set up and approach and all that, you know.

They would just 'drag' a sandbar, they called it, by flying over it about 20 feet off the ground and if it looked half-way good enough to land on, they would take her down. It was sort of a game up there and now, looking back, I had more white-knuckle landings and takeoffs in the time I was there than in all the rest of my flying career after that . . . .

So, on with the story, to my amazement, one of them had a prop that fit my plane and they brought it along; another guy brought a primus stove and in about an hour, they had rigged a 'dead man' to the plane, dragged it out of the water, flipped it back over and onto its wheels again. Two spars on one wing had been dented a little, but the fabric was all intact, except in one spot where I had slit its belly in that one last vain attempt to get some survival gear out before going to shore.

Water came gushing out of the wings so we emptied the gas cans, and refilled them with gas someone had brought. One guy filled it up and another jerked the propeller off as it had a slight curvature, like, they went *that-a-way* the wrong on landing. Another guy pulled all the spark plugs and set them on the primus stove to dry out completely. Another was drying out the points on the mag.

Crawling inside, I looked at my instrument panel, which was dripping from every point. The seat squished cold water up onto me in the worlds most uncomfortable bidet . . . . the tires weren't even flat and the gear was OK and the tail, although dented a little, looked serviceable. In two hours after they first got there, I was sitting in my plane and one of the guys was propping it to get it going. Amazingly, after a few tries, the motor spun over and started up! It ran rough because we found that there was crankcase damage, but run it did!

The plane was worth about $4500 and after all this work by everyone, I wasn't going to just let it sit there. I had ten gallons of gas and I was 80 miles from home. I could take it all apart and boat it out one piece at a time or I could screw up my courage and fly it out. The decision was made and I taxied down to the end of the sandbar and while it didn't perform like a new plane (duh) it DID act like it might just fly! I took a mental check to ascertain that I had, 1) been to the bathroom, 2) paid up my life insurance, 3) paid my tithing and said my prayers. This being done, I revved it to full power and it flew right off the sandbar.

That was the highest I had ever flown. I climbed just as high and as fast as I could, thinking any minute that poor old, waterlogged engine was just going to stop short, in midair, so I wanted to get as close to home as I could before that happened. I had my seatbelt on as tight as it would go and the rough ride was causing vibrations that was loosening knobs and buttons left and right, and I was kept busy pushing them back where they went. It looked like it was just disintegrating before my very eyes!

Forty of the miles to home were over the ocean; I made it all the way, with one of the guys in the rescue party following me. I landed at the airstrip and taxied the eight blocks down the road, right through town, to my back yard. A couple of weeks puttering on it in my spare time and it was in the air, as good as new!

Now, I want to clear any misconceptions up now: I didn't spend all my time futzing about in planes while I was in Kotzebue. I routinely did 24-hour shifts and was on-call 24-7 because I was the head of the hospital and just flew enough to give my Guardian Angel ulcers!

"ME DROPPING CANDY BOMBS AT SCOUT CAMP"

'MY BEST FRIEND AND QUITE POSSIBLY MY GUARDIAN ANGEL, BILL REMBER, POSING WITH ME AND ONE OF HIS STUDENTS'

CHAPTER 11

"4ᵀᴴ OF JULY, ALASKA STYLE"

Traditionally, and for who knows for *how* long, the Kotzebue area has been the summer gathering place for trading and for socialization, for hunting the Oogruk seal and for large-scale fishing and fish-drying. Indigent tribes came from up and down the seacoast, across from Russia and from inland, to spend a few short months adding to their larders and enjoying the too-brief warm weather. Probably, up through the last thousand years or so that people have gathered here, there was not a set time or a particular day or week that a real celebration was held. Since being made a territory in 1913 and achieving Statehood in 1958, the Alaskan Inuit, Eskimaluet, or more commonly called Eskimo people have adopted the 4ᵗʰ of July as the official yearly celebration event for the region.

There are so many dialects spoken and so many sub-cultures that speak differing languages, I didn't even try to learn each one completely. Instead, I tried to get a passing knowledge of enough of them that I could be understood and respond, as translators were not always available and even when I brought my own translator, sometimes we still were not able to understand all that was being said.

It can be compared, in an exaggerated degree, to what we in the lower 48 call 'accents', as in Texican, Southern Drawl, New England Bostonian, and Midwest, and so on.

As they did in centuries past, people gathered from all over and they came for the fun, the contests, the traditional games and the new American customs that were fast becoming Alaskan customs, too. A large number of the photographic slides and pictures we took are from this colorful, boisterous time.

It was the walrus hunts that marked the beginning, or invention, of probably the most well-known event, the blanket toss; it was not recreational, in the beginning but a vital part of the hunt. The 'blanket' was actually several walrus skins sewn together by the women who were very skilled at working with sinew. When the men were out on the pack ice hunting for walrus, they would travel the leads between blocks of ice. Often, the ice floes would close the channel, so the hunters would get out their walrus skins and get the smallest guy and flip him up in the air where he could see around, and point out the direction to go.

The men holding the blanket have to run underneath and keep up with the 'toss-ee'; I have seen them flip a person thirty or forty feet in the air! If they missed catching him . . . well, let me just say that every time we had a blanket toss at a big celebration like the Fourth of July, at least one person would break a leg or ankle and occasionally, I was told, there had been fatalities. And that was understandable as all it would take was someone coming down crooked and twisting his neck, or the toss-ers not being able to get under the toss-ee in time and having a bad fall to the ground. The event sure was popular and it went on all day and evening, with different people and groups trying their luck, learning or teaching.

I never did try the blanket toss myself: I guess I figured I had better ways of hurting myself, like flying planes . . . . besides, I was about twice as heavy as the preferred light-weight toss-ee's! Judy Wyatt, the wife of one of the other doctors, broke her tibia in a toss.

One of the popular and interesting contests was called a Knuckle Hop; the men would get down on their hands and knees and have to hop on their feet and knuckles and race. This doesn't sound as brutal as it is; you have to see it to believe it, but I've treated guys after a heated Knuckle Hop who've ended up with their knuckles abraded right down to the tendons. It would take months to heal.

Another popular game was the Rope Pull; variations of this can be found all over the world in other cultures, but the difference between other rope pulls and the Eskimo Rope Pull is that the rope is held between the teeth! I never did see anyone lose teeth in one, but it HAD to be painful!

Another was the Knuckle Pull (lots of games involving knuckles, huh? Must be a reason for that!). Two people sat facing each other and they would each put out a hand, as if they were going to shake hands, but instead, they would grab the middle finger around the middle finger of the other guy and pull with just this one finger. The loser, of course, was the one whose finger flipped open. I have played that and my forearm hurt for a week! It practically just pulls the muscle out of the insertion into the arm. Kinda dumb for a guy to do when his living depends on his hands . . . .

Another contest I had never heard of was called the Niksik Throw. Niksik is Eskimo for 'hook' and in fact, a lot of the people called me 'Doctor Niksik', which is about as close as they could get to saying 'Hooker' in Eskimo. The niksik was about the size of volleyball or a little smaller, perhaps; it is made of skin with a bunch of sharp hooks sticking out of it. The idea was, when hunting, if a seal is killed, the hunter can throw out this niksik in the direction of the seal . . . like throwing a lifeline to someone who is drowning. The niksik is dragged over the slain seal and the hooks grab on and the animal is pulled back to the kayak. Realize, there was no such thing as swimming in after the dead or wounded creatures . . . the water was so cold and the hunter was so heavily clothed that he would just sink like a rock if he fell over, so skill maneuvering a niksik is essential to successful seal hunting.

In the *game* of Niksik, however, a ball of fur or something is representative of the seal and it would be tossed out on the ground. The contestants would take turns trying to successfully 'hook' the ball in the least amount of time. So many games are representative of survival skills, aren't they?

Oh, but, the 4th of July Celebration! There was always a muktuk eating contest, I was informed. This year, one of the contestants was a fat tourist kid who said, "Oh, yeah! Sure! I'm gonna win this!"

Muktuk is whale skin and the layer of fat just under it's about the consistency of a rubber white wall tire and looks like it, too as the skin is black and fat is creamy white. It's a little like gum, bacon rind and leather . . . all rolled into one. Yum!

Everyone who enters the contest is given pieces that are the same size, to be fair of course, and the guy to get his piece down first, wins! With a cash prize and the notoriety winning brings, there are usually a godly amount of contestants. I think the prize was $2 that year . . . . must be the notoriety, then, I guess, because the white stuff is really disgusting as it tastes just like lard.

I kind of like the black part, though . . . I think it has a earthy, nutty flavor . . . reminiscent of the plankton the whales diet is made up of, I guess. What does plankton taste like, anyway?

Phyllis wouldn't even touch it and the two little boys didn't like it, either, but they tried it; little Kelly was the only one who kept her piece and she worked on it all afternoon.

Anyway, this naive tourist-kid made the mistake of grabbing up a big chunk and he chewed and chewed and chewed. Wrong approach. The way to win is to cut the portion into small pieces and not even bother with chewing . . . just chug them down! And, try not to even *think* about the next 24-or-so hours when these pieces will make their inevitable way back *out!* Poor kid! He looked so stuffed full, if you stuck him with a pin, he would blow up like a balloon and pieces of muktuk would just shoot out everywhere!

What the natives do with the stuff is as follows: pretty simple details, here, for the slabs are cut from the whale in long strips and put down in perma-frost cellars, then carved on and eaten until gone. One fellow took me down into his cellar and there it was, hanging in long rows . . . big slabs of it. The slabs were veiled in long strands of greenish-grey mold but it didn't penetrate the muktuk at all, the guy told me; they were just wiped off before eating . . . . no cooking, no smoking, no marinating . . . and no accounting for taste, I guess, either. To me, it's just old lard on strips of musty boot-leather . . . .

A fellow named Art Fields ran the celebration while we were up there; I took the time to get to know him and admired all I saw. He was Eskimo but had a strain of white blood in him, he said. He was married to a full-blood Nulato named Josephine who worked as a secretary at the Hospital and she was super-sharp. They made an exceptional couple; Art was a professional outdoorsman, which means he flew his Super Cub airplane for guests, led hunting expeditions, and hunted for meat for his family on the side.

If I had to pick one person to be stranded in the wilderness with . . . choosing the one individual who was the most outdoor-savvy and likely to help us both survive, it would be Art. He also seemed to be very personable and would have made a good politician, had he chosen that as a profession.

Tommy, Art and Jo's son, was in charge of the 'Kicking Contest'; let me share the details of this unusual game to you. First, a ball of tightly-wrapped strips of fur about the size of a volleyball, was suspended from scaffolding. It started hanging down to a length about 6 feet from the ground and as the contest continued, it was raised until it appeared to me to be an amazing eight feet off the ground! The object was to kick the ball with one, or both, feet, and not lose one's balance . . . . now remember, these little Eskimo guys were an average of about 5' 5" or so. This made the contest very interesting; it almost seems that it would be impossible to do and I might think so too, had I not witnessed it! Their 'Kickball' was by far the most popular contest of the celebration, with people gathered around 12-deep to watch and a long line waiting to play.

There was a dogsled race too, but because there was no snow, the sleds had wheels . . . the dogs were just going crazy, excited it seemed, just to get out and run.

The Air Force Base was nearby and always took part in the 4th of July Celebrations. I think they sponsored a beauty contest . . . no surprise . . . a lot of those military guys had only one thing on their minds . . . . but they also put on an Air Show that was really well done and made for excitement and patriotic feelings all around.

As I look back at the slides and pictures we took, I am struck by the incongruity of the younger Eskimo kids in straw hats and blue jeans, eating cotton candy while all around were the Elders, dressed traditionally in summer parkas, the workmanship of which was exquisite.

Then, of course, no celebration would be complete without the presence of the *homos horribulous tourista*. Even on non-celebration days, tourists milled around asking inane questions, going into people's yards and even homes without permission and seemed to think the whole party was just for them . . . like a living diorama or something, and that they were welcome anywhere and everywhere.

The Weins Airline had a Hotel in Kotzebue and flew these groups in and they stayed the night, or sometimes just for the day. The Eskimos sold them 'instant artifacts' that they had made and then 'aged' them to perfection, or, more distressing, sold the tourists really authentic items they had dug out of the old dwellings on the beach ridges.

There was a 'Beautiful Baby Contest' or some such thing, too; I almost had to believe, after seeing it a few times, that the actual judging was not on the beauty of the babies, but on the handmade parka's they were presented in. Some of them were so well-made and exquisitely decorated that they would have been worth hundreds of dollars! What an art form!

Couldn't help but notice a patient and acquaintance, May; she and her husband were enjoying the Fair, riding herd on their little boys, all dressed up in cowboy outfits and looking just too cute for words. I attended May's last delivery; they had three little boys already and wanted a girl *so* badly. When I pulled out a boy, the disappointment was obvious, but, a few minutes later, as I reached up to help separate the placenta, the placenta *kicked me,* so I hollered, "Wait a minute, there another one in here!" Hope ran high! I pulled out another baby! It was twins! Another little boy.

There was actually some talk about adopting them out, but, of course, they wouldn't, and ended up with their own little baseball team and loved them and took really good care of them all.

My little boys remembered for me that there were two pigs at the celebration, reminiscent of Lower-48 State Fairs. Someone brought them up from the south and brought a flatbed of baled hay for the enclosure, too, and hosted a greased pig contest for the under-12 crowd which was just too funny to watch and the proud winners got something of real value, too. I think they got to keep the pig!

There was an old bootlegger nicknamed, Stubby, who always raked in the cash during this time, and other times, too. He prospered most of the year, bragging to me one time that he made more money than I did, which was probably true! His illegal whiskey was the backbone of his monetary prowess; when the Eskimo firefighters got back into town after a long, dry season, their pockets full of money, instead of taking it home or spending it on things their families needed for winter, they would buy $20 bottles of hooch, get drunk and damage themselves and others, all the while, lining Stubby's deep pockets!

On the other side of it, I was up all night, stitching up busted heads and pushing innards back where they were supposed to go after knife fights. The whole town was drunk and partying, it seemed. Stubby said he made $2000 in two days, which was more than I made in 6 weeks! If I had been charging by the stitch, I would have made some serious bucks, too, but I was on shift work, not piecework!

He also owned and managed owned a regular bar, called, appropriately enough, 'Stubby's' and it proved to be a popular watering hole for a certain type of clientele . . . namely, 'not fussy'. It caught on to such a degree that he even went and had tee-shirts printed up to sell over the 4th of July Celebration one year; they were available in several lurid colors and sported 3 different caption, for unlimited fashionable clothing choices and versatility in gift-giving. There was "I Like to Go to Stubby's" . . . not original, perhaps, but correct and to the point. Then, to make the selections even more universal, there was "My Daddy Goes to Stubby's" and, not to leave anyone out, "My Mommy Goes to Stubby's".

The year that we saw these, when we were at the Celebration as a family, I almost rolled with laughter at the shock and disgust on Phyllis's face as she 'tsk-tsk-ed,' wondering what kind of parent would buy a shirt advertising a cheap, nasty pick-up bar for their CHILD to wear! In some sort of perverse, twisted attempt at humor, I took the time and patience to teach the baby of the family . . . . Kelly at this time who was just learning to talk, to say: 'my momma doos ta 'thub-iees!' Kelly actually remembers saying it (I called her on the phone while proofreading) and the boys remember it too . . . . Phyllis was not amused . . . . I never could understand just why . . . .

One of the features of the celebration that we really did enjoy, Stubby tee-shirts notwithstanding, was exhibitions of Native dancing. I knew a guy named Paul Green and he was in one and wore some authentic old-time clothes. He also had on a mask he'd made himself and as he slowly moved about, making his way around through the crowd with it on, in addition to a good costume, he was making a strange buzzing noise with some sort of mouth-device . . . like a harmonica with only three notes . . . made an interesting and impressive spectacle.

We didn't buy any Eskimo masks because they were not authentic; they were only made for the tourist dollar. The US southwest-states' Indian tribes hold pow-wow's and dance in traditional ways, wearing masks, and I guess the tourists just expected the Eskimos and Inuits to have dance masks, too. Even though they were not authentic . . . kind of like the Seminole Indians . . . . We enjoyed a dance by a beautifully dressed woman accompanied by drummers who were playing the traditional driftwood and stretched-skin drums. A narrator chanted and interpreted her movements and it was an exciting and pulsating spectacle, yet simple and endearing at the same time.

When the first Christian missionaries visited the Eskimo and Inuit people, they taught them that dancing was sinful, so, much of the traditional history and legends that had been kept alive for centuries upon centuries was lost. Now, with the resurgence of traditional ways and ethnic pride and the upswing in popularity of honoring the "Old Ways", these dances are being recorded by those who still remember. It would be a terrible shame were it not so . . . .

The Hospital had a float in the Parade, which we'd made to represent First Aid treatment for a snow machine accident. Very original. We put a snow-jet in the bed of a pickup truck and sort of slopped out-dated blood filched from the blood bank all over . . . add a nurse to show how to take care of the obviously badly damaged patient and you have a real prize-winner! I don't recall the float *winning* a prize but the bloody thing was quite popular with the onlookers and we circled the parade route three times so everyone got a good look at it. It would hardly have been worth it to go around just once . . .

After the parade, it was time for the races. They started out with the kids, grouped according to age and weight. Kit won a dollar in a race, and boy! That was a big deal! Kyle, being the oldest, usually won everything he competed in, but that year, Kit brought home the prize. I think I remember winning a dollar myself in the race for men under thirty. Phyllis won the same race, for women under thirty.

'We wuz long-legged, lean and lanky!'

"FLYING NURSE ON BLANKET TOSS, 4TH OF JULY CELEBRATION. THE BIG BUILDING BEHIND AND TO THE LEFT IS THE LOVELY WEIMS TOURIST HOTEL"

"FRANK AND MAY SHELDON WITH THE TWIN BOYS I DELIVERED. TAKEN AT THE 4TH OF JULY."

CHAPTER 12

MORE PEOPLE STORIES

Traveling to Alakanuk was something I looked forward to, mainly because of the friendly couple Clem and Daly. They had just one child, a daughter, who was very wild. Clem had a pistol and always said he was going to shoot any guy that got his daughter pregnant. The running joke on him was that he might not have enough bullets on hand to do that, and, where would he start?

I was preparing to turn toward home on that Friday evening, when it was discovered that there was no gas in any of the villages, so I couldn't even get a ride at all out of the Tri City metropolis of Chevak, Emmonk and Alakanuk. The weather was kind of pluses-and-minuses and hard to navigate in anyway. I had gotten minimal TB indications there in the past; in other words, although I really liked to travel there and really liked the teachers, I didn't have a red-hot reason to go. Once there, though, no matter how much I enjoyed it, ultimately it turned into time to leave.

Chevak was such a poor village and so lacking in entertainment, cultural pursuits and almost any kind of diversion, my infrequent stopovers were more like Papal visits and less like a working medical stint. The children would run up to just touch me and tug on my coat and chant 'Doc-tor, Doc-tor' They would then follow me around constantly . . . . a little train of them, usually height-calibrated, with the tallest in the front, closest to me and the accompanying miniature Eskimos trailing behind, keeping up the rear. I felt like the Head Lemming. That kind of hero-worship I didn't need, but it was touching and sweet, looking back on it now.

After routine exams and treatments were complete, and it was clear that I was not going to be able to head for home at that juncture, I spent the evening with a Father Nawn. I mention him several times in this book; he used to be a Physics professor. I pumped his fertile mind for several hours, gleaning information from him and absorbing all I could about electronics, ham radio aerials, and things like that. He was just tremendous . . . a real font of knowledge. Just wish I could recall everything learned from him each time I got a chance to visit. When he finally looked near worn out, I padded off to bed, a cot in the supply room of the school; I said my prayers, curled my gangly frame into a ball, hugged my pillow and zonked out, my head still spinning with all of the new knowledge. Believe me, my prayers always included a plea that I would retain all the things learned that day . . . any day.

The next morning however, the worm turned, as it were, and the whole day was just a series of frustrating elements, one after another. First, it seemed there was little chance of getting a plane out due to inclement weather; then, there was no gas in the village yet, so I couldn't even get a Snow Traveler. I sat around and read a book I luckily had packed and waited for delivery of gas so I could be on my way.

Now, my personality has changed somewhat over the years . . . mellowed, if I am to believe those closest to me . . . I suppose most everyone does calm down to some degree, as they age but few things frustrated me more then *and* now than wasting time, both seeing others do it and being 'forced' to have *my* time wasted as well.

The later it got, the more I felt righteous anger at being stuck in that boring, smelly place with nothing I could do about it. Understand, please, that as much as I had enjoyed the visits and enjoyed the area, it was time to leave and I had 'places to go and people to see' and it was very frustrating being stuck there. Early in the afternoon while I was caved-up in a bright corner of the schoolroom with my almost-finished reading matter, unbeknownst to me, the villagers had organized and planned a dance in my honor.

The whole town was there, I believe, as I came out of the building, blinking in the mid-day light, and let myself be guided toward the circle, 5 or 6-people deep, surrounding the village center; there were probably about 120 people of all ages.

There was a raised platform-ed area in the center of the village; it was flanked by the schoolhouse/Chapel/medical clinic, the general store and a gas-and-go-service-garage. Everyone had gathered around it and formed a half-circle facing the stage. The tribal leader got up in front, pounded his walking stick on the stage floor to get everyone's attention and announced, "This is dance for the Doctor Hooker".

My paperback got rolled up and shoved in my inner parka pocket in a hurry.

The traditional dances of the Inuit are hard to explain without sounding inane, but the dance seems so simple, it makes it hard to understand how that simplicity somehow is translated, without words, to such elaborate, magical stirrings that pluck the strings of a soul-deep, inner instrument. I felt very small and mean for having harbored frustrated feelings over the last few hours. It turned out to be an epiphany for my soul, and very humbling for Great White Doctor.

Mary and Edna were two village girls around 16 years-old, who spoke very good English and who had helped me before with the clinics. They took it upon themselves to translate and explain the dances to me, parked one on each side. Both were round-faced, and giggly and their black eyes sparkled as they spoke but the more they spoke, the less giggling there was and I could watch them and the dancers and drummers, too, and they gazed at the performance through young eyes but old souls . . . as the whispers became those of their ancestors who had witnessed and participated in this ancient ritual—time after countless time . . . . murmuring softly of the hunt, the unity, the family, the tribe—for centuries passed down. DNA memories so rife and powerful, even the non-enlightened felt the pull.

It has always been a regret of mine that I was not equipped to record the event. The overwhelming, sensory payload would be hard to completely describe, however, even with pictures and sound. It was an experience and not just an event. Filming might have only served to dish it up in bland black and white with a matte finish that wouldn't give proper credit to the illumination of it all.

I came back to the states with some movies we filmed at other times but I had to satisfy myself with memory only to share this particular occurrence with others.

When the drums began, I became totally engrossed; from where I was seated, it looked like the drums varied from ten to twenty inch hoops of driftwood with seal gut stretched over them. The men knelt in front, three or four of them and five women stood behind them, swaying without moving their feet. They told the stories, and with Edna and Mary translating loosely yet helpfully, I watched the intricate movements of the small hand-held feathered circle-shaped objects.

The leader, the older man who had called the gathering, stood out in front, holding a supple willow wand with feathers on the end which he shook at the dancers. Meanwhile, the 5 original drummers were joined by 5 more until all 10 drummers now chanted as they played the drums held between their knees. The additional drums gave a deeper, bass tremolo which seemed to cause a reverberating echo in my chest.

The sky had become overcast and although it was early afternoon, we were encompassed by twilight and it was very dim and hazy. The surrounding mountains were garbed in grey mist which was settled around their base and muted the sharp angles of the jagged rock cliffs. As it got later in the evening, the fires became central and the 3 fire pits were the only source of light. It was a mystical, very moving and spiritual atmosphere, aided by the crackle of the surrounding fires, and the occasional whine of sled dogs tethered a few yards away. Even the littlest of the children gazed at the scene raptly, not squirming or pulling away.

When someone came over and tapped me on the shoulder and said a plane was coming in now and would be ready to fly me out, I really hated to leave.

As if to make up for making me wait almost a whole day, not one but 2 planes had flown in! One was piloted by Fred Nolte who showed up and showed off with his usual acrobatics. This guy was a real nut: he would swoop in and do a barrel loop with passengers in the plane. He did other things that added up to poor flying in my opinion and since my opinion was the only opinion that mattered in *that* certain set of circumstances, I chose the other plane and pilot. We tossed my gear into the waiting cockpit and settled in, my heart and mind still reverberating from the drums. I had taken time to thank the Elder and asked him to relay my compliments and appreciation to the villagers; I told him that I was deeply touched and he nodded and smiled and, still holding the willow whip, wished me safe passage back to the Hospital and home.

Curling up and pillowing my head on my duffle bag, my body told me what I already knew: I was really sick of traveling. This had been a 12-day trip and it was hard work because I would end up treating people late at night when it was convenient for them: after they came in from hunting, and then in the mornings they would come in before school started, maybe 6 or 7AM. I never got enough sleep. There was so little daylight at all that I lost my day-night, early-late orientation and went to bed and got up when the notion struck rather than what the clock said. I just couldn't get the hang of it.

Also, I felt pressured; looking back, I realize I was probably not that secure in myself about my medical knowledge. Knowing a fact or a procedure is one thing but putting it into action was another and there were a LOT of first-times for me, medically speaking. I'd see things and be guessing half the time when I diagnosed someone, placating myself with the correct assumption that 80% of the people were going to get well eventually, with or without medical intervention and assuming a doctor didn't screw them up. But, the averages were just not good enough for me. The ever-present realization that failure was a very real part of medical care sometimes: it is a profession with no guarantees, neither for the Doctor nor the patient.

Chevak and the other sister villages were really cool; the teachers there soon were good friends and I always tried to bring enough produce for them . . . as much as I could. I did them favors, sending them back things from Anchorage, but despite the good people who lived here and the good people that came here to teach them, the little hamlet of Chevak was really poor: the whole population was on welfare, I was told. There was no natural source of wood and they had to collect and burn willows which were just smoky little sticks at best. The people were really good-hearted and appreciative and it was a pleasure to be able to help them any way I could and I tried to visit often and ease some of the medical burdens of the people, if I could. I can still see that place in my mind, after 40 years. I will go back someday . . . .

MISS MARY

Mary M. came in to see me and told me she thought she had the clap again. She was a sweet little thing with a very pronounced, marginally-corrected cleft palate and she had the speech pattern that this deformity brings with it. Had I had the expertise to repair her smile, I would have done it gladly, just because I admired her spunk and outlook on life. She had a sense of humor that guaranteed that she would brighten the day of anyone she came in contact with . . . and 'therein lie-eth the riff,' as Shakespeare would say . . . or is it, 'a rose by any other name . . . ?' Oh well!

Mary was a . . . . a very *popular* girl but, as an unfortunate result, she was also a chronic carrier of assorted and sundry STD's as well. She always had a venereal disease of one kind or another every time she came in. She'd been to the Clinic so many times and had such a thick file that instead routinely entering the diagnosis as Such-and-Such STD, I would just make a notation of: "Rerun" or "Curtain Call", or "See page 11."

"You went and did it again, didn't you Mary?" I said to her as I saw where she was waiting this time; I put on a frown and a stern demeanor, trying to appear un-forgiving and angry as I came into the small room carrying her outsize file and the latest lab results. She was sitting on the examining table, swinging her legs, popping chewing gum and just grinning.

"What you mean, 'again', Mister Doc Hook?" She lisped, and beamed at me, the wings of coal black hair framing her merry face.

"OK, who happened to you now . . . do you have a name?" I inquired pen in hand for the annotation I was obliged by law to ask, although I knew she would not be forthcoming.

"Oh, Mister Doc, I don't know no NAMES!" She giggled blithely, giggling into her hands.

So much for fact-finding.

Generally speaking, the way it was with STD's, at least the non-lethal, run-of-the-mill, smorgasbord of easily-treated venereal diseases in Alaska in the 1960's, there weren't too many apparent symptoms for the women except for vaginal discharge. On the other hand . . . well, not *hand* exactly . . . the male got a case of burning and stinging right away in that small but greatly esteemed area, and it was the exquisite pain upon urination (I am told) in this highly-regarded nether-region that brought them in to see me, pronto, post-haste, hop-to, quickly and without delay! I used to call it the 'gift that keeps on giving' that made peeing 'going more and enjoying it less . . . . '

As far as getting the names of the man/men involved, that was the easy part. It was a small town and there was only one clinic. I would get to see Mary's paramours soon enough. I just wish there was some way to lock Mary up for a few weeks . . . maybe get a chastity belt . . . just long enough for the wide-sweep antibiotics I was using to do their job before she introduced another new strain into her system and into the systems of next weekends' love-at-first-sight. The nurse prepared the injection and gave Mary her usual double-rump-full of penicillin, which would hold her for a couple of weeks, anyhow, and we sent her on her way.

Mary's mother worked at the Hospital kitchen and she sold Avon products on the side. She was an exceptional lady and well-thought of by the staff and others workers. She was, as they say up there, 'soft-footed' which translated, as closely as I can figure out, means she has a retiring and pleasant demeanor. Mary usually drove her mom to work and picked her up after her shift was over. Mary was NOT soft-footed . . . every time she came to the hospital area where her mom worked, she would stick her head in the door and holler, "Ding, dong. Avon calling", and then giggle into her hands and crack up everyone within hearing. Our family still treasures this phrase and when one of us uses it, it still makes us laugh . . . and reminisce. Only Kit and Kelly would have been old enough to remember, but of course, they were never around Mary . . . yet, all eight of the children heard the stories so many times, they have a memory of the memory . . . strange as that may seem.

Another story involving Mary started with a Clinic visit by a big, brawny young fellow who reminded me, in later years, of the icon, barrel-chested lumberjack in those paper towel commercials: plaid shirt, suspenders, a spectacular and big reddish-blond beard and a bigger voice. One morning, as I came to open the clinic, he was waiting around outside the yet-unlocked clinic door, wasting no time wanting in. I greeted him and ushered him inside with universal body-language motions, as it was apparent that his grasp of the English language left a bit to be desired.

We tried mightily to accomplish the exchange of information when I took him back to examine him. He was able to tell me that he had been transferred from Sweden here by his construction company; he even had an introduction letter of sorts from his new boss up here, telling anyone who needed to know his full name, company address, and personal information including his medical write-up which I made notes from.

Being new in town and probably a bit homesick and lonely, Sven had sought out the warm places of food and drink and instant friendship: he did not remain friendless very long.

In his strong Scandinavian accent, he answered the generic list of questions I asked, in addition to the information in his letter. It was not only vital but against the law *not* to try and get answers for the personal inquiries, in order, hopefully, to enable us to perhaps stop or at least slow down the Venereal Musical Chairs, Kotzebue-area version. Now, when I asked who he had been with sexually, he just shook his big head and frowned down at his big boots, his wide forehead wrinkled with effort.

"No name, Doc," he finally said, grinning. "Joost pretty gurl, long hair, round face, 'bout dis high", gesturing to about mid-chest on himself. I was 6'4" and he even had a few inches on me, which made him a veritable giant in the community.

"Ya, ya, dis tall," continued gesturing, "long hair," gesturing, as if repeating the answers would make them believable, "round face", as he drew a circle in the air.

That fit most of the young ladies in Kotzebue . . . or Alaska. Becoming more adept at the game of charades we were playing, he elaborated: "Beeg boops", he grinned, and signed with the universal double-handful, bosom-area-weighing-motion that meant she was well-endowed.

"Was she easy?" I inquired. I tried to think of how to form the question without being too raunchy. "Easy, Sven?" There were simply no words or actions that would be forthcoming from me on that one. He simply wrinkled his brows again and looked as perplexed as I am sure he was.

"Did she talk funny, Sven?" Then I mimicked her, silently asking forgiveness, for I would never be cruel or poke fun at anyone, and certainly not someone as delightful as our Mary. I ducked my head and put my hands over my face and mimicked Mary's high-pitched feminine giggle as best I could.

"Ah, yes! Dat hur!" A big smile ear to ear and he nodded so hard, his blond bangs were flapping up and down like a sheet in the wind.

"Call Mary back in", I directed the attending nurse. "She struck again!"

~~~~~~~~~~~~~

ONE FLEW OVER THE CUCKOOS NEST

The Kotzebue hospital owned an International Travel-all, which is like a 4-wheel-drive-tank that's used in snow-covered places as it travels easily in the snow. The road to the DEW line was about 5 miles; we could use it winter and summer, but if the road was closed due to blowing snow, when that happened, we traveled by Snow Machines.

Almost every night, one of the officers, who were the only ones authorized to drive the truck, or one of us physicians or the pharmacist, or the Sanitary Engineer, would go out. The nurses on midnight-shift could be back in time and the day shift nurses had plenty of time, so only the ones on the evening shift could not use the Travel-all to go and shop at the PX, or go to a show. In this relatively featureless place, the Military PX was like the Mall . . . .

Actually, I was not supposed to be medically responsible for anyone over the DEW line; it went without saying, though, that they were there if we needed them and because of that, we were available when they needed us. We always came through. Usually the only time they needed us was when someone went berserk. Sounds strange, but it happens more than one would think.

One night we got a call that one of their men had just gone off his rocker. He was absolutely bananas, they said, ranting and raving and screaming and tearing things up. When I got there, after traveling the snowy miles in as great a haste as the conditions allowed, they had him under restraint, so I got some Thorazine, an anti-psychotic tranquilizer, into him. Now, I had never had a reason to give this medication in this large of a dose before, and I didn't realize about its peculiarity at that level. Once in a while, a patient's blood pressure will just plummet and go phuuttt, south, to nothing. I will never forget when I put the needle into his vein, before I even withdrew the needle, he just went 'boink' and his blood pressure dropped to zero. I thought, "Omigosh! I've killed this guy!"

Over the next few moments, I don't recall anything happening except that everyone present, including the Noble Doctor, just stared at the non-responsive fellow, openmouthed. He finally came around, shaking his head and drooling a bit, and they put him in a straight jacket. By that time, the radioed message had gone through and produced what was necessary and there was a plane on the way from Anchorage. We loaded him into the carryall and went back across the tundra over the horribly rough road and met the airplane and trundled him inside.

All ended well.

Another time, a 2AM call came through from Cape Romanzof, a DEW line site about 200 miles north of Kotzebue. One of their civilian employees had gone crackers and was forted-up in the kitchen, stocked with plenty of big knives and nobody was going to go in there and touch him no matter what, because, as reported, he was a big, mean Mamoo! So, I grabbed some tranquilizers again and chartered the Ferguson brothers to fly in. Four of us ended up going and because it is an 8-place plane, we whipped up there pretty fast! When you're used to flying a Cub, this 200 MPH airplane was really something. AND they let me fly it! Almost worth the early-early wakeup call.

We landed at this rugged airstrip and since it was summer, it was still light at 4 in the morning. There was still un-melted snow up there and the ice was all crunched up, like it gets so far North. With the co-operation of the military guys, we gathered up a lynch mob of about ten big uniformed-hulking bucks and headed to the mess hall.

I directed the maneuvers.

"You two grab his right arm and you two, grab his right leg and you two on his head, but watch that he doesn't bite. You two on the left leg and you on the right and then when you get under control and all quieted down, then call me in and I'll give him a shot."

Sounded like a good plan to me . . .

There were two straightjackets on hand, and we somehow got him away from his weapon cache so, the Bowery Boys rushed him with a Hail Mary play that would have made Steve Young proud! They held on good and tight and I bravely stepped in and was intent on locating a likely vein in the bulging veins-on-top-of-muscles that were his massive biceps. Up to this time, he had been cursing up a blue streak, even some graphic imagery that was new to *me*! I thought I had heard it all in the ER's of LA . . . .

"You dirty, rotten sons—you guys are gonna get it—just wait'll I . . . . " and then he just seemed to run . . . down . . . . slowly . . . . like an old clock. His eyes crossed and his face took on a peaceful countenance that made him look like a choirboy. A very *large* choirboy. We put him in one straight jacket forwards and another straight jacket backwards and it seems the tag team military boys had brought manacles, too, just to be sure. He was BIG, I'm tellin' ya! And none of us wanted to take a chance of him working himself loose when we got him in the airplane at about 3,000 feet, and then have to deal with him doing his darndest to carry out his dire promises to take us apart and kill us all, although I am sure I would have bravely stepped in . . .

Well, he *did not* take us apart I am please to report and we all made it to the hospital where he got *really* tied down and *really* docile. He woke up the next morning absolutely normal and as nice a fellow as you would want to meet. He had just had a psychotic break and the medicine-induced coma straightened him right out.

NOME, AND OTHER MIS-NOME—ER'S

In August of my first year in Alaska, I went down to Nome on an official visit, wearing my dashing Health Services uniform. I accompanied a Dr. Lee and he did most of the talking during a meeting with the directors of the Hospital there; some policies were agreed upon and they initiated a lot of positive changes, and while I usually hate, loathe, and despise meetings, this one was productive and warranted.

It was awfully hot in Nome . . . . probably 75-degrees, and on the strong easterly wind, there was a sweet, pervasive odor of burning pine from the 57 forest fires that were blazing out of control in the interior regions. This had been a dry year with lots of fires and when the wind blew the smoke in, it was reminiscent of happy times, camp fires and the like, but it sure represented a dismal loss of the wilderness aflame. All the available men from the BLM and as many as could be rustled up from the villages were on active duty, fighting the flames and hoping to control the spread.

Nome-the-City was certainly an out-of-control fire of a different kind: financial ruin was a plague that just kept getting worse. Nome was never meant to *be* a town for the story goes that it was mistakenly put on the map during the Gold Rush days in 1898 when gold was found right on the beach. There was no town there, so a cartographer put "none" meaning it had no name and somebody misinterpreted it and put it down as Nome.

At least Kotzebue has an easily discernable reason for its existence: it was and is a natural meeting place owing to its many assets. But, Nome has no salmon runs in any river that go by and because that is such a vital industry, without that, Nome had little in the way of an economy. Actually, you might say that it's a white man's town, settled and populated with higher-than-average income-ed non-Native residents.

Eskimos moved in but most of them couldn't find any of the almost non-existent work there, so were on Welfare, and with the Public Dole which breeds the triplet curses of drinking, drugging and VD, the story just continues to play out with negativity. The rates of these cases were three times the rate of similar places in Alaska. Prices for almost everything were exorbitant, too. I used to get $50 a day per-diem for Nome when it was usually $30 in all the other places up there. These facts, of course, are from my 1967 journal.

There was a Hospital in Nome, built in the early 1940's called McDougall Memorial Hospital, triple-M for short; it was run by some church, Episcopal I think. They decided they would keep funding it as a service to the poor because it did not pay its way by any means; it ran at a huge loss because few of it's patients had money to pay for care. Public Health had an obligation to provide health care for the citizens, though, as so it did.

The Hospital recruited it's own Doctors from wherever they could . . . hired its own doctors and it's Director, in some cases, from Anchorage. The first Director in Nome that I came to know of after I took over Kotzebue, was just there to make some money . . . to turn a profit it seemed to me. He'd put people in the Hospital for just about anything and we, being Public Health, had to pay so much per day for every Native beneficiary there, and it came out of my Kotzebue budget. This caused problems as one can easily see: they wanted to keep the hospital full of our patients and we didn't want to drain our already-strained budget to pay for any more, other than ones who really had to be hospitalized. Finally, my boss in Anchorage insisted that the patients be sent up to me because we had a fixed overhead anyway with all the Doctors on salary. Why not get their money's worth?

The Nome facility was all run by a bunch of white guys . . . kind of a conspiracy that I was never really able to figure out. There was political structure and backing and there was a *lot* of Federal money like OEO and VISTA and all those overgrown governmental agencies that can have a very complicated and twisted set of inner workings. I was glad to be on the outside of that.

Heard a story that was widespread around town about a fellow by the name of Leonardo who had a café and it was said that he was a tremendous Chef. You didn't dare call him a cook or he would have a hissy fit; he really put out some great meals, but along with the cuisine, patrons were served his brand of philosophy as a side dish. He had a lot to say and was very outspoken about the political situation in Nome. After just a short time of him voicing his opinion, he was run out of town, I was told. Too much negative talk about too many powerful people . . . . typical but tragic.

The Health Aide told me an odd, local story about a man and his six-year-old boy who were fishing in his boat when he fell overboard somehow. He never did surface again, but the little boy was able to guide the boat through the ice floes to shore and then walked three miles back to town, crossing a deep, fast-running river on the way! The boy, when found, contended that a "man with wings" helped him cross the river; a party then went out to see if the man had made it to shore and could be rescued, and they found a clear set of the boys footprints on both sides of the river! After hearing the story, I wanted to meet the boy and found him perfectly normal in every way and as guiles-less and forthright as he could be! One of the things that make you go "hmmmmm."

All in all, this particular trip to Nome was pleasant. Nome, at that time, had a small but active population of LDS people and I got to know some of them. I had a nice Sunday afternoon there in the little meeting room. They laughingly told me that their congregation didn't warrant the LDS term for a small group of Mormons who are organized, usually called a Branch. This one was so small, they called it a 'twig' instead!

When my ride home was delayed (for the millionth time), I was able to attend Church at Chamberlains in Nome. George and Nita Halleck took me home with them after Church; he was very knowledgeable and shared his expertise freely, so I spent several delightful hours there, then went down to the Dan Johnson's later that evening.

Them, I liked at first sight . . . had an almost immediate 'draw' to them both that doesn't happen to me often upon meeting someone. I guess I was, and still *am*, a bit backward in that department, in that it usually takes me quite a while to warm up completely when I first meet someone. There was another couple, the Outwaters, who were there, too; she was quiet but most pleasant. They had been on an LDS work mission to Portland. Brother and Sister Brown were the group leaders there and I enjoyed their company, too. The Johnson's were planning to move to Kotzebue and I could see that this would sure be a huge plus for the social life there as they seemed stable and are strong in the Church and all. I learned that some LDS folks named Christiansen's lived nearby, too, in Shismaref, a little village up the coast, but I did not get to meet them.

It may sound odd to non-Mormons to talk about who is LDS and where they live and so on, but being out and away from the 'heart' of Mormonism in the west, the people who practice their religion always try to reach out and friendship other LDS folks, as well as non-member neighbors. It was a nice day to be in contact with friends and meet others.

When my Health Service Aide and I left Nome, we took a F-27, a good-sized prop jet that flew 250 miles an hour and is the regular workhorse of the larger towns. For the smaller places where the airports are minimal and the airstrips and landing areas are dirt, the Otter or Beaver or Cessna 185's are usually the most adaptable and see the most use.

One of the Health Aides, Harriet Wongitillon, gave me a nice pair of carved seal earrings for Phyllis. She has a young son who was born with a cleft palate which had been repaired quite well. She was an interesting person to visit with; most of the time I don't ask too many questions about people's past . . . they just open up.

Often, a woman would have a child or two and no husband/ mate seemed in the picture. Some of them were divorced, I knew but some just had children without marriage; it seemed more common to run into that lifestyle up North than it had in the states and I surmised, rightly or not, that a lot of Eskimo men would feel inadequate marrying a woman who had more education that he had . . . that was my opinion of the situation, at that time and place.

In one village, back near Kotzebue, I fit 43 people for glasses, saw and examined around 200 kids and about 45 adults in the 48 hours I was there. Finished my work by noon on Saturday and went out on a house call some miles out away from town. This is barren land and it's rare to see nicer, larger frame houses for they are the exception rather than the rule, but I learned that these bigger homes were also inhabited by two or three families, sometimes, in order to afford the upgraded housing.

One house that I stopped at was home to an older native man, whose money-making activity was obvious by the number of pelts that I could see hung up in a built-on addition that was open on one side. There were dozens of pelts, mostly fox, but I saw one that made me ask him the story behind it.

"Well, I had this trap and I checked it every day, like I do all my traps, and it had a white fox in it. As I pulled up, he somehow pulled himself out of the traps jaws and took off on a run; he was hard to see and I was chasing him, throttle open on my Skidoo machine, when he lost his footing and I ran right over the top of him!" He chuckled at this point in his rather violent (for the fox) story. Then he went on: "By the time I got the thing stopped and turned around, I couldn't see him. I went back, following the track of the snow machine and finally, there he was, sort of squashed down in the snow . . . somehow, the tracks on the snow machine had pulled him in and really chewed him up and this . . ." he said pointing to the ragged fur, " . . . is all I that was left. I saved the pelt to remind me of that stubborn, determined, hard-to-kill fox".

Not a story to tell around the dining table but certainly indicative of the harsh way of life and death that Alaska was at that time, and probably is still.

Once, Perry Green, a furrier from Anchorage, went in and out on the same plane with me. We got to chatting and he expressed his support for the administration of the then—Senator Greening. He was also in the business of buying and selling not only furs but ivory, too. He was very informed and interesting to talk to; I told him a bit about myself and he expressed his opinion as to my intention to move to Anchorage and work in the Hospital there.

Then, we got into a discussion of religion and when then the subject came up again about me taking over a leadership position in the Kotzebue Hospital, he expressed the notion that he thought I wouldn't have a problem making a go of it, as he said, "even if I *was* LDS."

He never mentioned his own religious beliefs but said that he, quote, 'came into contact with several Mormons,' in the past and he said and had a high opinion of them as a people. We knew some of the same folks and the flight was enjoyable, even if I did without my usual nap while in-flight.

We started discussing his observations and experiences he had since spending so much time in Alaska. He had a unique opinion for the high rate of Schizophrenia in the outback country: he thought it had to do with people listening to the radio stations that played 100% of their programming time with the Radio ministry-missionary, hell-fire and brimstone-type preachers who had programs that were run almost all the time and were exclusively of this type. He said that if all you had for company was a radio (and that is true for many folks in Alaska's outback) and all you heard, over and over, was the fact that you were probably going to Hell to burn for eternity unless you repented of sins you didn't even know you had and came around to the way of thinking that particular Pounder of the Good Book proffered, it would make anyone nuts. I chuckled along with him at his unique theory . . . it kind of made sense but I didn't buy it . . . .

~~~~~~~~~~~~~

An excerpt from my journal, indecipherable as to date, but apparently written from the thriving metropolis of Elim, tells me that I flew to Nome and waited to meet up with a Pediatrician named Jim Herschfeld, from the Hospital in Anchorage; I wanted him to accompany me and one of my best nurses, Lori Juteau, on a field trip. At that time, the teachers at the State funded school there, the BIA teachers were Richard and Mary Francis. They are a cute couple, always patting each other, holding hands and such. It is a delight to see that kind of joy in marriage.

Because they are both teachers in that town, they are great examples of my pet theory that good BIA teachers are solid gold and bad ones can damage not just the students that have to try and learn from them but the whole town and the ambiance, if you will, of the entire village. Richard and Mary are of the '14-carat' variety and do just that in the uplifting and positive manner they take with the children and all the villagers, both.

Well, anyway, Jim, Laura and I flew into Elim . . . just 'slipped in', rather, as the weather was zero-zero and commercial flights had been cancelled. We decided rather than postpone the long-planned trip, we would try to get a Charter and sure enough, we dug up a pilot *and* a plane that would chance it. This was a new area to me . . . I found it exhilarating to be up in the air . . . when somebody else is flying, that is . . . . and they are super-good pilots who know the country and are trying to sneak through under the radar as it were. It sure lends a certain air of suspense and challenge into an otherwise dull flight.

So, all filled up with suspense and challenge, we got into town on a weekend night, there and I encountered something I had never seen: there was a *city-wide* card-party going on. I can't recall the name of the game but it seemed that practically the whole town was there, everyone of them either playing the card game or just socializing. Seems that folks pitched in with a quarter or whatever they could and they served some punch and cookies and just had this great small-town old-fashioned Social! The idea and organization had begun with Richard and Mary and *that's* a perfect example of what I was expounding on before: a good BIA team can make or break a town. I hadn't heard of this socialization before or since: everyone enjoying each other's company and it didn't matter if you were white or brown or green . . . rich or poor . . . everyone had fun!

These teachers didn't just teach during the week and then disappear and hide out; they feel that the school is an integral part of the town. I wasn't alone in my opinion, either. If a traveling Doctor has a good experience in a village and is welcomed by happy people, it makes the grueling task of *travel and treat* worth it. It can be a fun place to go and to look forward to going to again, so the docs make every effort to go back to that little village again and often.

The worst case of just the opposite happened to me toward the end of my sojourn in Alaska. I was at one of the other villages where the atmosphere was certainly *not* conducive to a pleasant stay at all. From my first visit there, it seemed that the people were almost all hostile and resentful and rude to me, which was most unusual, but then, I came to realize that's the way I then witnessed the teachers handling the people: with resentment and ill-disguised hostility!

I actually left that village in the middle of the night and traveled over 20 miles by snow machine over pack ice to get *out* of there and back to a town where the teachers were not ignorant misogynists. SO unfair to the citizens. I performed my duties and helped whomever I could, but that was all . . . I can't recall the name of the town . . . wish I could . . . or maybe it's best I *don't* recall. It sure does make people like Mary and Richard Francis really shine in my eyes.

Well, back to the story and the reason for the visit from all three of us, and that was the report of a strange case involving a local boy: he presented with reports of frequent seizure-like behavior. We flew in as a team and got settled, then he was brought in on appointment as his family lived quite a distance away. We had him wait in an area, with some toys and distractions, next to the examining room at the School while the mother met with us and described his actions. Luckily, she had some English and she told us that the little boy would "scream and holler and get so mad, he'd turn blue and pass out". This behavior had been going on for over a year and getting worse each time, the mother reported.

Getting *that* information was not how the initial report read and not the thing we came all the way out to the middle-of-nowhere-Elim to witness. Listening to her, Jim and Lori and I exchanged puzzled expressions as, according to the mom, it sounded like this was just a spoiled kid having temper tantrums with breath-holding spells Unusual, too, for I'd found, in the Eskimo culture that most of the children are shy and polite.

Not little Mamoo.

When we called him to come into the room and join his mother and we three, he looked to me to be about 8 years old . . . a little pudgy and overgrown for his age, perhaps, scowling and with a pouting lower lip he was in danger of tripping over. Jim helped him hop up on the examining table and I headed in with my stethoscope. Mamoo took offense at this apparently, and started a screaming recital louder than I would have thought his child-size vocal cords could produce.

Mary and Richard, since they were the ones who initially reported his strange behavior, were there too and were open-mouthed as well. I glanced over at them and they seemed uncomfortable about instigating this whole, involved trip. Jim stepped in about this time and tried to talk to the boy; Lori, whose specialty is to treat little nose-pickers like this, was standing back with a shocked look on her face, and simply witnessing the event.

She'd told me earlier that Jim, who had initially responded to the first report of the lad by phone, had suggested to the child's mother that she just ignore him and that eventually the temper-tantrum would blow over. Jim related earlier during our flight that he found it almost funny to watch other situations of this learned-behavior and the effect it has on the loved ones, compared to other bystanders, of horror, laughter or deep concern.

At this time, the mother stood aside and was just wringing her hands and openly tearing up; we had been told that she was a widow and this was her only living child, her only chance at posterity, and she had been desperately trying to implement the advice Richard had given her, but with no positive results.

After about a minute of screaming vertically while seated, it seemed Mamoo decided to take his act horizontal and the little rascal fell/jumped off the examining table and onto the floor for Act II. It consisted of the same decibel of screaming but was further embellished with feet kicking and heel banging . . . then, silence fell.

Time for Act III.

He glanced around, his bright, beady brown eyes taking in his audience, and it seemed he was checking out their responses. He next proceeded to hold his breath . . . at least that is what it looked like to us. He was not gasping for air nor did he seem in distress . . . he just pouched out his ample cheeks and turned a lover-ly shade of blue! Jim was still chuckling and shaking his head but I was alarmed at the cyanotic turn of events and I turned to Jim, and with facial expressions, eye-rolling and body-language-shrugging, non-verbally, asking him something like, "How long are you gonna let this go on?" Words to that effect.

Mamoo's mommy, all this time, was still crying but it didn't keep her from chattering a mile a minute, in her variation of English and her native tongue. I was completely unfamiliar with some of what she was saying for there are so many dialects in Alaska . . . she was pointing to the little guy and nodding her head vigorously, almost jumping up and down similar to what her son did in the early stages of his Tony-winning performance. After a couple of minutes into it, Jim broke the spell by turning to the sink, filling a glass with cold water and tossing it in the kids face.

My kind of cure. But no change.

In fact, after another minute into Mamoo's Circus, it looked to me like the little bugger might actually be having an honest-to-goodness seizure! Jim must have drawn the same concolusion, because he was on the floor beside him and in the next instant, I was down, too, assisting in giving him mouth-to-mouth. We got him breathing and stabilized him; the little fella had been genuinely afflicted, then after a quick consultation, we three agreed that boy and mom should be on the next flight to Anchorage, and so they were.

As it turned out, I heard much later from Jim, that although Mamoo was still a brat who threw temper tantrums, he was also a brat with a brain tumor. Operable, I am pleased to add. What a dull world it would be if there were no Mamoo in it . . . .

~~~~~~~~~~~~~

I spent a week at Point Hope during whale hunting season one year; the night before I got there, a guy had been out on his snow machine, riding along the beach doing something or the other and his wife was riding behind him, pulled on a sled. The throttle stuck on the snow machine and they kept going faster and faster until, finally, he jumped off. His wife was scared stiff, I guess, and was too frightened to do anything but stay on. The whole kit and caboodle headed for a snow-drift with a house underneath it. She tipped over, still clinging tightly to the sled and when it stopped suddenly, she banged her face into something hard and grew a good-size mouse on her right cheekbone. She came into the clinic with her face swollen so shut and I couldn't even see the eye all. I treated it as best I could; the next day, the husband showed up and, by way of a 'thank-you', I guess, brought me two masks made from the neck bones of a whale . . . I immediately knew I wanted them because one looked just exactly like his wife's swollen face! I paid for them gladly and I still have that one today.

The only wood that far north and all around Point Hope is driftwood, so the only building materials they had available to use, then, were whalebones, especially the ribs. The bones are sometimes ten or twelve feet long and the people set them upright and pack sod around them to build their homes. An interesting method . . . and a good example of how ingenious mankind can be.

~~~~~~~~~~~~

One of the teachers who was assigned to Wales built a boat; he was LDS and I had a chance to visit him several times when I was up that way. He was originally from Rigby, Idaho and he and his wife worked in Wales for three or four years. He told me that if both members of a couple were teachers, they could make between $25 to $30 thousand a year and that was a lot in the 1960's; not too shabby! He enjoyed teaching and seemed to love Alaska and all it had to offer and was really keen on the old-time ways of doing things.

He decided he wanted to build a whale-hunting boat, called a Umiak, and he wanted it to be as authentic as he could make it, so he got some village women to teach and help him. The boat was made of walrus hide stretched and sewn together with sinew to give it some elasticity so it would stretch: after these boats get soaked, they are water-tight. They are extremely light but able to hold a huge amount of weight . . . they are truly a fascinating thing to see.

As the story goes, it had been 25-years or more since the villagers of Wales had gone on a whale hunt . . . they were just too lazy to get together and build a boat, in my opinion. However, when the teacher finished and the boat was built, the village guys and the boat builder, too, got excited about the whole deal and did all that needed to be done to finish it and then made the preparations to go out on the ocean hunting!

They actually got a whale!

And . . . wow! . . . what a boost to community spirit! It just went sky-high!

The cooperation needed to not only build the vessel but then to man the thing and to be successful, then get the whale back on land and prepare it in the 'old ways' brought generations of villagers, all ages together in an endeavor that was a tremendous lift to everyone involved. What a wonderful occasion for everyone involved! . . . . well, not the whale, I guess.

Generally speaking, there are usually only one or two days a season that whales can be hunted in that particular area, and that's because they only pass the Point during a short and specific time. Well, the next year, everyone wanted to do it again, so the whales passed the point and were spotted, and the spotter came back to the village on the run to report! Problem was, it was on a Sunday and this LDS-teacher-guy would not go hunting on the Sabbath.

Now, for a small village of around 200 people, one whale can provide a huge amount meat and there are dozens of other uses Eskimos can make from it and there will be plenty for everyone.

This fellow was so devout that he wouldn't let the *villagers* take his boat out on a Sunday at all, even without him. The whales passed by that one lone day and the boat stayed on dry ground. The whole village was mad at him for a long time, I heard. I felt badly when I found this out, but you can't fault a person for having standards and sticking to them, I guess. Makes you wonder, hmmmmm?

It was interesting the way I heard about this incident . . . I was up at Point Hope which is about 300 miles from Wales. I was up doing doctor-stuff, and from the building where I was, I saw this little fire and a guy sitting out toward the point so I eventually took a break and went out to talk to him and found out that he was trying to keep from freezing to death while watching for the whale run. We chatted for a bit and then the guy up and said something like, "Well, Wales would have gotten a whale this year if it weren't for that darn Mormon teacher!" All the positive stuff was ignored for the negative stuff . . . . too bad.

∿∿∿∿∿∿∿∿∿∿∿∿

"FATHER NAWN AND HIS SCHOOLCHILDREN IN FRONT OF HIS
CHURCH AT CHEVAK"

"RUEBAN HILL AND HIS LITTLE GIRL, VILLAGE OF
HOOPER BAY. NOTE THE WIND-POWERED CHARGER."

"PAULINE SCHUERCH AND 'HOOK' IN FRONT OF THE
VILLAGE STORE IN KIANA."

'DOC HOOK AND OLINDA GREGORY. . . SEE THE
HEADS POKING OUT OF THE DOOR?'

CHAPTER 13

BASKETBALL (YES, THAT'S WHAT I SAID)

Basketball is close to my heart: I've always loved the game . . . both to play and to watch. I was on my High School team in Phoenix and we played in a State Championship team my senior year. Enrollment was around 2,500 so it was quite an honor to work hard and then be chosen out of the 500 or so guys in that grade who could've tried out.

There is a small town attitude that I brought with me, of: "what's happening to me? who in the world am I?" I felt that way a lot when I was younger and even today when I see myself flying around in my own plane and giving talks and presentations and making a good living and having people respect me and all, I feel I'm just a small town kid that nobody could ever be impressed with. But up in Kotzebue, I was a Big Fish in a little pond . . . I was THE Doctor, and a lot of folks knew who I was and whoever I was in my own mind, I was with the hospital and since basketball was popular up there, I got involved with it, too.

I guess that's who I was then.

Those were some pretty rough games. Some of the guys were really good and some were mediocre—I was just an over-the-hill player with *memories* of being quite good. Most of the Eskimo guys were between 5'6" and 5'9"; we had a BIA teacher on the team that was 6'8". The Eskimo guys were fast and just almost in-fatigue-able . . . they just *never* seemed to run out of gas. The majority of the BIA teachers were good players too, like Bill Rember and Gary Hebert . . . they were only average height but

KEITH HOOKER, M.D. AND M. DAWN BENTLEY

built like brick outhouses and they were skilled players in addition to their physical strength.

We organized a little roster and played a Barrow team, charging like 50-cents for spectators to watch our rural team league games. We sometimes got around 100 people out to a game, usually family of the players or when there was just nothing else to do! The little bit of money that came in was used for travel funds to get us to games in Nome or Barrow or to the big trip of the season, the Fur Rendezvous Tournament in Anchorage.

At one Barrow game, I think it was the first year I played up there and at half time I was utterly exhausted because I was in such poor condition. The only time I did any running was hurrying to the delivery room to catch a baby, or running between my house and the Hospital to keep from freezing en route! At half time, I would just collapse on the bench, feeling like a squeezed-out sponge, trying to suck up enough energy to make it through the game . . . through that long, long second half that seemed to stretch on into infinity and beyond.

Those flippin' Eskimo midgets would run up and down on a fast break ALL the time. There was no way I could run to both ends of the court during play . . . I'd end up walking back most of the time. SO the White Giant ended up being the White Cream Puff for the second half, heck, for the second quarter!

During tournament half time, the Eskimo team members would go outside and relax with a beer and a few cigarettes, while even in our little home games I was gasping and dying . . . 'what a fine kettle of fish this is', I thought. "Here I am a good, clean-living Mormon boy, treating my body as a Temple, and these guys probably were partying the night before and are still hung-over and they're running me into the boards!"

Not only that, but I was at sea level where the oxygen is so thick, you have to push your way through it and I couldn't seem to get enough of it into my lungs to keep me vertical.

The first game we played, the Barrow team really waxed us on that Friday night and then we had a Saturday night game, too. They had one white guy with them . . . I forget his name, but he was about 40 years old and if I thought *I* was over the hill, *he* was right beside me in the next *valley!* We ended up getting to know each other quite well and he was a good player and more importantly, a good sport. He was a charter pilot, flew a two-engine plane and was an Aero Commander. I admired his skill and sometimes envied his career.

The second night of the tournament, one of the other teams best players dislocated his little finger . . . his hand pointed north and his little finger was pointed that-away-east. They were ahead of us by a bit, at that time, so play was stopped while I took a look at his finger, as I was the only medically trained person there. I put on my professional 'hat' and took a look . . . I knew that I could fix it, to some degree, right then and there and have him get an x-ray later to make sure it wasn't broken; I could have given it a little tug and snapped it back into place. But for the fact that the rotten little stinker was killing us in the game! Although he was only about 5'5", he'd been driving right through our defense and had already made about 25 points, while I was breathing my last breath! Probably, if I'd done the right thing and tried to pull it back into position, I wouldn't even have had the strength to do it, so, I waited until the game evened up a bit, point-wise, then adjusted it for him and let him play the last few minutes . . . . we just barely beat them. I have always felt a bit guilty about this so will take this opportunity, publicly, to apologize.

"Sorry about that."

There. I feel much better.

A bunch of us, nineteen I recall, went down to Nome to play; we left Kotzebue three hours late, two hours of which was due to a hole in the airplane's engine strut. They expertly repaired it (used duct tape I'm sure: this was Elastic Airlines, of course). After winning the game, at 11:30 PM, we found out Phyllis and I and the boys didn't have a Hotel room, so we called up Dan Johnson and his wife, some friends of ours from Church, and we stayed with them.

This team was comprised of a couple of FAA fellows and a couple of school teachers and the rest were local guys. Usually, for away-games, we would charter a plane and then separate up and stay with friends. I always stayed at the local Hospital.

Basketball is not a gentle sport but it's not supposed to be a contact sport, either. Another truism is that when bush-leagues travel to the hometown of the other team, they need to be at least 20 points 'better' to make up for the 20-point advantage that the local referees are known to give. This isn't fair, but it *is* bush-league ball; it's also known as a 7-man team. When the games get going, my good nature really takes some hits early on, and after a quarter of play, I'd even elbow my mother if she was out-rebounding me.

On this particular game, the center for the opposing team was a lawyer for VISTA; he was a pretty nice guy and we actually considered ourselves friends. Everyone was kidding me and telling me how much they'd bet that I wouldn't foul out and we were all laughing and joking about it.

Well, so the VISTA guy was pretty good that night. He was a hockey player, too, so he was more rough than skillful and I was getting the worst of the deal. Ten minutes into the game and we both were getting a little hot. I'm a somewhat good natured fella and I wasn't really mad yet, but getting that way!

This particular guy and I were fighting it out for rebounds. Getting rebounds is all a matter of position—whoever gets to the right place at the right time and can keep the other guy from pushing him, well, he is going to get the ball. You might want to watch this on TV next time you are tuned into a game: ignore the ball and watch all the fights—literally—underneath the basket.

All the other teams members were giving us room and the only thing I had to watch out for was this slimy VISTA lawyer-snake-ex-hockey player (him) who was giving the Noble Public Health Doctor (me) a LOT of elbow and hip.

So, while we were tripping and kicking each other like Jr. High girls, trying to get into position for the rebound, the referee threw us *both* out for dirty playing and we both spent the rest of the game on the bench, in the end.

So I didn't get as tired that night . . . .

The guys on the teams didn't take any of the winning and losing stuff too seriously . . . it seemed that basketball was just a way for them to get some parole-time from home and have a good time drinking and hanging out with their buddies. At half-time, I went over and shook hands with the lawyer and we exchanged mutual back-pats.

What I didn't know was that the local radio station was broadcasting this momentous event throughout the airwaves of the whole Artic and some parts of Siberia . . . Mighty KICY . . . the Voice of the Arctic. Everybody in Kotzebue heard that *their* dear Doctor Hooker had been kicked out of the game for fighting with the other teams center . . . what was NOT broadcast was that the center got kicked out, too!

When I got home, I really got the raspberry from friends and the people at the Hospital looked at me differently after I got back, thinking that I must be a na-as-ty guy. It really was a funny situation looking back on it now. The disgrace was that the very professional, upstanding Doctor-type person would stoop so low as to get into a fight with a low-down, dirty-playing VISTA lawyer, (read 'cobra' here). VISTA wasn't looked at too kindly in some camps at that time.

It was toward the end of our stay in Alaska that I had an experience related to basketball that marked me forever.

At Kotzebue, if Phyllis and I had outside activities to plan, we tried to have them on Saturdays while Sunday was saved for visiting friends or just being together as a family. If I was out of town, I went to Church meetings if I was somewhere I could or if I was not on duty at the Hospital. My days were so much alike that Sunday didn't seem much different from the others, really. If I got bored in the afternoon, I went over to the recreation hall where there was bound to be a pick-up basketball game going on and I often played. Not having Church to go to, we were a bit lax about Sabbath-keeping out in the bush.

The big event is, as I mentioned, the Fur Rendezvous in Anchorage, held in February or early March. Historically, the fur trapping was pretty much over and the trappers came in to sell to the fur buyers. Nowadays, a lot of them fly up, if I recall, from Seattle. In the old days, the 30's and 40's, it was a fur auction but anymore it ended up being about a 3-day blowout, involving the whole state. People would come in from all over and there would be contests, dogsled and snowmobile races . . . kind of like a below-zero State Fair. The Fur Rendezvous started having organized basketball tournaments years before. As time went on, their 'A' Class tournament had some excellent players, even some ex-pro guys who were up there working on oil rigs and playing the city leagues near Anchorage.

When we lived in Anchorage, the LDS Church league would get the best of our Ward and Stake teams together and we'd do fairly well. We had the advantage of not beating up our bodies with liquor and tobacco. Sometimes we won on perseverance instead of expertise; with a lot of luck, sometimes we could pick up a missionary or two who had been college players, but only if we could play within the Mission rules.

From Kotzebue, then, we took our best and most eligible players to go down to the Fur Rendezvous tournament. These were usually on a Thursday-Friday-Saturday and occasionally Sunday schedules. The Health Service would always combine a Health Service regional meeting with the Rendezvous which meant all the doctors got to come in free and most brought wives, so they could enjoy a little R & R, too. Phyllis and I were looking forward to this particular getaway; many of the others on our team were less financially solvent and were excited about the tourney, too, so we would all chip in for the guys who didn't have the money. It made for good team spirit.

This particular time, we were entering the last year of the Hooker Alaska experience; I knew it would probably be the last basketball team I'd play on . . . at least the last with the level of competitiveness we were contending with. I really *never* expected our team would do so well and make such as good showing as we did, however.

The first game we played was with the team that had taken the Championship last year and we trounced them royally, right off the bat! I made close to 20 points and, remember, I was a broken-down old man of 30 by then! But I'd been training myself for the tournament with the realization of it being my last and all. The other guys on the team had worked hard, too, and we were all playing well together . . . it's rare for this kind of chemistry to be at such a level . . . it was kind of like the Perfect Storm of Old Man Basketball and we just slaughtered the other team!

On Friday we played another team that was supposed to be good, too, and by that time, it got to be embarrassing. We rotated guys in from our side that were mediocre enough to make it an equal match! We had one of those rare, crackerjack teams that some players compete for a lifetime without playing on and feeling that incredible exhilaration. When we were together on the floor, it seemed like there was magic in the air.

On Saturday, we played for the Championship, but it was a double-elimination tournament and if we lost on Saturday, we would have to play again Sunday. Well, that was the problem. Here I was: I had lived in Anchorage for two years and had been fairly well known in the Church circles there. I was also a traveling doctor and I was quite active and met many people; even more folks knew OF me and what standards I stood for, especially the youth.

If we won the third game, it would mean we were in the Championship and that ran into Sunday. It hit me like a ton of bricks: I couldn't play on a Sunday. It went against my beliefs and the people who knew me knew it did. This put not only me in a bind but the whole team, too.

It was not right to have two sets of standards, one for Church-friends and one for non-Church friends. I really did not know what to do . . . oh, I knew I couldn't *play*, that wasn't the issue at all, I just didn't know how to avoid it without letting the team down.

Well, I ended up calling all the team together and telling them that I had a medical situation come up at home and I had to go back. Right or wrong, that was my decision. It was not a total lie, but it was not the whole truth either . . . .

'Devastated', would maybe come close to describing the way I felt . . . I didn't know it would affect me so strongly and for so long, however. I listened to the radio and the play-by-play description of my team losing and I hated myself. Part of the self-flagellation was because I had been dishonest. I should have just told my team the truth and not have been such a coward. It was painful but I learned a valuable life-lesson from it: I never break the Sabbath anymore! It took me over a *year* to quit stinging from it every time it crossed my mind, but it did ease eventually.

An interesting sequel to this experience: there was a man that I considered my best friend at that time and his name's Larry Brown and he held a position of leadership in our Church; he's about my age and a guy with whom I have always been able to be brutally honest. When I was in Anchorage a few months later, visiting him, I confided in him, my dear Mormon friend, how absolutely miserable and disgusted I was with myself for hanging up on a standard and for being a hypocrite. Keeping my eyes on the floor, I opened my heart to him, and afterwards, fell silent. He had not said a word, but had been listening intently the whole time.

Finally, I looked up at him and he was smiling slightly.

"Well," he said, "I knew you were in a bind because I knew you were playing basketball at Kotzebue now and then on Sunday. I hadn't said anything to you about it, figuring you would make your own way with your actions someday. You know the difference between right and wrong. Now, I want to tell you what your decision *not* to play made here in Anchorage. You are pretty well-known and people know that you are 'that Doctor that lives in the bush' and there had been some interesting comments I'd heard around the area . . . comments like, "Wonder what Hooker is gonna do about playing basketball," because *everyone* knew you were down here and playing well on the team that was just whipping every one that came along.

"The word had spread like a wildfire," he continued. "The kids, especially some of the Scouts you've worked with, were wondering if you were a Sunday Basketball player or not . . . just a Sunday Mormon or not."

He went on to say, "You may not be too thrilled with yourself for being somewhat of a hypocrite or for making the wrong choices about playing on Sunday in the *past,* but on the other hand, you can never know how much attention was being paid to *this* game and by whom.

The decision you made when you choose not to play on Sunday had a very profound effect here, especially on the young people."

Those people, of course, will never know what hell I went through. For me, it was a very maturing experience that taught me two things: one, choose what you are going to do before you have to do it, and, two: don't dodge issues . . . face them head-on. In all sincerity, I try to do just that . . . .

'ON THE BANKS OF THE KOBUK ROVER WITH PUPPIES; RAY
BLASTERVOLD AND FAMILY TENT FOR FISHING CAMP.'

CHAPTER 14

FISH STORIES . . . Looks Like a Lot of 'Em Got Away . . . .

Lots of times, I would get into a village, do whatever it was I came to do, and then the weather would bum out on me and I would be stuck, unable to fly, sled, ski, or walk home. A lesser man would curse and shake his fist at the sky, but not the Noble Doctor Hooker: I always felt it was better to just relax and make the best of a bad situation. My biggest regret when these infrequent and unappreciated holidays cropped up was that they kept me from my little family at home.

One time, I was stranded at a village very near to a likely-looking, fast-running river so, making the best of it, and although brokenhearted as I *always* was on these forced hiatuses', but beings-as-how it was pleasant weather, cold but sunny and all, I decided if I couldn't get out of there, I may as well fish. I talked a local guy I'd met into taking me hooking on the river about 20 miles downstream in the tundra. I put on my mukluks, wool bootees, down underwear, my parka and covered up my ears well. All that preparation served me well and I was able to stay comfortable for at least an hour or more as we traveled by sled over the tundra.

We found a spot he approved of and started in. The ice was about 2 feet thick and we took turns pounding it, using a long sturdy stick with a sharp end on it: picture a shovel handle with a deadly-looking tip attached. It took a considerable amount of time to break through the ice at all but once we did, it was phenomenal! Absolutely stands out in my mind as the most frenetic, action-packed, fast-paced fish-catching adventure I had ever been on, before or since! Comparatively speaking, if regular fishing was a Sunday Drive, this trip would be the Indy 500!

We would drop a jig on a line into the water and bam! They would hit and we would drag them in, taking turns at dropping in the jigs.

For the unenlightened, a jig is simply a hook without traditional bait, and in this case, a small piece of red rag was tied on to attract them and the fishies would just bite instantly. We'd pull them out, pulling hand over hand, and toss them on the ice. They would flop about 3 times, and then become frozen solid. Amazing! The wind had been blowing the whole time but the sun kept shining bravely, but as it began to get toward late afternoon, we loaded all the fish onto the sled and made like sheepherders and getting the flock out of there.

The pile of fish was so high and unstable, I was hardly able to ride on top but ride I did as Jim didn't care: *he* was riding the rails and the dogs were doing all the work. It was a glorious way to travel. As we were bucking across the tundra, I took a few spills, though, and by the time we reached town, I had about all the fun I could stand.

It was about 6:30, and getting dark and I still had to pull a meeting that evening to make up for the weather-cancelled one the day before. I had grown a rotten headache so I gulped a few aspirin and grabbed a 30-minute power nap, got up and went to work. The fish were much appreciated by the eaters thereof and had divvied up quickly.

Never will forget that trip. My grin was ear to ear . . . under wraps, of course!

Saturday came and the weather was still bad and it was obvious that I was going nowhere I needed to be, so, rather than call the day a bust, I talked to a guy who was going fishing in a nearby river and I could go and "hook' through the ice again! We went down the same river I had been the day before, and as before, but this time by snow machine and sled, instead of dogs. Once again,

I had dressed in my warmest, putting on my down underwear, my wool bootees, mukluks, and parka and then I covered my ample ears really well, but I still barely managed to keep from freezing on the hour and a half trip over the tundra. When there, however, we caught over a hundred Pike, and they were nice ones, too, around 24" in length; the method was the same: we used heavy metal poles with metal spikes on them to bust our way through two-foot deep ice, going straight down, as if we were drilling for oil. We dropped our line through the small hole we had made; the line had a red rag tied onto it and the fish struck on it instantly: just like my trip the day before, it was a most exciting experience! My arms were aching but good, early one, however!

We fished like this until we were tired of it and we had about all the fish we could tote back; the wind was whooping it up so we piled all the fish on the sled he had tied to the back of the machine, I sat on top of them, just like before, and off we went, headed back. My thermometer registered -20 below. It was an unforgettable way to travel, perched on top of a mountain of dead fish and bucking along across the tundra with a 30 MPH headwind. Deja Vu! Gosh, I love fishing!"

Come to find out, the teachers and villagers had become concerned for us as it got close to dark and were organizing a search party when we pulled in. The fish were divvied up and I went back to my cot with a real thumper of a headache, swallowed a pill or two to kill it, warmed up and slept like the dead.

Sunday morning came up cold but clear and I said good-bye to Lower Kalsag and made it over to St. Mary's by plane before noon. This was a large Catholic Church and School and was run by the Jesuits. They showed me the kindest hospitality that had yet been afforded me. I had a big room all to myself with a very comfortable and warm straw tick in one corner. I set the x-ray machine up in another corner and enlisted a couple of the school boys to change the cassettes for me and with a regular RN plus the town Health Aide for extra help, it was really neat and efficient and a pleasure to work it!

Fishing was pretty common and everyone did it, summer and winter, but I still looked forward to hunting as something special. On a free day, I would jump in the plane and take off, flying maybe 200 miles or so to the Willuk River where there were Char; they look like big minnows, 18 inches long or more, and they would hit like crazy on #2 Mepps . . . they were just frantic and couldn't let one go by without a strike. I'd land on a sandbar, alone, and fish by myself, letting the relaxation and soul-mending environment wash away the cares and stresses of the week.

Sometimes there were only cruddy places to land, full of logs and rubbish that the spring runoff had thrown up there. I would fish for about an hour, until I had a plane-full of fish, then stop fishing and gut them all out, leaving the scraps to the seagulls who would be watching me as if they knew what I was going to do. They would come in, swooping down in big flocks, squawking and tussling over the fish innards. Now, I'm convinced they memorized the number on my plane and recognized me . . . . knowing they would get an easy meal . . . . what do you think?

There were other scavengers, too, waiting for the crowd to clear. I'd throw the gunnysacks full of cleaned fish in the back of the plane and take off for home. One time I was fishing that same spot from the shore of the river; the water was only running about 4 or 5 feet deep and it was sharp and crystal clear. I snagged my spinner on the bottom and decided rather than lose my favorite lure, I would just strip down and wade in after it. Now, believe me, that water was cold, even though it was July, but I was over 200 miles above the Arctic Circle so the bone-chilling temperature came as no surprise. So, there I was, in my birth-day suit, and up to my bellybutton in that frigid water, trying to retrieve a darned spinner that cost maybe a dollar.

Nickel-pincher extraordinaire I was in those days, sometimes to my detriment! Now, just about the time I got the spinner loose, I heard the engine of one of the exploration planes the big oil companies were always sending out and around. It probably had four guys aboard and the pilot kind of waggled his wings at me and I'm sure they had a good laugh about the tall and skinny skinflint, standing in ice-cold water, trying to save his favorite lure! Gosh, that has been 40 years or so ago and I took it for a fact that I was the only person within 100 miles of that spot. I wonder . . . . if I revisited it today there would probably be a resort built on that spot: the state is getting the notoriety it deserves and more and more people are coming up.

I was taking a chance, going off like I did . . . not even realizing until later that I hadn't told anyone where I was even going. My mind would get so full, I would forget things like that. It was a strain on Phyllis and I have felt badly about putting her through that, in later years.

We went to that nice spot several times with my wife and the little boys and with Phyllis's sister Wendy when she came up to stay for a while. The Willuk River has great fishing for Char . . . they are an Arctic saltwater fish that migrate upriver to spawn. From the air, when we would fly in, they would look just like a school of minnows, sparkling in the sun, but they weighed about 2 or 3 pounds! I would land as close as I could safely and we pile out of the plane and get out a # 2 fish net and some spinners and it would take us maybe a half hour to get all the fish the plane could carry, then the real fun started . . . . trying to get back up in the air! With passengers and 200 fish at 3 pounds apiece or so, it was a challenge because the sandbars were so rough. I would *never* be that daring again, especially with a 108 HP PA12 airplane.

Ice fishing is common, of course, as iced-in rivers are covered for so long in the year. One of the largest fish caught with this method is the Shee fish: they were keepers at about 3 feet in length . . . any smaller and they were unhooked and tossed back down the hole. When they were pulled up, they were rapped on the head to keep them from flopping back into the hole from whence they had been pulled. They would freeze solid in just a matter of minutes.

The Eskimo fishermen must have known the exact places to open the ice and put in their nets; their ancestors had probably been pulling fish from those spots for hundreds and hundreds of years. They seem to know where the fish would be heading and they would put their nets down before the ice got too thick. They check the nets every day or two, clearing the ice and pulling them in. They also netted salmon, trout and grayling. I really liked the salmon then and miss it now, as what can be bought stateside is just so inferior to those freshly-caught healthy fish.

Dr. John Lee, the Head of the Alaska Native Health Services in Anchorage was a guest of mine one fall and I took him fishing. We had a few days or so to enjoy, so we would work during the day and ice fish in the evenings. Every time we would cast out, we would get a strike; it was just super fun and he enjoyed himself immensely.

A 25-pound salmon would make a large meal for our family and plenty of guests. There was a commercial salmon cannery just downriver from where we fished. They just came right in onto the beach, cast out huge nets, and pulled them in. I don't know what they did with all the roe, as the fish they were harvesting were spawning and full of eggs. We used some of the eggs to catch trout by keeping the eggs in cold salt water. The tides didn't amount to much there on the shoreline, and since the sea posed no danger from high tide, everyone lived right on the edge of the ocean.

One time, Larry Brown who was a VD/Measles control Officer went with me on a 168 mile drive to a lake called Mae West Lake because of the dimensions and shape when viewed from a plane. After driving as close as we could to the spot we had chosen, we hiked in for half a mile, slashing our way through a solid wall of mosquitoes. We floated a life raft out and caught our limits in a half an hour!

We were fly fishing and the grayling just went nuts over that bait. That half-mile hike through the Great Wall of Mosquitoes discouraged lesser fishermen from going there, so our huge catch was the reward for our hardiness . . . there is another word that my wife used instead of 'hardy' when I related this story to her . . . . let me think . . . what was that? . . . . hmmm.

~~~~~~~~~~~~~~

On another trip, there were four of us along and we hiked in two miles to Lost Cabin Lake and fished five tough hours and caught only four fish between us . . . Oh well, it was good exercise and one fish apiece is just about right for on-the-spot eating.

One rare week, the conditions were ideal for Alaska: not hot, not cold, not buggy, not tourist-y . . . so our little family went out almost every night of the week and Phyllis and I taught our Juniors about primitive food gathering. We picked berries, after reading extensively and getting all the advice from others that we could get; we found mushrooms, too, and had a fun time just being together and experiencing how a tiny slice of life must have been for the natives of this land who had gathered these same treats from Nature during the short warm season. Drawing close to the end of our Alaska experience, the two oldest boys have a lot of memories . . . a lot of good memories, thankfully!

One trip with some buddies, Norm Trapan and Red Morely in Juneau, was a real vacation for me. These two guys were consummate fishermen who reveled in the sport so much that it actually dictated their moods: I learned that among expert fishermen their ego, their demeanor and their disposition was either great or awful, depending in direct proportion, on the amount or quality of fish caught!

They had their own boat and it was a treat for me to fish with two such knowledgeable guys. We were in a great spot and the autumn weather was perfect . . . just a little bite to the air and the aroma of campfires along the beach with tantalizing smells of bacon and coffee.

We were all in Norm's boat that time and he had anchored in a perfect position. They both thoughtfully took time with me that I know they would rather have been just close-mouthed, eyes-glazed over, and casting, but actually explained their choice of bait, why, how to move the rod and so forth . . . stuff like that from expert fisherman you just can't pay to get! I felt like a 10-year-old little leaguer playing ball with Roger Maris . . . !

After the preliminaries, we got right down to fishing and our lures hit the water in unison . . . Norm pulled in a nice fifteen-pound salmon in about 5-minutes, then I got the next two; old Red just sat there quietly and didn't say much as the hours wore on. The nice salmon had seemed to boost Norm's mood and he was even more talkative than usual, pointing out interesting bits of the passing scenery, telling fish stories and so on. On the other end of the boat, Red was getting quieter and quieter, not his usual ebullient self at all. Any attempts at conversation were met with, "Shut up and fish." Words to that effect.

When I (almost reluctantly) pulled in the next two fish, Red started to talk about turning around and going home. He was kicking at his bait can and snarling words under his breath that actually sounded menacing. I glanced over at Norm, he was just sitting really still, and when I started to speak, shook his head and frowned, as if to warn me off.

Then, all of a sudden, Red got hot and brought in the next three nice, big salmon. Oh, boy! He was on fire and talking a mile a minute, a total transformation, courtesy of 85 pounds of fish.

We wound up with six nice ones, the best day Red and Norm said they had had in a long time. Me, too.

The best fishing trips were the ones I went on with my kids. The anticipation, the looks on their faces and the pure joy they exuded out every pore was priceless. It was a sweet sensation that I'll never forget. The last summer we were there, Kyle was 6 and Kit was about 5 . . . what perfect ages for the First Official Guys-Only Fishin' Excursion Extravaganza! We packed all the fishing gear, first-aid, snacks, drinks, bug-dope, hats, sunscreen, jackets, and every other conceivable notion their mother could think of to send with us: we were equipped to stay for a month or two instead of just one day. The little guys were so geared up! Their confidence level caused them to insist on packing up a dozen or more gunny sacks to bring home all the fish they were going to catch . . .

Finally ready, we took off up river and instead of planning where to go, exactly, I used a trick I'd learned from my airplane buddies, and that was to fly along above the river about 20 feet until you'd see a good school of fish. They were surprisingly easy to see from up in there in the clear water; the most common were Char. They are ocean-going species of trout and because they have not been used to being fished on a river in relatively shallow water and with food being more scarce than it was in the ocean, they would strike at almost anything. By using spinners on our poles, it made the perfect kind of fishing for the little guys: lots of non-stop action!

We landed on a sandbar after spotting a good-sized run, and as we were coming in for the descent, I remember thinking to myself, 'You know, I could really screw up here; I've got my boys with me and if put the plane down wrong and hit a rock or something, we could be up here for a while.' Of course, I had a full complement of emergency survival kit supplies, but that wasn't the point, really. We'd be stuck until someone found us. Well, the really light plane I had at that time managed to land OK on the sand/rock bar, and we unloaded our gear and started. I found it best to go ahead and make the cast out for the boys and just let them reel in; about every other cast, they'd hook a fish: one would start to reel his fish in, then the other boy would get a strike! I was working hard keeping the two lines clear and in the water, for, almost as soon as the spinner would hit the surface, an eager Char would hit. They boys would pull 'em in and I would boink the unlucky Char in the head with a rock to keep them from dying a slow death . . . mostly to keep them from flopping back into the water and escaping, really, but the other way sounds so much more humane . . . .

The boys would fight the fish on the line and after there were a dozen or so on the beach, I would call a 'time out' and gut them, rinse 'em off and put 'em in a sack in the water to keep cool. Before too long, the excited shrieks the boys were putting out were sounding a little hoarse and a lot of the initial thrill was gone. My heck, we had a big old mess of fish, so I thought it was time to head back as it was getting towards sundown and the little guy's arms were in danger of being pulled right off!

I recall needing to take off while looking into the sun and since I couldn't see very well, it would be hard to dodge the holes and indentations and rocks in the sandbar that kept me from being able to take off smoothly, or at all. So, I hatched out a plan and Kit and Kyle helped me cut willows, like 1/4 inch thick and I pushed them down into the sand until they made a little path for me to follow, showing the way that avoided the large potholes and rocks too big to move . . . things that would have messed up the landing gear real bad. We put down about 100 yards of these, and it the plan worked quite well: I followed the Willow Slalom and was able to get us airborne in no time. Before we got up 50 feet, the birds that had been patiently observing us gutting the fish swarmed down to gobble up the bonanza we'd left for them. I circled around a couple of times as the boys were getting such a kick out of seeing the birds squabble and fight as they swooped and dived over the unexpected bounty. They were bouncing in the seat and laughing so hard!

The boys couldn't wait to show off their catch to their mom, and good mom that she was, she made the appropriate exclamations of delight at the size and quantity of Kyle and Kit's success on their first fishing trip. Plenty to eat and plenty to share! Their first trip, maybe, but not their last by any means . . . . they grew up with a love for the great outdoors just like their parents. I take my grandchildren fishing now . . . . it's just as sweet.

"FISH DRYING ON A RACK ON THE KOBUK RIVER"

"WHITEFISH CAUGHT BY UNIDENTIFIED LUCKY GUY
ON THE YUKON RIVER"

"ON A FISHING BOAT, HOISTING KING CRAB!"

"DOWNTOWN KOTZEBUE, FISH-DRYING RACKS ON LEFT"

CHAPTER 15

SNOWMOBILES AND SLED DOGS

Let me begin this chapter by saying that some readers will bristle at the next little bit here, and if you are a dog-lover, you might want to just skip this Chapter. However, I am telling you the way it was in the part of the country and the time of history when I was there and saw what I saw.

Now, if you are a snow-machine lover, you will appreciate all the technical talk about speed and RPM and motor size and such-like but HATE the other parts about parts . . . parts strewn all over and back again: snowmobiles run into the ground, machines taken apart brutally by big, grimy hands and tossed to the side and left to rust away on some forgotten ice floe . . . . it's not pretty, folks, but it's real.

We got a rude awakening in Alaska about sled dogs; we had read Jack London's contributions to modern literature as well as all of the classic dog stories we'd enjoyed as kids, so I guess we were expecting loyal, highly-intelligent, furry-coated pets with loving dispositions who adored their owners just as much as they were loved in return.

Unfortunately, most of the ones I saw were half-starved, unkempt and savage beasts which were kept tied or chained up at ALL times. I can recall only a handful of dogs-kept-as-pets; it was as strange to the natives to have a dog as a pet as it would be to us to see a horse in someone's living room. The dogs I saw in Alaska were an unfortunate product of the times . . . a machine, if you will, that had outlived it's usage as a machine and was abandoned and tossed aside . . . along with Buggy whips. Wringer washers. Dictaphones.

My little guys were never allowed to even be in the vicinity of, let alone *pet*, the dogs we came in contact with throughout our whole Alaska stay: one ER experience working to restore a child's face will do that to a person.

There was a lot I learned from listening to the people talk about the sled dog; much of what I write here is the knowledge I gleaned from just listening. For obvious reason, animals who are not nurtured but live on a day-to-day survival of the fittest life reflect their savage environment. There is only one person they tolerate and that's the guy that throws them half of a dried fish each day. Even he never takes chances with them.

Too many times, I had small children as patients who had been terribly injured by a dog; they would get too close to the team, disobeying their parent's stern reminders, and the dogs would attack before anyone could get to them.

Sled dogs were not raised as pets or to be playful or have pleasant dispositions . . . they were work animals and their owner only fed them what the owner had to, keeping them marginally alive and in marginally good health so they could work.

To just say that 'that's life' and that reality is often harsh does not excuse, in my mind, cruel treatment of animals. But, this is an *account* of what we saw there, not a commentary on right or wrong. Once, some animal-rights writer saw a bunch of sick and dead dogs and wrote an article, complete with heart-rending pictures that got a lot of print about how these poor dogs were starving up there in Alaska. When he got home, he joined with some Humane Society folks, got a whole bunch of money, and decided it would be a good idea to ask people to MAIL dog food to all those poor, starving dogs, First Class!

Well, good intentions aside, First Class mail gets priority over everything else and I got bumped off of several emergency airplane runs because the plane was packed full of emergency dog rations, sent by concerned animal lovers. If you think *I* was put-out and angry, you should have heard the Eskimos. They didn't need dog food; they were simply switching over from dog sleds to snow machines. The well-meaning folks in the Lower 48 effectively clogged the mail delivery and the bottom-line economics people of Elastic Airlines, naturally taking the cargo that paid the most, bumped people off flights and held up the regular running of mail for weeks.

Dog food was packed to the ceilings in warehouses while packages containing warm winter clothes, food supplies and even medicine were delayed. I was told that some people went and got the free dog food but their animals wouldn't touch it. I also heard it was finally carted off by some poor governmental agency that had a hard time explaining the mongo-big expenditure for a bulldozer to bury rotten dog food. Maybe the Polar Bears or Grizzlies ate it . . . I am sure it smelled just fine to some kind of varmint!

A bit of background: After the Eskimo people started moving into the Interior, and firefighting in the summer, or working the oil pipelines and wells or just working anywhere for good wages, they started buying snowmobiles and got rid of their dogs. There are two (maybe even more) schools of thought on this. One: the older people mostly, said that the snow machines were not as good as dogs because if you got stuck, you could igloo-up with the dogs and they would help keep you warm, and, you could walk back home in less time that it would take you if you rode a snow machine and it broke down. The other course is that people would just rather travel at 50 MPH than 10 MPH so snow machines were rapidly taking the place of dogs when we were there.

NOTE: Now, by this printing, the return to the old ways and the cherished traditions of time gone by resurrected the use of dog sleds and the resurgence of all the lore and magnificence of the historic imprint left by the animals and the drivers who carved out an existence in the hostile environment of Alaska.

There, that's said.

There are still sled dog races at Kotzebue and we went to see some while we were there. It was truly something to see, alright, albeit the very little "seeing" that was involved. You got to be there at the starting line, or, you got to be there at the finish line. It was the in-between stuff that was interesting, I am sure, and some people did station themselves along the route.

We didn't.

The dogs get so excited at the beginning of the race, all barking and jumping around and acting doggy . . . it took a lot of muscle to control them . . . and it was really cool to watch.

These dogs are strong and they have been bred back generation upon generation for just those attributes; they weigh in at around 70 pounds; most are Malamutes or Huskies and the Samoyed are popular, too. The wheel, or 'lead' dogs are the most important . . . they are the Alpha Dogs and the rest of the pack are just the equivalent of drones in a beehive. If the lead dog is good at what he or (rarely) she does, it is worth the value of the rest of the pack alone. They just follow the lead. Kind of like a quarterback.

One of the doc I worked with, whose name I forgot, decided that he would make a dashing figure on the back of a dog team, so he bought some dogs here and there and picked up enough finally to rope a team together. It was a monumental disaster, I heard, with no real lead dog and the either inexperienced or senile dogs that he hitched up were not enough to pull a sled properly.

Fascinating as it is when done correctly, in the beginning of any sled journey the dogs jump around and bark like crazy when they start out; when they get going, they pull in unison and it is an amazing thing to watch. The owner rides on the back of the sled that has runners much like skis and he stands on the back two feet or so of runner. If he loses his balance and falls off, he tries like everything to hang on to the sled because the dogs will just keep running: eventually, dragging him is harder that pulling him on the sled was and the dogs get exhausted and stop . . . then he can catch up and get back on.

There are no trees at all in some areas up there, you know, and nothing to tie the dogs to—well, you've heard the old adage that in Texas they tie their horses to a hole (they bury a big knot on the rope and that holds the horse) and they climb for water (the windmills) and they dig for firewood (cactus roots). Well, in Alaska, they tie their dogs to a hole in the water, which sounds even stranger, as they chop a hole in the ice over a river or lake, throw a stake in the hole, then do the same some yards down, tie a rope between the two 'holes', and then tie the dogs at intervals to this rope. The dogs dig out holes in the snow where they are staked and cover themselves up completely, with only the very tip of their noses poking out for air and in this way, and thanks to the efficient fur coats they have, they don't freeze to death.

One time, I was tooling down the road on my snowmobile and all of a sudden the throttle got stuck and I couldn't reach the key quickly enough and I lost control of it for just long enough to jump a bank and go right down the other side and smack right into this bunch of sled dogs, all tied in on the long line. It was a pretty strong rope, I guess, for all of a sudden I was going 20 MPH across the pack ice dragging 10 sled dogs behind me.

The power of my machine pulled the anchor stakes out of the ice and the poor dogs were scrambling on the ice, trying to stand up and run as best they could. I'll never forget the feeling I had, standing up and trying to use the brake but every time I slowed and braked the speed down, the dogs would catch up with me and they were snarling and snapping and lunging at me when they got near enough, red-eyed and growling like the Hounds of the Baskervilles. Sweet creatures.

The owner of the dogs had heard the ruckus and he was running behind me and my train, shaking his fist and swearing at me in Eskimo. I couldn't understand him but then, I didn't have to . . . his expression was enough to portray his feeling at the situation. I am sure he was calling me a 'gussuk' in a rainbow of colors. Gussuk in Eskimo can be compared to the term 'howlie' in the Islands . . . .

When I finally got loose of the rope and the dogs gave up trying to eat me, I circled around and gave him a ride to collect Fido and Fifi. They wouldn't bite him: he was the one that fed them their half-a-dried-salmon every day, remember, so they let him pull them together and return to the camp. I probably had just as much allure as the next fish to them and I was happy giving them a wide berth.

Dog races were fun to watch . . . at least, getting the teams lined up and ready to go was interesting . . . the rest of the race was quiet as a church compared to the tumult of the start of the race. I can't remember the Eskimo words for controlling the dogs and calling out the way he wanted them to go left or right, but I did perfect the noise they make to get the pack going. It's a sound I worked on until I could do it right and we use it in our family still today. If I am fifty feet from one of the kids (grandkids now!) with a lot of people in between, I can ssskkkkusssss! and they will hear it, turn around and know it is me and I can get their attention without raising my voice. Nobody else uses that sound and it is kind of odd but it works!

Most everyone was using snowmobiles when we were up there. I am glad to see that the tradition of the sled dogs and the huge importance it was in the lives of the Native peoples has gained interest and been preserved. One winter, there was a 100 mile snowmobile race nearby Kotzebue. It got a lot of publicity and there were a lot of people that came to watch and to enter.

There were not a few Polar bear hunters in the crowd, too, filling the Hotel where they and the tourists stayed. One of the racers took a wrong turn—the course was marked well, but he missed the flag somehow; it took him 3 days to get back. He was a white teacher that I had met and seemed to be a very sensible guy as he made himself a snow cave while he waited until the weather cleared and he could find his way back or be found by the search party. He came out alive . . . a little case of frostbite on his fingers but OK and so was his fragile wife who I had to tranquilize until he was found safe.

The "Pro-Dog" contingency would now say if he had been running a line of dogs, he could have just built that snow cave a bit bigger and stayed warm while he waited . . . .

The snow machines are a really good way to get frostbit in a hurry. It was a good idea to keep moving your face . . . making hideous faces at invisible foes was my favorite, and it keeps the skin on your cheeks from getting nipped. We always dressed very warmly because the chill factor, I am sure, would lots of times be -100 degrees below while we were riding the machines.

In my gear, I used to carry a thermometer and wind gauge; carrying gear wasn't too much of a problem because we always towed a sled with five to 10 gallons of extra gas, tools and lots of spare parts, including, but not limited to, spark plugs, axle, and plenty of wire, oil and fuses. It was always better to try and repair the engine than it was to walk back from wherever you came from. The tracks made in the snow would blow over in a half hour or less; at the beginning of winter, some of the fellows who traveled the trails would bring in tree branches and stick them up in the snow, here and there, along the trails. Sometimes, they would tie a rag on the top so they could be spotted and lead out of danger unless there was a white-out in which case, all traveling ceased.

A couple of the teachers, Russ and Rose Gilbert and Phyllis and I went Caribou hunting in the winter of 1968; we took two snow machines because we learned it was not safe to go out with just one. First, we went out on the pack ice which is about 12 miles across the sound and then we went up into the tundra where the Caribou were. For some reason, Caribou are not afraid of snow machines. They will spook easily by someone on foot but will let a noisy snow machine get right up within an easy shot of them. Russ and I prepared well for the hunt and were looking forward to the trip.

We left early in the morning and made good time on well-marked trails; the weather was perfect and our spirits were high. We all were feeling cabin fever and the winter-blahs and getting restless at being cooped up for so long. Before long, we were in strange country and spotted a nice herd of Caribou in a clearing ahead.

Phyllis liked to say that she enjoyed hunting, just not the shooting part, so she and Rose started to cheer for the Caribou; Phyllis yelled and jumped off our snow machine to try and scare them away. Russ and I growled at them both and told them to zip it, but every time we would go a few more miles to catch up with the herd, off Phyllis would go . . . cute as it was, it got irritating as Russ and I were out for winter meat. Eventually, the hunters won out and the cheerleaders were silenced . . . the hunt progressed in tranquility and all was right with the world again.

Despite the cosmic balance being restored, the rest of the hunt just sucked. The original small herd had dispersed . . . and to where, we knew not whence . . . . and tracking the strays wasn't working out as everything was white . . . just white all over and you couldn't even follow the footprints without going really slow and the caribou were moving much faster than that.

On the way back, half of us crestfallen and the other half totally exhilarated, we stopped at John Nelson's fish camp and they fed us a much-appreciated hot meal. Russ had somehow sheared the axle off his machine as we getting close to the camp, so it was kaput and we just left it there. All four of us got on our Sno-Sport and the sled. Phyllis rode on back of our machine to give it traction and we just hitched their sled behind ours where they rode in cramped, but not really bad, style.

The Nelsons lived at their fish camp year 'round and home-schooled their kids. They were only about 15 miles from

Kotzebue, but across the Sound, which was of course filled all winter with pack ice; we stayed at their place until after dark, getting warmed up and rested, and then took off for home base. Now, as I look back it was a little chancy to risk traveling that slowly in the dark but we were all well dressed and had a lot of gear in the sleds and rationalized that, should we have problems, we were well-equipped to handle them. It had the flavor of adventure and we were rather young and foolhardy . . . I can make that declaration because *now* I am old and wise. Well, wise . . . .

The sleds were about 13 feet long and Russ and I had built them ourselves; they were not pretty and just screamed 'home-made' but were functional and we had room in them for extra gas and food, too. The ice and snow was packed and we could easily maneuver over it, but there were two glaring problems . . . one was getting lost because if we were to lose sight of the tree-limb-marked trail, we'd be toast. Then too, it was getting toward Spring and the ice was bad: as the pack ice in the sound starts to melt, it is forced up into ridges by the tide and I never understood if it was the fresh water that eroded away the bottom of it, or there were springs in the lagoons, or currents from the River.

Regardless of the reason, the ice had begun to melt out underneath so that instead of four feet of solid ice you would hit a place with only a couple of inches of slush with snow over it. The next thing you knew, you were swimming and it would be very dismal!

So, we were laboriously picking our way through these pressure ridges with Phyllis behind me watching out, too. We came around Pipe's Spit and suddenly saw something odd ahead; it looked like a light flashing but that was just so improbable that I thought I was just getting hallucinations from being so tense and so tired. I kept telling myself there could not be a light out there. As we went on, suddenly a kid ran right out in the middle of our path, waving his arms and shouting, trying to stop us. We pulled up and he told us that he and his grandfather had been hunting in the same place we had been and as they were coming back in, the boy was on the sled, being pulled behind his grandfather and the snow machine, when suddenly, he said his grandfather and the machine just disappeared! The Skidoo the old man had been driving had fallen right in one of the thawed areas. He told us that they managed to horse the machine out of the shallow water but they couldn't get it running again.

They could have walked back to town, I am sure, and would have done just that except that we happen chanced along. The real blessing was two-fold, as we loaded them, too, into the sled and crept into town with the throttle wide open, making about 5 miles per hour. The Guardian Angel that had taken up residence on my shoulder so many times in the past provided us with a great escape from what could have been a disaster, for as tired as we were, we probably would have missed the signs, too, just as the old man had, and toppled right in . . . .

Snow Machines can be a lot of fun; I've owned dozens of them over the years. We tried to use the one we had in Alaska for fun and leisure, but the winters were so bitterly cold and dark, it wasn't easy to *have* fun. One time, we decided to take the kids on a winter picnic . . . warmly dressed and wrapped up, we went about three miles down the beach. Most of the gear we were carrying was just things to keep warm with, especially our big old red sleeping bag I tucked the kids into.

We had decided on a picnic as the weather had stabilized a bit and the wind wasn't blowing, for once, and we were all tied of sitting around the too-small house with nothing to do on a rare day off. We put a bear skin and a Caribou hide in the sled, then the red sleeping bag and the kids were dressed in so many layers of clothes, they could hardly walk. Phyllis had donned deerskin pants, caribou top and sealskin button mukluks and her muskrat coat, beaver hat and leather gloves . . . I got to wear my fur hat and my Malachi, along with similar fur clothing.

We coulda been a zoo!

It wasn't a very smart thing to do, I guess, because we couldn't even get the kids out of the sled; they were whimpering and so miserable and cold. It *was* about 30 below . . . I guess we were rushing Spring just a bit . . . . so after riding around for about an hour, we gave up and came home and warmed up the lunch we had packed, put a blanket down on the living room floor and pretended we were having a picnic . . . and waited a while for real warm weather!

"FUR RENDEVOUS SLED DOG RACE"

"FUR RENDEVOUS, DEAUX"

CHAPTER 16

BOY SCOUTS . . . "ON MY HONOR"

Early in 1966, I met with George Brennan, the Boy Scout Supervisor for Northern Alaska, at Salmon Lake and together we made plans to set up camp for the coming season. It is quite a process but it provided the kind of activity I seemed to crave; I've always been a very physical person and the 'Doctor Duties' I generally performed were time-consuming and exhausting from that angle, but my body naturally seemed to need more of a work-out, so to speak.

As I had, and have, a deep concern for youth, the Boy Scout organization was something I encouraged my sons to be a part of and I have a strong belief that it not only improves the lives of young boys and molds them into fine young men, but that it actually is the life raft to which some cling to save their very lives. Boy Scout Camp was something I really looked forward to each year.

Since becoming a state in 1958, Alaskans have embraced many American traditions and holidays and so forth with enthusiasm. The Boy Scout program was one thing that the people really enjoyed and supported and camp was greatly anticipated all year, at least in this area.

1966 was only the second year for camp; Gary Hebert started it and when he left and I just sort of inherited it. I didn't have my own plane that first year, so some of the other pilots filled in and a plane flew in every night with a fresh supply of food. That may sound strange, but it is really quite simple and necessary under the circumstances.

Those boys ate every meal like it was going to be their last. We had about 70 kids up there the first year and they could be considered truly under-privileged. You hear a lot of people talk about being poor and bandy-about the phrase, 'under privileged' at cocktail parties and there are endless fund-raising events to aid this very complicated and debated portion of our population.

The fact is that the majority of Americans have never experienced real poverty and don't really know what poor is, at least those who have not traveled out of the lower 48. Worldly goods, these kids had seen very little of, now, but what they DID have was the wide-open, relatively unspoiled and unpolluted country and their heritage, and, they were not displaced like so many in the urban areas. Poor in worldly goods and comforts? Yes, certainly. Rich in other ways? Yes, certainly.

At this time in history in Alaska, there wasn't much crime and such like, but there *was* a lack of fundamental programs and things for the kids to do, so during the winter, we tried to organize activities that included feeding them simply because we knew most of these kids didn't often get any good meals except what we could beg, steal or borrow for them from the BIA storehouses, the DEW line sites and the hospital and from private parties who donated and from Scout Headquarters in Fairbanks.

During Scout camp time, some of my colleagues would just *co-incidentally* shoot more meat than they could use and before you knew it, here they would come, hauling up the hind quarters of a moose or caribou; those kids went through food like a bull dozer through fluffy snow and they especially liked *meat.*

Everyone looked forward to the daily 'goodie drops', some more than others . . . . that 100 or so pounds of fresh meat would be cooked rare, dripping with flavorful juices and the very little fat sizzling away and as soon as it was even close to being cooked, knives came out and hands and fingers served quite well. Cutting and grabbing away and making the happy sounds of those young, healthy eating machines trying to fill the bottomless pit in their stomachs was a pleasant experience!

To safely store the large amount of perishables on hand, we would dig pits into the permafrost. Since we were so close to the

Arctic Circle, we merely had to dig down about 18 inches or so before hitting permafrost. We could just cover the raw meat well and put it in the pits and it would last the week of Scout camp quite safely. Well, it would last if it had to but it never lasted more than a day or so, it got eaten up so quickly!

During camp, I taught First Aid and qualified badges in rope-tying and we fished until I was actually nauseated by the smell of fish, a position I could never have imagined I would be in.

We climbed the mountains, swam in the Kobuk River and learned to shoot with a bow and arrow. What a time! I feel confident that there are men of the 40 to 50-year-old range in that particular part of Alaska that fondly recall the camping trips we took and the great times that we had! In looking back on these years, I remember the names of some of the leaders: George Brennan was there and Russ Gilbert and Gary Hebert, Gil Calls and Lester Richardson. All the BIA teachers were there, coming and going; some of the residents of Kiana came up, as did the Blastervolds; a family the name of Henrie had a fish camp near by and we went over and visited with them occasionally.

Our tents were pitched on a bluff overlooking the Kobuk River which was about 100 yards wide at that point. We were in the middle of moose and caribou country and knew there must be bears about also, but we didn't encounter any, thankfully. It was truly beautiful country; almost perfect. The sandbars were long and firm and we could easily land a plane on them, and so goings and comings were frequent. None of the native boys swam a stroke, which I found interesting, so some of the adults who could swim well roped off an area of the beachfront and tried to teach the young guys to swim . . . . without too much success. The boys just did not take to swimming.

If you are a believer in the DNA Cell Memory theory, then it's clear why they didn't: they had uncounted generations of their ancestor's cell-memory screaming at them, "What, are you CRAZY!?! Get out of the WATER!!"

The last day of camp, of the first year I was there, the boat I was riding in while fishing swamped unexpectedly and left me stranded on the wrong side of the river. The right side of the river, the one with the plane on it, was about 50 very wet yards away and how cold, I could not say, but nonetheless, I stripped to unders, tied my boot-laces together and slung them about my neck and swam the river; I did . . . more of a dogpaddle, really, while holding my clothes up out of the water the best I could.

All who witnessed it thought it was an awfully funny sight. It became kind of Scout Camp Lore and entered into the realms of campfire stories for years to come. The first year, I did it out of necessity . . . in the years after, I did it as sort of an ego trip for myself, the temperature of the water being about 50 delightful-degrees and THAT particular bit of folklore was a big factor in my show of Pluck and True Grit and Stamina for me, myself, and I.

The second year I helped with Scout Camp, I had my own plane and I'd fly in fully loaded every night. My usual load with that type of plane was probably five or six hundred pounds but when we had a little wind and it was cold, I could get about 7-8 hundred pounds off the ground.

The cafeteria and kitchen staff at the hospital would bake up fresh bread and goodies; the kids picked cranberries and blueberries on the tundra for me to bring back on the return flight as a kind of trade. Some of the boys belonged to the women who did the cooking at the Hospital so it was a win-win all around. I'd work the clinic and run the Hospital in the daytime and at night I'd dash out and either stay all night with the Scouts and other adult leaders, or else I'd just go up and stay for a while in the evening and fly home. At this time of year in late July, the sun didn't go down anyway and so I could just come and go whenever I could and flying in the dark was not an issue.

Sometimes, my boss would come up to camp, too, and after the boys were bedded down, he and I would go fishing. The describing of how the fishing was nearly brings me to tears; it was just fantastic. We used a #2 Mepps with a lure and drop it into one of those little streams from the tundra into the Kobuk River and we'd bring in grayling or trout. We never did get salmon up there; oh, they were in the water all right but they wouldn't hit on lures.

Sometimes we'd hook pike, which used to be considered rather a trash fish and not good eating, although the sled dogs seemed to eat it OK; pike were a challenge because they would chew the leaders right off unless we used wire. Pike were terrifying to see when you did land them . . . real living dinosaurs with a frightful mouth full of teeth. Right up there on the 'ugly' scale with Gar fish. Gar are no good at all to eat, but I've heard that there is about one ounce of delicately-flavored meat right at the base of the skull; I have never been tempted to try it. Taking the 10 or so biggest Pike back to camp so the kids could enjoy them was fun, too. Not fun for the Pike so much, I guess . . .

~~~~~~~~~~~~~

There was a Sergeant West from the Air force Base who helped us with the Scouts one year. He requested time off to come up and help run the camp. There was a guy I shall refer to only as W R, an Eskimo fellow who was there all three years that I was with the camp. I hunted a lot with WR and associated with him outside of Scouting, too. He loved to referee ball games, which was unusual because Eskimos generally didn't like to judge people. His personality was unusual, too, and was MOST unusual because you rarely found many Eskimo/Inuit men with those particular personality traits. He was cocky and a bit of a braggart and he had multiple girlfriends, I was told, and managed to juggle them along with his wife. Not my idea of a role model, but an interesting individual and he seemed to have a real commitment to the boys.

It was remarkable to see the old Eskimo games and skills that he taught the Scouts; they did the knuckle-hops and knuckle pulls which are true Inuit games. I showed them a couple of games that were new to them. Tractor Pull was a favorite and it began with two boys tied together with a rope and the one who could pull the other over a line was the winner.

Another game was Stick-Pull, a real old Mormon pioneer game: Two guys would sit with their feet together and take a stout dowel or stick about six feet long, and both of them would hold on to it. The first guy to get pulled off the ground loses. In showing them, I was matched with this guy who was really strong and he challenged me to stick pull. You are supposed to count in unison, 1-2-3-pull! But just as I got ready to count, he gave a yank and flipped me—literally picked all 200 lbs. of me—right up off the ground! I must have jumped a bit when I saw what was happening, for he threw me and I landed by the fire, facing the opposite way.

It was so darn sudden that I just sat there and looked around, probably wide-eyed and surprised as an old owl! Here I sat, 8 feet over on the other side of where I had begun.

The boys' eyes sure popped and then of course, everyone wanted a try after that and it went on for hours. Lots of sore muscles the next day! Another thing I enjoyed was buzzing the camp with my plane and tossing out treats. I'd fly in and drop five-bucks worth of bubble gum or some other wrapped treat like that, just throw it loose out of the plane window. It was great fun for the boys . . . kind of like an Easter Egg Hunt on steroids!

The only really bad thing about camping was the terrible mosquitoes, but they were everywhere in the summer anyway, so we just had to adjust to it. The gnats were worse as they would just gather right in front of your face and fly into your mouth or nose . . . . no heavy breathing!

After camp was over and everyone went home, the very few kids who had learned to swim wanted to show-off their new skill so when the temperature of the lake got up to about 50 degrees at Kotzebue, they went swimming. I never saw the grown-ups in town get in the water willingly, though; there was a lagoon in the middle of town but everybody stayed away from it in droves. Seems there was a local legend about a mermaid who would grab you and take you down under the water and drown you, so instead of swimming in the relatively safe lagoon, the few people that did swim would go and swim in the ocean and drown.

Made no sense.

In the wintertime, Willie Jones, a driver for the hospital, and I took the boys out on the pack ice and taught them to make igloos. Yes, you read right. A tall, skinny white guy and Willie, a full-blooded Eskimo were attempting to teach young Inuit boys to make igloos. Willie knew how and had done it many times, but all I had were directions on paper. We both started out, leaving about 10 feet between us.

He got his snow blocks cut and packed and up in about 2 hours. He had 4 boys on his team and I had the other four.

My team's fell in . . . There is a real trick to it; it was 25 degrees below zero on the day we prepared for this lesson: a nice temperature, really. We went out far enough into the plain to have *good* snow, wind-blown and full of air. In this condition, it could be cut into chunks. Back in the villages, people piled chunks like this around their houses to cut the heating bills. With being full of air, the blocks had fantastic insulating value; they molded together and held tight and handled almost like adobe.

The idea is, I would start out on top of a snowdrift that I could cut down into and when I cut out the first row of blocks, then I could cut another layer of my vertical cuts and get double duty, so to speak. Besides that, I was digging out the center using the snow I excavated for blocks. When I got it up so far and to the desired height, the kids handed me blocks over the walls. Then it came to a pivotal point: the center block, the king-pin or whatever the proper term is for it. First one was a no-go but on the second attempt I got one set before the igloo caved in.

We went around the outside and cut out little chunks of snow and chinked it here and there, much like mud—daubing. Then, we punched a couple of holes in the top for ventilation. I told them the story of the Franklin Arctic Expedition where it was thought that they died of asphyxiation for when their bodies were exhumed and autopsied there was no other explanation of why they had died. They had built an igloo for protection and simply sealed it up too tight and ran out of oxygen while they slept, it appeared.

We checked the temperature outside and it was 25 degrees below zero when we started and warmed to 19-below in the afternoon; on that particular outing it was done for instructional purposes but, at that temperature, if a person is camping, voluntarily or in an emergency, he is really working for his life. If it is not done properly, he's in real trouble. We'd gone out with a lot of gear but the basic, simple igloo was still important and it made me feel good to teach this elementary and vital concept to the youth, who seemed fascinated by it.

After finally constructing one large enough and with the correct ventilation and everything, all eight of us got into it and pulled the door block in behind us to keep out the wind. We lit a candle and watched the temperature rise on our thermometer, and in just a matter of a few minutes, the temperature had climbed to zero. Now that still doesn't sound too cozy but when you've been outside in

25 below and a wind-chill blowing that took it down another 20 degrees, zero is almost tropic! We were all comfortable and we weren't dressed very warmly, either.

When I sleep in a sleeping bag in an igloo, I often undress down to my skivvies, for if a person gets into a sleeping bag with a lot of clothes on, especially is he/she is a bit sweaty, (and we are *always* a BIT sweaty, whether we know it or not) the wetness just cools a person down faster. So, I usually layered my clothes underneath me and that makes for a good bed.

We had splashed some water over the outside of the igloo when we had finished it and it made a shell that was really solid. The next day, when we were ready to move out, we tried to tear it down and just couldn't. We could drive a snow machine over the thing and it wouldn't break, that was how solidly it was put together. It was a sight to behold. I wish now had taken pictures of the igloo and the boys that built it.

None of the kids we had at that time knew how to build an igloo up to that point, which is a cultural tragedy in my opinion. For generations, the native people had lived WITH Mother Nature and not fought against Her. When the early missionaries began converting the Eskimos to Christianity, they told them to stop living underground in igloos, like animals. "God's children live above ground", they were told. They had to begin building their dwellings above ground and then they had to worry about heat and since there is no firewood, they had to use coal oil in stoves, which was expensive and unhealthy. It was a vicious circle and was NOT in their best interests but, unfortunately, it was a common situation.

Now, thanks to editing, I realize that I have brought this up before, but, although it seems I harp on the subject, it really is a sore point and must have been important enough for me to mention it numerous times in my journals . . .

One example of tradition being more than just culture for culture's sake was the story of a teenaged boy who was out on his snow machine when he went flying over an embankment. He was lost about three days and when he was finally rescued he had lost toes and part of both his feet to frostbite. An old man who was telling me the story said if he had only known and followed tradition, he would have been OK, but he was dressed in white man's clothes and had on new rubber boots that he had paid a lot of money for as they were more 'stylish' and cool than traditional mukluks with fur liners. If he had had those proper boots, sealskin pants and probably a muskrat coat, the furs would have kept him warm. and, if he had learned how to build an igloo, he would have not suffered at all. I know 6 or eight Eskimo-Indian Boy Scouts who can build an igloo! I wonder if it's still taught . . . .

Probably not in the right chapter for this short tale, but reading this reminded me of a guy I knew named Will. We met at the hospital and I think he was a janitor or a systems engineer there . . . but we talked a lot and one time I made the comment to him that I had a hard time remembering my patients' names. I went on to say, without thinking, that 'all the Eskimos look about the same up here' and he didn't miss a beat, grinned an said, 'Yeah, ok, but we think all you white guys look alike, too.'

So much for political correctness.

SOD AND WHALEBONE HUT

BOY SCOUTS COMPETE

CHAPTER 17

RANDOM SAMPLES

So much of what I recorded on paper and on tape while living in Alaska doesn't fall into any particular category or chapter heading. There are dentistry stories and hunting stories and people-stories and the biggest space-taker is the practice of medicine. So often, a typical day would include all of these things and more. I'm just going to lump together the stuff that is interesting to me and things I do not want to be forgotten: some of the following happened early in our stay and others, right at the close. If the stories were dated, I included that and they DO jump around a bit but in and of themselves, they are little vignettes of our adventures there.

February 1 1967

Went up to Hooper Bay, stay extended through to the 11th. Bethel was the destination on Wednesday morning with 20MPH wind and a temp of -20. Delightful. It was so bad, my Village Aide and I were stuck in Bethel for most of the day, able only to work out of the clinic. Had 150 people to see during the Chest Clinic. Helen Lake and Albertina Hale were the two health Aides and they were a great help in getting through the backlog of work. My stay in Hooper, planned for 3 days maximum, extended to Tuesday of the next week due to the weather. It was always blowing during this whole time, sometimes very hard; when the winds get around 40MPH or more, all activity shuts down. You can't be out in it for you can't see and the frozen snow is pelted into you so hard, it feels like buckshot.

Well, we did get 70 sputum tests done out at the clinic, most by the induction machine, and about 75 X-rays. Those were pretty good numbers for a village of 500 people. I stayed right in the clinic; all I needed was a bed and water to wash-up with. There were two beds in the clinic two examining rooms and a waiting room with a bathroom and cold/cool running water. A veritable palace!

The only grocery store yielded a stale loaf of bread for 95-cents, a big box of rice and a small box of dry milk. With the hotplate on a counter in my suite, I lived like a KING! I had two invitations to eat out with the people in the Church there and the teachers. Rueben Hill, the maintenance man, took me down to the Bering Sea on one of the days before the equipment was delivered.

We visited an old fish camp that was completely snowed over and we could see nothing but mounds under the snowdrifts. We must have made an interesting sight: an Eskimo mush-ing his dog sled along with a white man riding on the sled, towing a kayak behind! The kayak was to be used to get seals if we were to shoot any that were out in the water.

Most of the time, I found that the village called Hooper Bay was filled to the brim with absolutely nuthin'! Then when the missing gear I needed DID arrive, it was mayhem trying to get caught up. I only read one book and half of another in the time I was there.

Word had gotten out that I knew how to fix teeth, too, so while the wait was on for the TB scanning stuff, people lined up for dental work. I used 27-gauge needles and knew how to do dental blocks and was pretty good at numbing patients up, just like real dentist's do. The small needles I used cut down a lot on the pain; in the past, apparently, some of the locals had come in for extractions and whoever it was doing the extracting would have been more at home in a butcher shop, or so I was told.

It didn't take long to run out of Lidocain for injections so I had to use some Demerol I had on hand; I would just zonk the patients until they were almost asleep . . . it still hurt but they just didn't care. This was a big village with many medical needs so my supplies on hand were exhausted. These folks were really stoic and it was hard to tell how badly I was hurting them . . . that upset me but there was no other option . . .

Since Monday was a 'snow day' and complete bust, on Tuesday I couldn't stand to be stranded any more, so hired two young fellows with Snow Travelers to pull me to Scannon Bay which is about 40 miles up the coast. It took us 3 hours and a bit to get there; there was a particularly high tide and we couldn't go up the Bay directly but had to maneuver through a pass in the mountains to get to Scannon Bay. On the journey there, I rode the runners on the sled because I was afraid it was going to turn over and the drivers didn't disappoint me in that arena. Ron, my x-ray tech, rode in the basket on his sled and got rolled out several times. He frost-bit his thumb holding on.

The teachers in Scannon Bay were enjoyable people, very cooperative and helpful. We were able to get sputum's, and X-rays on everyone there, including four converters and all their families. That was my primary job: finding the 'carriers' as it were, and treating them as well as the people they had come in close contact with, thus wiping out TB in that village!

A popular tourist-type souvenir I saw for the first time there, and that was found in gift shops and so forth, was stuffed unborn baby seals. You just can't imagine how adorable these things are, if rather macabre. When pregnant female seals are hunted and shot, the mindset, I suppose, is that the kit was dead anyway, so what was the difference? As I say, macabre, but certainly cute. You never forget the sight if you ever see one.

All in all, the trip to Scannon Bay was successful, despite the initial problems. I bought two stuffed baby seals, some small baskets of unusual style and quality that I hadn't seen before, shot some fantastic photos of this very picturesque little village, nestled as it is at the base of a high mountain and the Bering Sea.

. . . . and got my first, and last, dog bite!

Walking through the village, my workday complete, I heard some yelling from far away and even as it got near and nearer, I couldn't make out what was being shouted and then out of the clear blue, I felt a powerful force hit me and then immediately, there was a seriously-feeling pain in an area that was not easily accessible to me . . . .

Just about one second after the bite from the invisible dog, the owner caught up with his errant demon-canine-from-Hell, but not before he had ripped through my Cruiser pants and if you have ever seen Cruiser pants, you know that would NOT be an easy thing to do. That cursed hound took a piece right out of them and, at the same time, out of me.

There was nothing to do except go back to the clinic and see what the damage was, so I got a mirror and sure enough, there was a puzzle-piece missing from my lily-white butt . . . still have the scar. Ah, Scannon Bay! Forever with me . . . .

The Health Aides, Gemma and Helen, were a huge help: we ended up with very near 100% turnout, which is great and what we needed to see. Some supplies ran out on the last few patients, however, and there remained a need for penicillin or the like for an ear infection.

There was a lady who was pregnant and had developed toxemia so I gave her a grain of Phenobarbital and her high blood pressure came down to 140 over 110; I ended up authorizing her into the hospital.

The last cowboy of this rodeo was a young boy with a bad cut on his leg which was not healing properly and was quite infected. Got him cleaned up and shot up, and I washed up and packed up and readied myself to fly UP . . . and out! The weather was not cooperating but we made it anyway; I had a 'down day' coming with nothing to do and I wanted to get home to my wife and children and do just exactly that!

SAVOONGA

This is a town with real charm . . . very friendly and upstanding people and one of the strangest affects I have ever come across in my travels: everyone is very quiet . . . right down to the youngest child . . . all speak in very hushed voices, barely above a whisper!

Every time my place flew in, there was a big group to welcome me; after several very pleasant visits there, I wanted to bring Phyllis with me and reported this to them, but for some reason, she was not able to come, and my next trip they expressed their disappointment as they had several diversions for her. How thoughtful! And what a 180-degree from a few other towns I'd been in . . .

They speak a different dialect here, too; this is one of the reasons I never bothered to learn to speak even the most prevalent Eskimo tongue because, for instance, down in the southern part of the area I was responsible for, Yupik is the spoken language. In the Nome area up higher, they speak another dialect and there are even more, and these people, all from the same state, cannot understand each other totally so it was interpreters for me! My brain was stretched quite enough. After clinic duties were complete, I had arranged to go walrus hunting with around a dozen other folks, including two BIA guys, five natives from Savoonga and a few others I did not get information on, and my friend, Patrick Wongigillilen. There were nine in our boat, which was a big 20-foot long skin contraption with a 40HP 'kicker' inboard motor in the middle and a tiller in the back.

It took over 5 hours to even find some to shoot at, even though several of the guys had observed walrus pods in the areas we tried first but with no avail. Finally, we came upon two pods of walrus with about 20 or so in each pod. Astounding! We ran the boat up as close as we could get to them without spooking the bunch and I started taking pictures.

The armed hunters in the boat started blasting away and finally cornered one on a room-size piece of ice floe. I got movies of the Great Hunt, though, and when I got back about 6 PM, I was cold but happy. The walrus would be properly honored as every ounce of its huge 1-ton body would be utilized. I have a lot of this hunt on film and it is neat for me to watch, as it lets me re-live the experiences I had that day. Sitting in a skin boat is just plain cold and there is no two ways about it. The Eskimos that were onboard were unfailingly cheerful for the whole trip; it is an ages-old custom for them to go out this way in boats. How fulfilling and satisfying it must have been for them to keep alive this generations-old tradition; if you believe this sort of thing, as I do, there were visitors from the other side who were sharing this right along with their mortal heirs . . . .

Before the days of helicopter and airplane that could be utilized to spot-hunt, this type of operation was extremely dangerous, for going out on the ice with the tides and winds moving the huge blocks of ice, football-field size and sometimes even miles across, could be and often was, deadly. The boats are frail-appearing objects that carry the hunters on the search for walrus, of which the boat itself is made of, fashioned by sewing the thick walrus skins together with sinew until they are waterproof. Hand-crafted driftwood frames comprise the vessel's skeleton; we had nine guys in a 20-foot boat that could be easily picked up and carried by four and would hold literally tons of cargo. Called 'Umiaks', they are truly amazing! I treasure a miniature replica of one that I brought back with me.

We were hunting among the ice floes and if the wind or tide had changed and we had lost our 'lead', or open water, we could have just picked the boat up and carried it across to the next lead. If we had gotten caught on a pad of ice and drifted out of sight of land, it is easy to see how easily disaster could strike.

The whole time, the natives from Savoonga continued to speak quietly, even in the heat of the hunt! When approached by villagers selling items, they would walk up very close and hold out the object they were trying to sell and say, "Yes, we got this. Why don't you buy one of these from me?" Talking in low tones was common in this village for centuries. After being there an hour or so, I'd find myself whispering back. I'd never been in a village where there was so much unity and such a lack of strife as well. On my second go-around there, one of the ladies presented me with a set of bone-earrings for Phyllis and another had made little carvings of walrus' for the boys. This is one of the best examples of where I felt like the people were really grateful for having me come out. It felt great to be of service and I will never forget the soft-spoken kindnesses I experienced there.

A story is told that several years back, acting on rather marginal information, a nurse and a pilot were dispatched out and their plane crashed, killing the pilot and crippling the nurse for life and it turned out that the patient they were coming to aid was not critical. Sad story for such a pleasant town; it sure tempered my enthusiasm with caution concerning 'emergency' flights.

When you circle in at a thousand feet or so, coming in to land, you can see the coastline of Siberia. People who had relatives in Siberia used to go over and visit back and forth, but around 1946, a group of family members went over to visit and just never came back, so no few dared go over since then . . .

Eventually I did leave Savoonga and when I got back to Kotzebue, it sounded like everyone was yelling, by comparison. They were gentle-natured folk, as well, and perhaps this led to the hushed voices. A sociologic study of that custom would be fascinating.

~~~~~~~~~~~~~~

Just a quick little story that still makes me smile even thinking about it after all these years. Bill and his wife Jo were near and dear to Phyllis and me during the time we spent in Kotzebue. They were both teachers in the school there and were cheerful, uncomplaining, and hardworking.

They had a daughter Kristie who was about 6 or so when we met them; I actually delivered their second child and it's this story that I want to relate now.

We'd known Bill and Jo Rembar from the first week or so of moving to Kotzebue; over the course of our friendship, he confided in me quite a bit. He opened up one time over dinner and expressed his dissatisfaction with his job. He felt he was just stuck there, trying to inspire kids who didn't want to be there and who usually didn't get much support from home. If he hadn't been so conscientious, he would have just gone along, throwing the facts out to the students with little concern whether he had successfully planted the seeds of learning or just taken up the time babysitting.

Once in a while, he told me, a kid would catch a spark and he would feel encouraged. Some of the teachers we knew there were good and dedicated but too often, the good ones usually moved on and up to another locale to teach. You can do something simply for the money and get it done, but if there is no satisfaction in a job, it detracts from the overall enjoyment of life.

KEITH HOOKER, M.D. AND M. DAWN BENTLEY

Bill must have known that, as we talked in that vein several times. Eventually, Bill and Jo discussed it in depth between themselves and Jo continued to teach, as she enjoyed it and it was fulfilling to her, but Bill left that field, and with some training, became a flight controller. It was shift work and although the hours were long, he would get two or three days off, he enjoyed the work, and he enjoyed the time he was *not* working because he could do what he really loved: flying. He and I did that a lot . . . .

Well, this particular event took place before he changed his profession. Jo and Bill had a little girl about six, I think I mentioned, and Jo had had a hard time with her pregnancies and her only delivery had been difficult; the couple had wanted more children for quite a while. When the time came for Jo to deliver, I was concerned that her pelvis appeared marginal in size and her delivery might turn into a C-section. We stayed near and watched her carefully and it took a long time, but eventually the birth was emminent; Bill was almost frantic at this juncture . . . he wanted a boy baby so bad it was pitiful. It was all he had talked about for the whole pregnancy and he had even painted the nursery blue . . . he was very, very much wanting a son. The baby finally delivered; now, this was in the days of 'no fathers in the delivery room', so he was out pacing in the waiting room when his son was born. It was just too tempting for me (darn that little imp on my shoulder that whispers these things to me!) and I thought about it and decided to play a trick on my friend. I just couldn't help it! I took a newborn Eskimo baby girl out of the nursery, bundled her up and walked out into the waiting room with her.

"Congratulations, buddy . . . you have a really cute little girl here," I smiled, as I held her out to him. Well, when white Bill Rembar looked at that obviously non-white, female Eskimo baby, his jaw almost hit the floor and it was all I could do to keep from laughing out loud: I can pull up the picture in my mind even now. After a moment or two, he caught on. He sure was mad. We all thought it was pretty funny in speaking of it later, but for just a moment there, I was afraid I had gone too far with my buddy . . . he finally had his son but only for a little while, and then could only watch over him from above . . . .

Tragically, Bill was killed in an airplane takeoff not long after his son was born. I still mourn for my friend . . . .

∾∾∾∾∾∾∾∾∾∾∾∾∾

One guy whose last name I will not reveal although he is probably dead and gone, was a fellow I'll call 'Berger'. He was a local bootlegger and he had the reputation as a guy who would do anything for a buck; he was also, I believe, an alcoholic of the worst kind: he adamantly denied he had a problem with alcohol.

At that time, I was the acting Aviation Medical Examiner; the FFA would certify a doc in each town with an airport and, since I flew and had an interest, I signed on. My motive was mainly that an AME got a trip somewhere every year and I got to take mine in New Orleans—a four day seminar on how to be an AME. Now, this Berger had both a commercial and an instrument rating, because he was a commercial pilot and a guide. He would go down to Anchorage and see a doctor down there he knew who would pass him with just the proper paperwork, filled out just so . . . and wrapped around a hundred-dollar bill, I believe . . . .

One evening, Berger was coming in one morning from poaching, which he did all the time; he radioed in that the front cable to his ski had broken. The danger in that was the ski, instead of pointing a bit upward in front, had dropped down so that when he landed he would go nose-over and flip. I was called out there in the ambulance in case he got creamed. He was a good pilot, I had to admit; and he was flying a Super Cub . . . if there is any headwind at all, it lands at maybe thirty miles per hour, so there wasn't too much of a problem. He had someone in the plane who could lean out on that side and push down on the back of the ski. So, he landed with no ill effects or danger to anyone.

Berger was a man of many faces and in addition to Poacher and Pilot, he owned a tavern and a hotel and ran a rather lucrative business by calling himself a Big Game Guide and Outfitter. One week, he had a whole bunch of hunters in-house and the story goes that as the kitchen help set up breakfast, Berger came in and put an unmarked, generic aspirin beside each plate on the dining area tables. When the guests filed in and were all seated, he called their attention to the pills and, in all seriousness, told them that the pills were a new treatment for VD, so, if they had been indiscreet the night before, they were to take them. He used to laugh when he told the story himself, because, he said when the guests left the tables, there was not one aspirin left. Speculation was that even the ones who had not done anything amiss took them along, 'for future emergencies.'

~~~~~~~~~~~~~~

Setting up a dual-purpose clinic, far away from the Hospital, demanded careful planning and execution. The Hotel I arranged to stay in for this long-planned clinic in Juneau had probably been built during the reign of Czar Nicholas. It had not aged gracefully. The windows were opaque with accumulated filmy dirt, the curtains were ragged and coming un-hemmed and the blankets smelled like their last 50 occupants. The mattress was mushy and the springs were sprung and creaked loudly when I moved in my sleep . . . and I use the word 'sleep' loosely here. The room next door had an occupant with a loud cough. A productive cough. A frequent, lung-rattling cough. In the five days I was checked in, the maid didn't change the thin, graying sheets even once. The tiny bathroom had no shower and was at least half the size of a standard one, so getting my long body clean in and my face shaved in a sub-sized tub and Lilliputian, cold-water-only sink and a one-inch piece of used soap was, shall we say, tricky?

The building had four floors and one ancient elevator that was running with the original equipment Otis Elevators must have designed fifty years before. The walls were festooned with layers of grime and adorned with clever sayings, phone numbers, squashed bugs and one spot that could have been blood spatter.

Late arrival of guests in the middle of the night was heralded by the creaking of the ancient wood floors and the terminal-sounding, groaning-grind of Grandfather Elevator, rising to the dizzying height of 40 feet. Other than these irritants, it was a delightful place known as the Hotel Juneau, where, "The Elite Meet to Sleep". That was their motto. Really. No kidding. It was an interesting place to stay, once. The fishing we managed after hours had been worth it, though, and I *did* get a lot of TB testing done during my work-time there; arrangements had been made to team up with a fellow-medical guy who had a clinic set up to screen for venereal diseases.

Larry Brown ran the VD Office for the State and he'd heard a tip that there were some virulent cases of syphilis showing up there, and there was a need for TB testing and updating in Juneau, and that was what had brought me to Juneau in the first place. Not the salmon fishing after all. Really.

Syphilis is an especially grim disease because, after the rather mild initial symptoms recede a bit, and the victim thinks he or she is all better, it goes into sort of a remission which can lie dormant and undetected for years, meanwhile spreading to others sexually. It's a real killer for in the late stages, for untreated syphilis attacks the brain and causes a myriad of problems there, from amnesia on to complete loss of bodily control and insanity. Many, many patients ended their miserable lives, dying young in sanitariums . . . for an unremembered act and nameless partner . . . and no answers to 'what, where, when, or even who' . . . . a permanent souvenir from the distant past!

Not really worth a 'roll in the hay', is it? Remember that!

Thanks so much, Uncle Arthur, for that bedtime story, huh?

Anyway, VD, or STD's in today's vernacular, was widespread in some areas and new cases seemed to be centralized in this one location, Fairbanks, and Larry Brown was determined to track it down and stop the spread if he could. In talking one time, we thought of an ingenious method of testing and put it into practice in Fairbanks: we set up a table and a testing area in a local bar, the Redwood Bar and Café, a popular hangout with the residents. We put up a sign that said, "Have a FREE TB test here".

We were well patronized, and as word got out through some of our friends at the hospital that frequented the bar, they started telling everyone about the "great TB Clinic" that was coming, so there were a goodly number of participants. The bar owner was pleased as his patronage increased on those nights.

This is how is went: when the victim . . . excuse me . . . when the participant sat down, our third member acted as scribe and took the participants abbreviated history and all contact information; he was swabbed on both inner elbows, then I would put a TB test in one arm and Larry would take some blood out of the other. Since we started around 9PM, by the time the line formed it was made up of pretty cheerful fellows. Most of the men were too drunk to care what we were doing and the fact that we were performing 2 tests on them didn't register.

This was about the time that topless dancing was getting popular. We had set up in the bar right before it opened and for the first 2 hours, there was live music, featuring a non-descript band that just barely warranted the descriptor of "live". They had a forgettable name and put out lame renditions of the popular rock songs of 1960's.

Meanwhile, in our little corner, The Larry and Keith Show was doing well, concentrating on the men who, in various stages of inebriation, were lining up to check for TB; all was well until the first two sets were over and the main act took the stage. The dancers did not go unnoticed by the bar patrons; from the area our table was set up in, it would have taken a bit closer examination to determine if, indeed the under-clad lassies were truly topless or just a pasty away from it. I am proud to report that The Larry and Keith Show did *not* stop to determine this vital factoid but continued, undaunted, on the Noble Quest which they had embarked upon. This tough assignment ended finally and although it proved futile as far as finding a syphilis carrier, the TB tests got taken . . . and we were able to study a lot of human anatomy!

~~~~~~~~~~~~~~

Sunday morning of the same trip, the sun smiled upon us again and I was able to go to St. Mary's by plane and got there about noon. This is a large Catholic school and Church, run by the Jesuits; they showed me the greatest hospitality I had ever experienced while I was there. I had a room to myself and it was a luxury suite, 16x16 with my x-ray tent and table in one corner; they aided in getting a couple of local boys to change the cassettes for me in the tent. I even had a bed with a surprisingly comfortable straw tick mattress. They fed me often and well and it hardly felt like work. I had a regular RN as my assistant in addition to the village Health Aide. Wow . . . things run so much smoother when proper preparation is made!

Phyllis and I flew out to Wales with the Christensen's . . . a great couple about our age that we sure enjoyed doing things with. It was the last of May and there was still plenty of snow and boy! Was it cold! When we got to the village, we saw that someone had shot a polar bear; a young fellow in the town had bagged it on an ice floe. I guess it was just not a very bright bear and didn't know enough to go north with the rest of them and got stuck in a Polar bear Catch-22: he had a choice of either jumping into the water with the intent to make shore, which he probably couldn't, or, just stay on the floe and starve. A well-aimed bullet was a much more humane end.

The ice was breaking up this time of year and this is where you see the walrus and seals in good numbers; they come up on shore to rest and soak up some sunshine. Walrus' are very intelligent, and protective, too, for if one is shot, the rest of them will actually go after the hunter! I found that fascinating and not the norm in the animal kingdom.

Walrus use their tusks for several things, two of them being they swim up to an ice floe, cock heir heads back and jam their tusks into the ice and pull themselves (nearly a ton, in some cases) up, and then crawl out onto the ice floe. They also use them to scrape mussels off the rocks, and then grab the mussels in their mouths as they drift down to the bottom. Actually, the tusks are just canine teeth; they are larger in the males but females have them too. I have a lot of pictures of them and you can easily tell the difference by the configuration. A mature female walrus weigh about a ton but the males can get much larger.

The four of us and a village acquaintance of mine went out in a boat and steered to an area that had a large group of walrus gathered together . . . moving along the solid ice floe like giant slugs . . . but very graceful in the water. We had planned to shoot a walrus if we could, and by 'we', I mean the male half of the Christensen's and me.

The other half was along for a ride and promised not to do anything to disrupt the hunt, as was done on another occasion in the past that we would just as soon forget. Hunting walrus was dangerous for the reason I mention previously about the herd instinct and the protectiveness of the animals for each other, and sure enough, when the villager who was heading up the hunt beaded in on a large male, another smaller female walrus, probably in his harem, and came after us right after the big one fell.

Carrying my 300 Magnum close at hand was crucial that day: that particular gun shoots out a shell about the size of my thumb, so as she came whuffling and snorting along in a direct path toward us, blood in her eye, I had no choice but to unload a barrage of shots to take her down. I couldn't hear anything out of my right ear for days because it turned out everyone in the boat who was armed, even the non-hunting 'pacifists', were firing at the hell-bent walrus out of sheer self-protection. We were in 300 feet of ice-cold water and would all have drowned immediately if she had gotten to us, and she was determined to get to us, it seemed.

Again, the animals were hunted and slain by the villagers in that particular hamlet would utilize every scrap of the nearly-two ton of walrus remains. It was illegal to sell raw ivory . . . it has to be carved. Hunting walrus only for the ivory is called headhunting because the walrus is killed just for the tusks, The meat is wasted and that is a practice I am adamantly opposed to, but it still happens. Someone from this village would get the tusks from these fallen mammoths and they would get into the hands of an artist who would turn them into something beautiful and valuable, but at great cost.

Some of the artifacts and natural things we brought home were valuable because of their workmanship or rarity. I wish now that we had been able to bring back more, for each item has a memory attached. The most wonderful souvenirs we brought home with us, we still have! Their names are Kelly and Kiana. They were born in Alaska and the precious and personal stories of their births are recorded elsewhere, in the same place I have recorded the birth of all eight.

'ALL THE LDS IN AREA GATHERED AT OUR HOME ON SUNDAY'

COUPLE ON STEPS OF CHURCH

CHAPTER 18

LEAVING KOTZEBUE
AND SAYING GOODBY

1970.

Eventually, of course, the time passed and all that is left of these four-plus years in Alaska are the items we bought while there, which are on display at our homes and some are in storage; at least, the tangible items. We've shared hundreds of these mementoes with friends and family when we got back from Alaska . . . many, many other items have been given away as gifts.

Some of the artifacts and other things we brought home are valuable because of their workmanship or their rarity. One of my favorites is a tiny replica of a kayak: it's only about 5 inches long; the ribs are so delicate and artfully made, it's a masterpiece! It's a I treasure it because I rode, many times, in the real thing while there. My Malachi, a Russian hat that's made of beaver skin is really neat-looking but I can't wear it much because it is just too hot, even during Utah winter storms, but I wore it a lot in Alaska and it was perfect.

The whale vertebrae masks have to be seen to be believed. I have a pair of wolf-face mittens that are wonderful. The backs of the mittens are the whole wolf face, with the eyes sewed closed—they are really fantastic gauntlet gloves about 20 inches long. We came back with beautiful furs, too, from white fox to grizzly, none of which I shot myself, and various other memorials of the years spent there . . . things that are unique and available nowhere else in the world. I doubt if some of the things could be found even in Alaska today. We were there when the culture was just beginning to change over from the Inuit-Eskimo to more white influence, with the native Alaskans becoming wards of the state. One of the most valuable items I own are . . . . ready? . . . . two walrus penis bones! They are called 'ouzik' and I saw and bought four and still have two of them. Interestingly, there are only four mammals on earth that have penis bones and the walrus is the largest by far. The ones I have are about 1½ inches thick and about *18" long.* They look like ivory but are solid bone; one of them has been broken and had *healed back* together before the death of the walrus-owner! This is the only one I ever heard of that had been actually broken: how? I don't know because there is so much flesh around them, it is hard to imagine that particular accident happening now does it? Don't try.

A special and humorous story regarding the ouzik . . . once, during some Regional Church meetings, one of the Mission Presidents in the Church came to have a meal with us and get acquainted. This would have been sometime in 1969; he was very interested in all of the mementoes we'd collected and I was relating as much about each one, in turn, as I could. He was a good audience and I enjoyed showing him our treasures. I thought I had asked Phyllis to put the ouzik somewhere out of the way, just for the visit, as I really didn't want to explain that particular item.

Well . . . . there it was . . . .

He picked it up, hefted it, and looked up at me expectantly, as if to say, "what in the world is this?".

"Well, Brother Hinckley that is called an ouzik . . . it's a . . . sort of . . . bone." I then attempted to distract his attention . . . . "did you see this great grass basket, Brother Hinckley?" I began . . .

He was still studying the ouzik . . . "What kind of animal bone is this, Brother Hooker?" he questioned.

"Well, uh . . . . well, now, it's a walrus bone, that's what it is."

He wouldn't let it go. "What part of the walrus does this bone come from?" The direct inquiry afforded nothing but the truth. "Well, Brother Hinckley, it's a penis bone, as a matter of fact . . . ." I finished rather lamely.

He hefted it one more time before placing it carefully back on the shelf he had found it on.

The silence was deafening.

Then he said, "Aren't our Fathers creations marvelous?" and then he smiled . . .

~~~~~~~~~~~~~

We bought everything we could afford to at the time, but now I wish I had gone without lunch more often and bought a lot more, although in some cases, I guess I was just a sucker to buy what I did. I just couldn't resist the crafts or, sometimes, I just couldn't resist the craftsman: no only for the nature of their art but for the need of the artist. We have some beautiful grass baskets and bark bowls that probably would be at home in a museum and there have to be decisions made about that stuff and pretty soon, I suppose.

~~~~~~~~~~~~~

My seven living children and 36 grandchildren (subject to change) will all have many things from their Grandma Phyllis and from me to honor and treasure, I hope, as we have done. I use a lot of 'show-and-tell' when I travel about and lecture; thousands of people have heard my stories and seen the pictures and honored me by showing an interest in the objects, which I wish I could give better voice to. Some of the things will go to a museum for that is where they belong, for all to see.

Phyllis and I had known for a year that the time was fast approaching when I would have to find a new location to "hawk my wares." Up to this time, it had been a really fun assignment for me. Phyllis got by and the little kids were too young to care much where they were, as long as they had mommy and daddy and each other. They were getting old enough to go to school, though, and we were faced with either educating them ourselves or sending them to public school, neither of which sounded all that good to either of us. We wanted to be where they could have all of the advantages of their culture, as well as the privileges and opportunities of our Church.

The LDS Church is family-orientated and its programs and services are far and away, in my opinion, the best environment for raising children. At this time, Kit and Kyle were old enough for school and Kelly was only around two and Kiana was a little bit of a thing. Some changes had to be made. I didn't feel any more ready to go into private practice than I had felt two years ago, but the situation that we were living in was closing up tight and we were running out to planning time very quickly.

Socially, for us, Alaska was not all that great, but there were a lot of very good times. Some people who lived there got out, did things, grew, were active, and took part in their surroundings and others who lived there went bananas, just sitting around. There were limits on the things to do in Alaska during that time; socializing often included drinking and we were not comfortable with that as a constant, especially around the children. We didn't fit that pattern. We had grand times with the friends we made, and what friends we made! Lifelong friends . . . Eternal friends some of them, I am sure. Playing games, having traveling dinners where each group went from house to house, eating a different dinner course at each stop. Enjoying the outdoors with other young families and flying planes around and so on was incredible.

The place could not be better if you enjoyed hunting and fishing and hiking, but, to be honest, only for limited months and even then, camping and outings were almost always uncomfortable for one reason or another and while having the plane was great (but expensive), it wasn't something we were able to enjoy with the kids . . . not practical at all for us, anyway.

So much had been so good! Some of the best times and the most memorable were the oddest, I guess: one of my fondest memories is of harvesting ice, as strange as that sounds. In the winter we would go to a lake where everyone in the region went to cut ice. When the lake was frozen over, we'd go out and get blocks of ice that we cut out with a saw and then brought home using a snow machine.

The distilled water we always had on hand for drinking was flat and tasteless, but the lake water had a certain amount of vegetable matter in it, some tannic acid, and it was just delicious. The Eskimos lined the cakes of ice by their homes, in easy reach, taking a cube at a time inside to thaw, anything from a sliver to a 10 pound hunk. You recall the story of the irate teacher and his yellow ice? Fond memories.

Some of the memories are bittersweet. We had a little girl named Joena who we took care of for many months and she was the two year old chum of Kelly's; we got to love her very easily, but she went back to family. There was also another little boy . . . . it often happened that when a family just had too many children to care for in their estimation, they just gave one away. This little boy was one I had delivered and as soon as the mother held him, she said she just didn't have room for him and did not want him, so, having little choice, I took him home just as soon as he was delivered. Tucked him under my arm and when I handed him over to Phyllis, I said: "Merry Christmas . . . 'Tis the season to be jolly . . . ."

We called him Jerrod. Phyllis loved him so much and although the plan had always been to find him a good home and adopt him out, we really got attached during the time we had him.

A nice couple from Fairbanks adopted him at 6 months. When they came to get him, Phyllis just went in the back room and would not come out, as she was crying too hard. She had collected the bottles and clothes and toys he liked to send with him, and then, suddenly, he was just gone. We often spoke, in later years, about how much we wish we'd kept him . . . but we had to turn our backs . . .

~~~~~~~~~~~~

TERMINATION DUST

It was time.

Phyllis was half-heartedly getting things packed and ready to go and I was dawdling around, straightening everything up at the hospital, when 'termination dust' forced our hand.

In the old days before rapid transportation, people had to take boats back out after spending the summer months fishing or mining or cutting timber or selling artifacts or searching for gold or whatever brought them to Alaska for the summer months. When the first light, fluffy snow started to fall, on and off, along about early September, it was called 'termination dust' because if the folks didn't immediately get going, they would be frozen-in for another year.

Now, although we weren't living in Anchorage anymore, that's an Anchorage terminology, but I liked the story surrounding it and thought it needed to be included. The last trip of mine to the far north was to Savoonga, after waiting in Nome for 4 days. When that trip was over, I got to thinking that I wanted to go back to St. Lawrence Island just one more time; there were good, warm feelings there because I had felt liked and wanted. It was worth sitting in Nome and reading for a day or two waiting for a plane to take me there and visit the people I wanted to see one more time. It would be a long time, I feared, until I would be able to come back.*

All in all, I felt good about my tour of duty. The clinics in the villages were going along pretty well and the Health Aides had good training and were capable and caring. We had really stomped all over TB: it certainly was not the killer it had been . . . in fact, it was no longer much of a problem at all.

Now, there was still a lot of follow-up work to do and constant surveillance to avoid its reoccurrence, but I felt good about my battle and was ready to hand the gauntlet over to someone else. Thinking about the stories told during Agony Hour still brought a smile to my face and a chuckle when I remembered all the high drama it produced. One or two stories are particularly choice, like the one about the 'bowels'. Now, bear in mind, all the Health Aides had some English . . . they had to in order to communicate with the Mother Hospital but, since the report went out via short wave radio, anyone who had a ham set and wanted to, could dial it in and listen to the back and forth conversations.

* **NOTE: flew back to Alaska in May of 2009 with my best friend and lovely wife of 6 years, Juanita, who had never been there but heard SO much about it from me that she was really looking forward to it. We took our own plane and went wherever as we pleased; it was certainly a satisfying and enjoyable time.**

It was impossible to keep everything confidential and most of the Aides spoke only simple English so we could not use the more precise technical terms that we would have preferred using so that not just anyone listening in would know what was being discussed, exactly. Still, there were listeners. Before I left, I had come to realize that a LOT of people tuned in to Agony Hour. Guess it was better than religion radio! I wish I'd saved *all* of the notes . . . hope you think so, too.

An Aide called me one evening, very excited. She said, "Dr, there is a 23 year old male here with an awful pain in his bowels!"

"Where in his bowels, in the upper right quadrant?" I queried. "Yes," she answered.

"The lower left quadrant?" I pressed, to which she just kept saying, "Yes! Yes!"

"Well, where?"

"Oh, Doctor," and she started to sputter again, then took a big breath and settled right down and said slowly and carefully: "He has awful pain in all his bowels—B-A-L-L-S!"

Sometimes, the best method to protect the privacy of the patient, especially those who happened to be on non-time-constrained or long term cases, was to write letters back and forth. They were always original and I found them to be charming, especially if the Aide didn't have much English. If I would have thought about it, I should have saved them all and made a book out of them, too!

My favorite was from a patient that I had never met who lived quite a ways distant in a town called Hamilton, which is at the mouth of the Yukon River. Apparently, she thought that by describing her symptoms accurately, she could avoid having to travel far to the clinic, or, be embarrassed about asking for the medication she wanted in person. It goes as thus:

"Dear Doctor: I finally got a nerve. Sorry if I bother you, Doctor, but I really need an ointment for my rash. Would you kindly send me one too please? I am so miserable from head to toe but it is all in the same place. O, I am so ashamed. It heals but then it starts to rash again and I use have to use big ol' napkins for bandages. Would you please kindly tell me what kind of sickness I got? Is it danger to others? I am me here, staying with my sister and I don't think I will ever go back to St. Michaels. No questions please just send the ointment. Thank you very much. You are kind and good. I will be waiting here in Hamilton for my ointment for my lady place. God bless you always, your on and off patient, L."

PS. If this letter bother you? If it is a crime just tell me to stop the writing and I will stop. Thank you and enclosed is $3 for the ointment and that is all I have 'cause I need it bad to soothe the itching pain on the rash"

Another winner: A letter from Skaktoolik and in this case, one of the Community Aides:

> Dear Doctor, I treat G.B, age 25 and J.S age 21 with procain penicillin. The boy got 2.4 and the girl 2.4 according to your orders. The boy have backache, burning urine, frequent urine, and the dis-charging yellow puss-y. I asked both if they had enter-a-course with anybody and they both say 'no'.
>
> Sincerely, M.C, Health Aide.

PS. they are liars I think."

This last one is choice: the first sentence had quickly become a by-word with the other doctors at the Hospital and when I showed it to Phyllis, it became a family joke. I love the tone of concealed accusation toward the doctor (me) . . . it's plain that this Health Aide feels that it's the doctors fault . . . my fault for sending her away from her home and allowing all this to transpire! Also, note the half-measure treatment for her spouse and how it points to her command of the situation . . . she will cure him alright, but not immediately! Good for her!

> "Dear Dr . . . . Oh, no, you gonna have a bad news from me. My husband got gonhoreeha and get sick from Selwik girl, D.S, while I was gone down to Kotzebue that you have me go with that Gallivan boy the one with the broken arm. That Selewik girl come here to (my town) and stay with my husband while I am gone. He gave me some bad sickness. We both received Procain Pen 4.8

and 2.4 bisellin and my husband get 2.4 Procain and 1.2 bisellin. I even write to Selwick Health Aide E.R. and tell her about D.S. and what she do to my husband.

Signed, Health Aid—L.J.

PS: answer me what you think about this?"

. . . . And then . . . . it was all over.
    . . . termination dust forced our hand and Phyllis and the kids flew out early while all of our tons of 'stuff' took the more leisurely scenic route by barge. I wanted to stay a few weeks longer and fish and hunt as much as I wanted to, without the hindrance of time. Rex Maughn, my old and good friend, who had been a classmate of mine from Arizona State and the man who baptized me into the LDS faith, made it big in oil, and was coming up and we had things planned for a real good vacation. I cached gas all over so we could go anywhere we wanted.

As soon as he got there, we took off and just fished and hunted every minute. We traveled up-river to fish; I landed on a sandbar and we filled up the plane with fish. It was an amazing trip and he was totally thrilled. Then bad weather hit us and looked like it was going to stay for a while, so we had to head back after only one week.
    The arrangements for the sale of my plane had already been made; I flew out of Kotzebue one snowy morning. The week of 'guy heaven' was over. My little 7779-H airplane had to fly for 10 air-hours to get me to Tok Junction, and since I only have a 3-hour bladder, I had two stops on the way. Getting there, I parked at the airstrip and stayed overnight with friends I had arranged with.
    I was missing my family badly . . . it was time to leave . . . time to follow the lighthouse beam that would lead me home. The lighthouse beam that had been guiding me in Anchorage . . . it had been guiding me in Kotzebue . . . . now, it had moved entirely, back to the Lower 48 . . . . we were too far apart and I missed them . . . .
    Alaska had left deep tracks on my soul . . . . tracks that would always remain on my heart . . . calling me back, to once again fly

her skies . . . scout her beaches . . . nurture her people . . . . the people I had learned to love and respect.

I taxied up to the tie-down at the airport and climbed out of my plane for the last time, grabbed my medical bag and knapsack and walked over to a gas station where I stocked up with a couple of bottles of soda pop and a handful of candy bars.

Then, I was Anchorage-bound . . . it was 250 miles away . . . my family was there and they were missing me, too, and waiting for me . . . . there was no bus to board, nor plane to catch here, so I did all I could do . . . I stuck out my thumb and hitched a ride with a long-haul trucker just as it started to snow.

Termination Dust. . . . .

"THE FAMILY: PHYLLIS, KYLE, KIT AND KELLY AND ME,
IN FRONT OF OUR OLD ARMY JEEP"

GETTING READY TO LEAVE ALASKA. PHYLLIS AND
KIDS LEFT TWO WEEKS BEFORE I DID. PHYLLIS IS
WEARING DARK GLASSES TO HIDE THE TEARS . . .